The Ethnic Enigma

The Ethnic Enigma

*The Salience of Ethnicity
for European-Origin Groups*

EDITED BY

Peter Kivisto

PHILADELPHIA: The Balch Institute Press
LONDON AND TORONTO: Associated University Presses

973.04
E 84

Associated University Presses
440 Forsgate Drive
Cranbury, NJ 08512

Associated University Presses
25 Sicilian Avenue
London WC1A 2QH, England

Associated University Presses
P.O. Box 488, Port Credit
Mississauga, Ontario
Canada L5G 4M2

The paper used in this publication meets the requirements of the American National Standard for Permanence of Paper for Printed Library Materials Z39.48-1984.

Library of Congress Cataloging-in-Publication Data

The Ethnic enigma.

Includes bibliographies and index.
1. European Americans—Ethnic identity.   2. Ethnicity —United States.   3. United States—Ethnic relations. I. Kivisto, Peter, 1948–   .
E184.E95E84   1989   973'.04   88-70317
ISBN 0-944190-03-0 (alk. paper)

Printed in the United States of America

Contents

Acknowledgments 7

1 Overview: Thinking about Ethnicity
  PETER KIVISTO 11
2 In a New Light: Italian-American Ethnicity in the Main-
  stream
  DONALD TRICARICO 24
3 Mixed Ethnic Identities among Immigrant Clergy from
  Multiethnic Hungary: The Slovak-Magyar Case, 1885–1903
  BELA VASSADY, JR. 47
4 The Attenuated Ethnicity of Contemporary Finnish-
  Americans
  PETER KIVISTO 67
5 Class, Ethnicity, and the New Deal: The Croatian
  Fraternal Union in the 1930s
  PETER RACHLEFF 89
6 The Interweave of Gender and Ethnicity: The Case of
  Greek-Americans
  ALICE SCOURBY 114
7 Constructing an Ethnic Identity: The Case of the Swedish-
  Americans
  DAG BLANCK 134
8 The Honest War: Communal Religious Life in a Dutch-
  American Protestant Community
  LAWRENCE J. TAYLOR 153

Notes on Contributors 178

Index 179

Acknowledgments

I would like to thank a number of individuals who provided support or advice along the way, including Dag Blanck, Susan Kivisto, Stanford Lyman, Martin Marger, and Kermit Westerberg. The Augustana College Faculty Research Committee provided generous financial assistance to assist with the preparation of the manuscript, and Alice Dailing did an excellent job typing it. The Immigration History Research Center supplied me with a timely Grant-in-Aid to pursue my research on Finns, and the National Endowment for the Humanities, via its Summer Seminar program, afforded me with the opportunity to get to know a number of the scholars who contributed to this volume. Mark Stolarik, at the Balch Institute, also deserves thanks. Finally, Susan, Sarah, and Aaron make it all worthwhile.

The Ethnic Enigma

1

Overview: Thinking about Ethnicity

PETER KIVISTO

Ethnicity in the modern world remains an enduring enigma, and debates, both acrimonious and dispassionate, abound concerning the origins, the present state, and the future of ethnic identity and ethnic communities. Especially if ethnic affiliations are seen, at root, to be essentially ineffable, understanding the form and content of communal bonds generated by what Max Weber (1978, 394–95) referred to as "'ethnically' determined social action" is an extraordinarily complicated and vexing undertaking. Indeed, he was convinced that the problematic character of this was such that in the long run "the collective term 'ethnic' would be abandoned, for," he felt, "it was unsuitable for a really rigorous analysis."

The dilemmas that attend the rigorous analysis called for by Weber are, perhaps, nowhere more evident than in the United States, that nation of nations, that great polyglot, that land presumed to be free from the impediments of traditional society. Indicative of this is the general lack of conceptual clarity informing ethnic theory as it is applied to the American landscape, which is reflected in the recurrent recourse to a wide range of metaphors to depict this ethnic experience, the most prevalent including the melting pot, the transmuting pot, the ethnic mosaic, the tapestry, the symphonic orchestra, and the salad bowl. Despite the wide attention devoted to ethnic groups in American society by social scientists and historians throughout this century (a claim disputed by Cinel 1969 and Vecoli 1970), and despite a veritable flood of work that has been published on the subject in recent years (Vecoli 1979; Ibson 1981), scholars remain uncertain over how to interpret the role of ethnicity in American social history. Thus, in the midst of a dramatic efflorescence of interest in ethnicity within the academic community as a whole, Harold Abramson (1980, 150) could write, in the *Harvard Encyclopedia of American Ethnic Groups*, "we have long been confronted with the major question: what happens to the groups and individuals who make up this diversity? What has hap-

11

pened in the past, and how can we describe what is happening in the present?''

The essays contained herein seek, by providing careful analyses of critical aspects of the life histories of various European-origin groups, to address precisely these questions. They do so with an awareness that the diversity and complexity of American social history makes it difficult to construct theories adequate to the task of interpreting the shifting patterns of ethnic-group affiliation. A consequence of this is that researchers working in this field confront and must come to terms with a number of competing theoretical traditions.

Compounding the difficulties, scholars have had and continue to have a hard time distinguishing and separating intellectual issues from sociopolitical or ideological ones. Thus, earlier in the century, the assimilationist theories espoused by sociologists affiliated with the Chicago School had a rather direct influence on social reform activities, such as the settlement house movement, designed to ease the transition of immigrants into the American mainstream. At the same time, the conviction of Columbia University sociologist Franklin Giddings that "consciousness of kind" was a pervasive and immutable bedrock of group affiliation led, when transmuted into racist ideology, to active involvement in immigration-restriction activities.

The infusing of scholarship with polemics has clearly not ended. In fact, beginning in the 1960s an outpouring of published work challenging the assimilationist thesis began to appear, coinciding with what seemed to be a resurgence of ethnicity among white ethnics. Greeley (1971) and Novak (1972) produced perhaps the most widely noted instances of the new genre of ethnic apologetics, arguing not simply that the melting pot had not occurred (as Glazer and Moynihan suggested in 1963) but that it should not. Not surprisingly, their arguments were challenged with equal verve by those who tended to see contemporary manifestations of ethnic affiliation as essentially anachronistic and/or reactionary. Though their approaches differed, their conclusions were fundamentally similar, whether one looks at the eclectic Marxism of Patterson's (1978) "ethnic chauvinism," Stein and Hill's (1977) vaguely Freudian analysis of the "ethnic imperative," or Steinberg's (1981) muckraking sociology of "the ethnic myth." In a somewhat different vein, Sowell (1981) sought to write a history of ethnic America that is, in effect, a morality play: those groups who have made it in America have done so because they have instilled in themselves and their children the proper virtues that make success possible—a willingness to work hard, to save, to invest in education as a means of upward mobility—while those who have failed have proven themselves to be lacking in such virtuous qualities.

While such writing tends to shed more heat than light on the subject, and it has had an influence on the way people think about ethnicity, an outpouring of high-quality scholarship has, nonetheless, emerged. This scholarship has had the desirable effect of opening up areas of inquiry rather than foreclosing them in the manner that ideological thought does. While adding to knowledge of ethnicity in America, such research has also asked new questions, questions that scholars are, in many instances, only capable of answering tentatively. The best of this work is valuable because of its desire to appreciate the particularities of the ethnic experience while simultaneously seeking to explore the common links among ethnic groups in America. Much of this work has benefited from the advent of the new social history that attempts to fuse historiographic research with the methods and theories of the social sciences. And researchers, in turn, have benefited by efforts to expand the stock of knowledge about ethnicity, whether it be by making use of quantitative data in creative ways in the manner encourage by social historians such as Le Roy Ladurie and Tilly, or by increasingly sophisticated ethnographic research. Benefits have also accrued from the mining of new archival data, and finally, from efforts to clarify and reconstitute the conceptual frameworks that can be used in the study of this enigmatic topic.

It is to this last topic that I briefly turn my attention, for it is my contention that confusion surrounding the theoretical models that are used in the study of ethnicity has contributed significantly to problems in coming to grips with the role of ethnicity in American social life, past and present. Scholars lack even an agreed-upon classification of theory types. This is not the place to rectify this, and as a consequence, what follows should be seen as a sketch of critical issues rather than a presentation of a technical demarcation of various theoretical approaches. For present purposes, I shall distinguish three major theoretical paradigms: the assimilationist, cultural pluralism, and variable ethnicity. They will be reviewed in order to place the essays that follow into a clearer theoretical context.

The origins of the three principle models used in ethnic studies illustrate the role of ideology in shaping orientations regarding ethnicity. The imagery of the melting pot that underpins the assimilationist model derives principally from the 1908 play by the Jewish immigrant playwright Israel Zangwill (Gleason 1964; Mann 1979). The message of his melodrama was explicit and unsubtle: a new harmony was possible in America because to become an American meant to cast off one's past, Old World identity and in the process to destroy the efficacy of divisive social and cultural barriers. In this, he echoes the argument de Crèvecoeur ([1782] 1957, 39) made more than a century earlier, namely, that "individuals of all nations are melted into a new race of men."

When Robert Park attempted to develop the melting pot metaphor into a sociological theory, he did so by severing questions of *is* from those of *ought*, by divorcing facts and values. This was accomplished by contending that the "race relations cycle," a four-stage process culminating in total assimilation, was a sociohistorical law that transcended human consciousness. Like gravity, the inexorable pull of the cycle was thought to make individuals incapable of resistance (Park 1950; Lal 1983; Persons 1987). If this were the case, there would be little point in studying the ways that people sought to make their own histories, albeit in circumstances not of their own choosing, for its sociological determinism promotes an ahistorical mode of inquiry. Such an approach, of course, was part of a larger drift in the social sciences toward severing their connections with history. Social change was treated as depending on forces that operated above the fray of historical contingency. The kind of research agenda encouraged by this orientation focused attention on measuring the degree of assimilation that had been achieved at various points in time, relying on such measures as those obtained from social distance scales (Park 1950; Bogardus 1928), rates of socioeconomic mobility patterns, and rates of exogamous marriages.

While the melting pot, or assimilationist, model has clearly been the hegemonic one in ethnic studies for most of the century, it has never been without a serious challenger: cultural pluralism. Indeed, seven years after Zangwill's play first appeared, Horace Kallen, a philosophy professor at the New School for Social Research, argued in the pages of the *Nation* that in the interest of democracy, assimilation must be resisted. As Fred Matthews (1984, 64) has written, he "coined the phrase 'cultural pluralism' and gave the canonic statement of the case for protecting immigrant cultures as oases of spiritual values." This viewpoint was reinforced two decades after the passage of stringent immigrant-restriction laws by Louis Adamic (1944) in his call for the preservation of "a nation of nations" (cf. Glazer 1953).

What is interesting is that this formulation returned history and human volition to the picture. If Zangwill was describing a superorganic process, Kallen and Adamic were issuing a call to action. Though the issues not infrequently get muddled, the cultural pluralist formulation, variously called "circumstantionalist" (Glazer and Moynihan 1975, 19–20) or "optionalist" (Gleason 1983, 919), is at odds with the primordialist position (e.g., Isaacs's "idols of the tribe" [1974] or van den Berghe's sociobiological approach [1981]), which views ethnicity as an immutable, bedrock given of personal identity and group affiliation.

As John Higham (1982) has suggested, beginning in the 1960s this position started to usurp the dominant assimilationist model, though he tends to exaggerate the lack of support for the melting pot thesis (e.g., Smith 1966). Scholars influenced by the new social history, particularly as it had been shaped by E. P. Thompson and Herbert Gutman, turned to the study of ethnicity as part of a larger interest in writing the histories of heretofore voiceless people. Zunz (1985, 83) points to the role played by the ethnic revival in the 1960s and 1970s in propelling scholars, especially young scholars, into this area. I would add that this was merely part of a larger intellectual attack on the legitimacy of the established social order. Zunz also notes, quite correctly, that this research was inclined to move away from measures of assimilation and mobility, focusing instead on the various strategies adopted by relatively powerless, exploited groups. In such research there was a distinct emphasis placed on the study of unique groups, with one positive consequence being the enhanced appreciation of the diversity and complexity of the ethnic experience in America; however, a pluralist theory divorced from a primordial interpretation of ethnicity did not contain a coherent explanation for change or continuity.

But that, precisely, was the focus of what can be seen as a third model: the thesis articulated in Marcus Lee Hansen's well-known essay "The Problem of the Third Generation Immigrant" (1938). Hansen's argument was presented not to an audience of scholars but to the members of the Augustana Historical Society, a group of Swedish-Americans dedicated to preserving their ethnic heritage. It received a wider reading when Nathan Glazer had it republished, with an introduction by Oscar Handlin, in *Commentary*. Responding to the widespread concern among the immigrant generation that their offspring were rebelling against the ethnic community and its culture, Hansen provided a view of generational change that suggested ethnicity was not consigned to steady erosion due to the process of assimilation. His oft-quoted parsimonious criticism of linear models, "derived from the almost universal phenomenon that what the son wishes to forget the grandson wishes to remember," suggested a view that could recognize the possibility that resurgences of interest in ethnicity—ethnic revivals—were to be expected. He argued, in effect, that ethnicity could wax and wane and wax again, given the proper circumstances. His explanation for the differences between the second and the third generation relied primarily on a psychological interpretation: The second generation is still uncertain about its relationship to the host culture, insecure in its status, and thus prone to compliance with the demands of Americanizers. The third generation, on the other hand, is so secure about its place in America that it can afford to explore its ancestral heritage without concern that manifestations of ethnicity will ipso facto entail a threat to its newly acquired status.

If Hansen is read literally, the overwhelming preponderance of evidence suggests that his thesis is incorrect (Appel 1961; Lazerwitz and Rowitz 1964; Nahirny and Fishman 1962; Abramson 1975). Similarly, his psychological explanation for this "almost universal phenomenon" is less than convincing. But if recognized for what it really is, a metaphorical statement rather than a literal one, it can be read as the first important expression of a viewpoint that treats ethnicity as much more flexible than recognized by either pluralists or assimilationists. Ethnicity is variable. Though Hansen is not always recognized as the source of this perspective, the imprint of his thesis can be seen, to note two rather divergent theoretical statements, in Yancey et al.'s (1976) "emergent ethnicity" thesis, looking, as it does, at social factors that contribute to the "crystallization and development of ethnic solidarity and identification," and in the phenomenological theoretical grounding of Douglass and Lyman's (1976) call for a recognition of the "situationally conditioned" character of ethnic identity. If the former tends toward a form of structural determinism, the latter attempts to recognize social actors as knowledgeable agents who make their own history, and, as such, play an active role in the construction, destruction, and reconstruction of ethnic attachments and identities. What such work has not done adequately to date is to specify the constraints, cultural and structural, on ethnic variability. As ethnicity comes to be seen as entailing a voluntary commitment on the part of the individual, to what extent can one continue to preserve the distinction E. K. Francis (1947) made long ago, when he treated ethnic groups as communities in contradistinction to associations? While this is most evidently a concern in analyzing contemporary manifestations of ethnicity on the part of the third generation and beyond, it is by no means an irrelevant issue for the immigrant generation.

Sifting through the strengths and weaknesses of these three main theoretical currents is problematic enough, and comparative assessments are difficult due to frequently differing foci of attention, methodologies utilized, and data analyzed. The complexity of the situation is compounded, however, by the realization that provocative attempts have been made to synthesize various strands from these theoretical stances rather than treating them as necessarily discrete. Perhaps the most elegant attempt to do so remains Milton Gordon's *Assimilation in American Life* (1964), wherein the author sought to link assimilationist theory with cultural pluralism. A more recent attempt to link perspectives, or at least to overcome some of the blinders imposed by each model, can be seen, from the historian's camp, in Higham's (1975) discussion of "pluralistic integration."

If in the study of ethnicity in America scholars distinguish the social histories of white, European-origin groups from all others, and there is obviously abundant empirical evidence to warrant such a distinction, a number of more delimited issues and concerns emerge (Ibson 1981). Oscar Handlin's *The Uprooted* (1952) codified an interpretation of the migratory experience of the varied waves of European-origin immigrants that dates back to views expressed by de Crèvecoeur about the emergence of the "new man" on the "virgin soil" of the North American continent. Central to this interpretation was the belief that what was entailed in the act of migration was, for better or worse, the thorough deracination of Old World mores and folkways. The jarring nature of the move and the clash of cultures in conflict were seen as destroying the bases of traditional modes of communal organization and values that were heretofore capable of providing a coherent, meaningful world view for ordinary people. If de Crèvecoeur focused on the positive, liberating aspects of this process, Handlin sought to depict the anomic state into which the immigrants were cast. This generation, he (1952, 6) argued, "lived in crisis" due to the alienating consequences of the move and, he suggested, while their offspring were able to establish roots in America, the first generation remained marginalized throughout their lives—in, but not ever fully a part of, the new American culture. Handlin did not emphasize the destructive effects of Americanization campaigns aimed at supressing inherited cultures, though his work dovetails with such an approach.

Instead, he offered a view that the entry of tradition-oriented, conservative, highly religious peasants into the maelstrom of a rapidly industrializing society was so disorienting that the immigrants proved incapable of hanging on to their cultural baggage, it being, in effect, swept overboard in transit. Though not altogether explicit on this point, his work gives the overriding impression that the immigrants were unable to hang on to the culture of their ancestors because it was a culture predicated on persistence, on natural rhythms, and, thus, simply did not resonate with the values of a society given to incessant change and to the dictates of that most unnatural time—industrial time (Thompson 1967; Hareven 1977).

While Handlin's thesis has had a profound impact on immigration history, the general thrust of the argument has not been without critics from an early date. Perhaps the most sustained early critique was that offered by Rudolph Vecoli (1964). He contended that the rather romanticized "ideal typical" portrait created by Handlin is strikingly at odds with the picture of one particular group that figures prominently in the pre-1924 wave of immigration, the Contadini from southern Italy. In stark contrast to Handlin's peasant, the Contadini had a weak sense of communal identity and allegiance, due to the fact that the family made demands for an all-inclusive kind of commitment on the part of its members. The harmony of the *Gemeinschaft* village that Handlin described is undone in Vecoli's account by jealousy, feuds, a code of personal vengeance, and violence. Far from holding sentimental ties to the land, the Contadini considered manual labor to be demeaning. Finally, it was magic, not Christianity, that played a central role in their everyday lives (Vecoli 1964, 404–415). In making these contrasts, Vecoli's point is simple enough: Handlin employed sociological theory in a manner that failed to appreciate the historical specificity of particular groups in particular places. He made one further point: despite the hardships that they endured, and he did not want to minimize Handlin's emphasis on the difficulties they encountered, the Contadini, nonetheless, proved capable of preserving cultural forms and institutional structures derived from Italy (Vecoli 1964, 409–410).

In the more than two decades since this article appeared, during the period when the new social history began to have an impact, the thrust of much of the best work constituted a challenge to Handlin. In the first place, this scholarship adopted Vecoli's stricture to remain sensitive to the particularities of distinct groups. It was hesitant to draw far-reaching conclusions about the immigrant experience in general. If not alway explicitly comparative, such research was often conceived in a manner that made comparisons possible; this was in many respects due to the fusion of historical and social scientific methodolgies. Second, Handlin's emphasis on the deracination of Old World culture has been widely disputed, though not from a perspective that views ethnicity as essentially primordial or immutable. Instead, the new scholarship sees the relationship between the Old World and the New as essentially reciprocal or dialectical, with the immigrants, far from being passive victims, playing an active role in shaping and weaving identities, values, and modes of relatedness. Thus, to cite a few somewhat arbitrarily chosen examples of recent scholarship, Yans-McLaughlin's (1977) excellent study of the Italians in Buffalo contends that the transition to a new environment was much smoother than the Handlin thesis would suggest, and that this was the case largely because these immigrants brought with them a culture that was flexible, that was capable of being adapted to new circumstances. This perspective is also reflected in Gjerde's (1985, 168–201) study of Norwegian migrants to the upper Midwest.

Although the transition "from peasants to farmers" was rapid, he illustates the ability of these immigrants to "learn anew" in order to take advantage of economic opportunities afforded by the American milieu. These assessments are reinforced by Morawska's (1985, 112–156) study of east central Europeans in Johnstown, Pennsylvania, with Morawska emphasizing what she refers to as the "strategies of adaptation" employed by the first generation.

Recently, in an effort to synthesize the thrust of the new social history of American ethnic groups, Bodnar (1985) has written a self-conscious repudiation of Handlin. Indeed, the title of his book, *The Transplanted*, indicates his desire to reformulate the understanding of immigration history. He faults Handlin on a number of empirical and conceptual issues. First, he contends that the societies that the immigrants left were not static, but were undergoing the transition to industrial societies, and thus Handlin's pre-industrial–industrial dichotomy does not hold up. As a consequence, it is misleading to speak about the clash of cultures. Second, immigrants were bound to the present, not the past (Bodnar 1985, 116). They responded not to the vagaries of industrialization but to its specific American form, capitalism. While clearly victimized by an exploitative economic system, they were not mere victims, but active participants capable of sorting out various options available to them. He (1985, 210) writes, "*Mentalite* for the immigrants was an amalgam of past and present, acceptance and resistance." In short, though larger societal forces propelled them to migrate in the first place, and they were unable to usurp the power of capitalist elites, Bodnar (1985, 184, 216) argues that they responded to America on their own terms. "Their lives were not entirely of their own making, but they made sure that they had something to say about it."

In reorienting ethnic social history in a direction that stresses the choices immigrants made, the strategies they employed, the resources they mustered, the ambiguities they felt, the coalitions they formed, and the constraints they encountered, Bodnar's work points toward unresolved questions and issues that need to be part of a research agenda for the future. It also reflects a marked departure from earlier work regarding the manner in which culture is related to social action. While Bodnar is nowhere very explicit on this score, he and like-minded social historians operate with a view of culture shaped by developments in sociology and anthropology, especially by the seminal work of Clifford Geertz. Implicitly this work views culture in a fashion very similar to that recently advanced by Ann Swidler (1986, 273). Treating culture as a "tool kit" of symbols, practices, and world views, this model sees culture not as a direct causal determinant of action but as a resource that has causal significance insofar as it provides "cultural components that are used to construct strategies of action."

This approach has proven particularly popular for studies of the immigrant generation. Nonetheless, to employ Swidler's (1986) terminology, such an approach is not only appropriate for studying the "unsettled lives" of the immigrants but the "settled lives" of their offspring, as well. While such work should not downplay the coercive character of the Americanization campaigns designed to rid the nation of the hyphenated American, scholars need to understand the lure that American mass culture had for ethnics. They need to better understand the precise role of the polity in the process of, to employ Archdeacon's (1983) phrase, "becoming American." How was the prospect of citizenship viewed? Why did American sports, music, and the like often attract the second generation to the detriment of ethnic culture? Why has intermarriage increased with each succeeding generation? Should intermarriage be seen as a rebelling against a restrictive ethnic community and its mores or as an unavoidable consequence of becoming part of the larger American scene? When embracing material values that encouraged the pursuit of upward mobility, were there unintended deleterious consequences of such an individualistic orientation on ethnic communal solidarity?

Related to these questions is the fact that ethnicity competes with other aspects of individual identity. In the words of Georg Simmel (1955), the individual in the modern world is entangled in a "web of group affiliations," each making varied demands for commitment. Part of the ambiguity that has characterized modernity revolves around the strategies utilized to wrestle with the competing demands of these multiple identities. Of particular importance for ethnicity are the competing claims of class, gender, religious, and, perhaps, regional identities. Research has all too frequently tended to avoid exploring the relationship between ethnicity and these other modes of identity, part of what Gutman (1977, p. vii) referred to as the "Balkanizing thrust in the new social history."

Thus, perhaps one of the most urgent tasks confronting scholars is to overcome the fragmentation that is a consequence of the separation of ethnic identity from other variables. Related to this, the agenda for the future must include dealing with another kind of fragmentation, that which results from a focus on the parts of American social history at the expense of analyses of the whole. It would behoove scholars, therefore, to consider Bender's (1986, 135) recent call for work toward a new synthesis in American history, one that is constructed with an appreciation of the "dialectic of center and periphery."

The essays contained in this volume are case studies of various European-origin ethnic groups informed by those currents of thought which see social actors as knowledgeable agents who make their own history, ethnicity as a complex and variable phenomenon, culture as a flexible tool, and ethnicity as a part of the total identity of individuals. The contributors, despite differences in methodological approaches and domain assumptions, share a conviction that research should be conducted in a manner that enhances comparative research. Their essays are not the products of a uniform theoretical model, but are part of what Herbert Gans (1985, 303) has described as an "ongoing paradigmatic change" in ethnic research that begins with the assumption that a new model must be "more situationally sensitive" than those employed in the past.

References

Abramson, H. 1975. "The Religioethnic Factor and the American Experience," *Ethnicity* 2, no. 2.

———. 1980. "Assimilation and Pluralism," In *Harvard Encyclopedia of American Ethnic Groups*, edited by Stephan Thernstrom. Cambridge: Harvard University Press.

Adamic, L. 1944. *A Nation of Nations*. New York: Harper and Brothers.

Appel, J. 1961. "Hansen's Three Generations 'Law' and the Origins of the American Jewish Historical Society." *Jewish Social Studies* 23, no. 1.

Archdeacon, T. 1983. *Becoming American: An Ethnic History*. New York: Basic Books.

Bender, T. 1986. "Wholes and Parts: The Need for Synthesis in American History." *Journal of American History* 73, no. 1 (June).

Bodnar, J. 1985. *The Transplanted: A History of Immigrants in Urban America*. Bloomington: University of Indiana Press.

Bogardus, E. 1928. *Immigration and Race Attitudes*. Boston: D. C. Heath.

Cinel, D. 1969. "Ethnicity: A Neglected Dimension of American History." *International Migration Review* 3 (Summer).

Crèvecoeur, H. de. [1782] 1957. *Letters from an American Farmer*. Reprint. New York: Peter Smith, 1957.

Douglass, W., and S. Lyman. 1976. "L' ethnie: Structure, processus, et saillance." *Cahiers Internationale de Sociologie* 61.

Francis, E. K. 1947. "The Nature of the Ethnic Group." *American Journal of Sociology* 52, no. 5 (March).

Gans, H. 1985. "Ethnicity, Ideology, and the Insider Problem." *Contemporary Sociology* 14, no. 3 (May).

Gjerde, J. 1985. *From Peasants to Farmers: The Migration from Balestrand, Norway to the Upper Middle West*. Cambridge: Cambridge University Press.

Glazer, N. 1953. "American Ethnic Patterns: 'Melting Pot' or 'Nation of Nations'". *Commentary* 15, no. 4.

Glazer, N., and D. P. Moynihan. 1963. *Beyond the Melting Pot*. Cambridge: MIT Press.

————. eds. 1975. *Ethnicity*. Cambridge: Harvard University Press.

Gleason, P. 1964. "The Melting Pot: Symbol of Fusion or Confusion." *American Quarterly* 16, no. 1.

————. 1983. "Identifying Identity: A Semantic History." *Journal of American History* 69, no. 4 (March).

Gordon, M. 1964. *Assimilation in American Life*. New York: Oxford University Press.

Greeley, A. 1971. *Why Can't They Be Like Us?* New York: Dutton.

Gutman, H. 1977. *Work, Culture, and Society in Industrializing America*. New York: Random House.

Handlin, O. 1952. *The Uprooted*. Boston: Little, Brown.

Hansen, M. L. 1938. *The Problem of the Third Generation Immigrant*. Rock Island, Ill.: Augustana Historical Society.

Hareven, T. 1977. "Family Time and Industrial Time." In *Family and Kin in Urban Communities*, edited by Tamara Hareven. New York: New Viewpoints.

Higham, J. 1975. *Send These to Me: Jews and Other Immigrants in Urban America*. New York: Atheneum.

————. 1982. "Current Trends in the Study of Ethnicity in the United States." *Journal of American Ethnic History* 2, no. 2 (Fall).

Ibson, J. 1981. "Virgin Land or Virgin Mary? Studying the Ethnicity of White Americans." *American Quarterly* 33, no. 3.

Isaacs, H. 1974. "Basic Group Identity: The Idols of the Tribe." *Ethnicity* 1, no. 1.

Lal, B. 1983. "Perspectives on Ethnicity: Old Wine in New Bottles." *Ethnic and Racial Studies* 6, no. 2

Lazerwitz, B., and L. Rowitz. 1964. "The Three-Generations Hypothesis." *American Journal of Sociology* 69, no. 5 (March).

Mann, A. 1979. *The One and the Many*. Chicago: University of Chicago Press.

Matthews, F. 1984. "Cultural Pluralism in Context: External History, Philosophic Premise, and Theories of Ethnicity in Modern America." *Journal of Ethnic Studies* 12, no. 2. (Summer).

Morawska, E. 1985. *For Bread with Butter: The Life-Worlds of East Central Europeans in Johnstown, Pennsylvania, 1890–1940*. Cambridge: Cambridge University Press.

Nahirny, V., and J. Fishman. 1962. "American Immigrant Groups: Ethnic Identification and the Problems of Generations." *Sociological Review* 13.

Novak, M. 1972. *The Rise of the Unmeltable Ethnics*. New York: Macmillan.

Park, R. 1950. *Race and Culture*. New York: Free Press.

Patterson, O. 1978. *Ethnic Chauvinism*. New York: Stein and Day.

Persons, S. 1987. *Ethnic Studies at Chicago, 1905–45*. Urbana: University of Illinois Press.

Simmel, G. 1955. *Conflict and the Web of Group-Affiliations*. New York: Free Press.

Smith, T. 1966. "New Approaches to the History of Immigration in Twentieth-Century America." *American Historical Review* 71.

Sowell, T. 1981. *Ethnic America*. New York: Basic Books.

Stein, H., and R. Hill. 1977. *The Ethnic Imperative*. University Park: Pennsylvania State University Press.

Steinberg, S. 1981. *The Ethnic Myth*. New York: Atheneum.

Swildler, A. 1986. "Culture in Action." *American Sociological Review* 51, no. 2 (April).

Thompson, E. P. 1967. "Time, Work-Discipline, and Industrial Capitalism." *Past and Present*, no. 38.

van den Berghe, P. 1981. *The Ethnic Phenomenon*. New York: Elsevier.

Vecoli, R. 1964. "Contadini in Chicago: A Critique of *The Uprooted*." *Journal of American History* 51, no. 3 (December).

————. 1970. "Ethnicity: A Neglected Dimension in American History." In *The State of American History*, edited by Herbert Bass. Chicago: Quadrangle.

————. 1979. "The Resurgence of American Immigration History." *American Studies International*. (Winter).

Weber, M. 1978. *Economy and Society*. 2 vols. Berkeley and Los Angeles: University of California.

Yancey, W., et al. 1976. "Emergent Ethnicity: A Review and Reformulation." *American Sociological Review* 41, no. 3.

Yans-McLaughlin, V. 1977. *Family and Community: Italian Immigrants in Buffalo*. Ithaca: Cornell University Press.

Zunz, O. 1985. "The Synthesis of Social Change: Reflections on American Social History." In *Reliving the Past: The Worlds of Social History*, edited by Olivier Zunz. Chapel Hill: University of North Carolina Press.

2

In a New Light: Italian-American Ethnicity in the Mainstream

DONALD TRICARICO

Italian-Americans are now well into a third generation, as more than three-fourths of the ethnic community born after World War II belong to a third or later generation (Alba 1985, 113). Since the period of mass immigration, there has been a steady climb up the economic ladder; the group has surpassed the national average for Protestants of British descent and whites in real family income (Greeley 1976; Alba 1985, 117–129). Younger members of this group are near the national average in levels of educational attainment (Alba 1981). A recent study of Italian-Americans in Bridgeport, Connecticut, shows that the third generation is well established in managerial, administrative, technical, and professional jobs (Crispino 1980).

These trends are accompanied by increasing integration within the society and culture. The old enclaves have either disappeared or are left with only a sprinkling of longtime residents (Tricarico 1984). Italian-Americans have abandoned the tenement neighborhoods for home ownership and the suburbs. They are, for example, the largest single ethnic group in the suburbs of New York City (*New York Times*, 14 November 1978). Younger generations, in particular, have adopted mainstream lifestyles and values (Fandetti and Gelfand 1983; Crispino 1980). They are also marrying outside the group. Indeed, as many as two-thirds are choosing a spouse who is not Italian-American (Alba 1985, 153–154).

It is by no means clear, however, what these developments mean for the future of Italian-American ethnicity. Using national survey data, Alba (1985) sees little ethnic distinctiveness among younger, third-generation Italian-Americans. He emphasizes a weakened identification with the group, the erosion of traditional cultural values, and the high rates of intermarriage as evidence of a "twilight" of ethnicity. The situation is seen as a classic case of "straight-line" assimilation. In the view of straight-line theory, the dominant sociological paradigm in the study of European-stock groups, "mean levels of ethnicity . . . tend to decline over generations" (Sandberg 1974, 68). The decline of ethnicity is construed as "deeply rooted in the structure of American society" (Steinberg 1981, 73). Furthermore, upward mobility is seen as predicated on acculturation and assimilation (Steinberg 1981, 257). It is assumed that by the time individuals reach the middle class, "in the second but mostly in the third generation" (Crispino 1980, 9), ethnicity has little relevance to identity, values, and group life.

It is clear that the Old World culture of transplanted *paesani* has not been handed down whole to subsequent generations. The above-expressed views, however, do not appreciate the fact that specific ethnic traits may be found alongside, and in combination with, core cultural elements, both being frequently modified in the process (there may or may not be a consciousness, on the part of Italian-Americans or significant others, of ethnic influences). This lived culture should be distinguished from the readily identifiable ethnic "heritage" (Greeley 1976, 310), although of course the latter is also subject to revision by later generations. While third-generation Italian-Americans are clearly more integrated within American life, it may be premature to write off Italian-American ethnicity. Indeed, as the following pages will suggest, it is possible to discern a "new" Italian-American ethnicity that is fitted to mainstream, middle-class circumstances in which being Italian-American is situational and congruent with higher socioeconomic status. In contrast with straight-line theory, which measures ethnicity in terms of adherence to traditional peasant cultures, ethnic groups should be seen as capable of altering boundaries and identity frameworks, cultural styles, and forms of expression (Barth 1969; DeVos 1975; Greeley 1976; Nagata 1981; Royce 1982). Moreover, American society may allow more room for ethnicity (although not the Old World version) than straight-line theory allows.

There has been relatively little research on Italian-Americans beyond the first and second generations and in settings outside the urban village. In his study of Italian-Americans in Bridgeport, Connecticut, Crispino (1980, 164) does acknowledge "the changing face of ethnicity" in later generations moving into the middle class. But this is given only passing consideration because it is regarded as "at most a detour on the road to complete assimilation."

Whatever lies down the road, ethnic factors are part of the *present* landscape. In the mainstream, however, ethnicity should not be expected to be lived "24 hours a day" (Sollors 1981) and, in particular, should not be viewed as entailing the cultural "world of our fathers." Ethnicity is *one* of the variables that affect identity, behavior, and group life, being a "matter of degree" (Cohen 1981) and "situational" (Etzioni 1959). In addition, there may be changes in the dimensions or manifestations of ethnicity (identity frameworks, forms of expression, cultural referents, and the like). In a complex, modern society, "ethnic identity is one of the many identities available to people" (Royce 1982, 1; Nielsen 1985, 137–38). For mainstream Italian-Americans, then, ethnicity is one layer of a "segmented self" (Tuan 1982). It may be consciously "developed, displayed, manipulated or ignored in accordance with the demands of particular situations" (Royce 1982, 1).

American sociology has historically viewed the experience of European immigrant groups from the related standpoints of assimilation and disorganization (Park 1950; Thomas and Znaniecki 1927). The gradual acquisition of American cultural patterns has been seen as undermining identification with the ethnic group and traditional ethnic institutions. Campisi's (1948) study of the "Italian family" emphasized the "incessant hammering" of American culture on core ethnic values. In her study of Greenwich Village in the 1920s, Ware (1965, 163–178) maintained that "American ways" had left the Italian community without traditions and "socially disorganized." Assimilation models, however, have paid little attention to the persistence and transformation of ethnicity and ethnic patterns.

In the case of Italians, there have been fundamental changes from the outset—in identity boundaries, institutional frameworks, and cultural content. These changes occurred as Italians absorbed the wider culture and became more integrated within the larger society. Immigrants from Italy came as *paesani*—not as Italians, but as townsmen as well as the inhabitants of a province or region (these origins gave overlapping identities). In the second generation, *paesani* identification gave way to a more inclusive concept of ethnicity based on nationality. It was sublimated as an intragroup distinction in the face of common acculturation experiences (melting dialects and customs) and sharper differences and conflict vis-à-vis members of other nationalities who lumped "Italians" together.

A restructured community reflected the capacity to absorb change in the second generation. Second-generation Italians were more Americanized: they substituted English for peasant dialects, formed social and athletic clubs, and became proficient in machine politics. Still, ethnicity and ethnic culture provided a major basis for their adaptation, combining with urban, working-class institutions (e.g., street-corner cliques, a defended neighborhood, crime syndicates, district political clubs). Americanizing influences, and the urban context in general, reshaped ethnic identity and institutions in the second generation, sublimating *paesani* distinctions and throwing into relief a common ethnic background and social situation.

Mainstream Frameworks for Group Identity

As part of a widespread ethnic phenomenon, Italian-Americans collectively mobilized beginning in the late 1960s (Novak 1972; Weed 1971; Glazer and Moynihan 1975; Nielsen 1985; Taylor 1979). They protested what was perceived as the continued denigration of the group in the larger society, especially in the mass media. Like other "white ethnics," Italian-Americans were responding to ethnic mobilization among blacks and other minorities as precedent and provocation. This response frequently informed a political strategy that reflected racial and class issues (Shostak 1973; Barbaro 1974). The "new pluralism" gave ethnic spokespersons an ideological framework and legitimacy (Nielsen 1985; Novak 1973; Stein and Hill 1977). While working-class "resentment" and status anxiety may have been involved, an expanding Italian-American middle class was a factor as well. The latter possessed the social resources to oppose bias and celebrate the heritage. Moreover, mobility and mainstream contacts may have made this group more sensitive to certain ethnic issues.

One of the more distinctive developments associated with the "new pluralism" was the attempt to articulate ethnic-group identity in positive terms (Novak 1973). For Italian-Americans, ethnicity was framed by a "backward" peasant culture and experiences in the new society (e.g., immigrant slums, proletarian occupations) that imparted "low prestige associations" (Child 1943). Following the examples of blacks and other minority groups, new conceptualizations of Italian-American ethnicity were advanced that included affirmation of the group, its ethnic "essence," and its heritage.

The family continued to be the primary way to express group identity (as with other aspects of traditional ethnic culture, ethnic family patterns came into conflict with the "core" culture and were specifically selected for reform by social workers, Protestant missions, and the public schools). Idealized family traditions rooted in the "old country" (Gambino's "l'ordine della famiglia") were submitted as the "soul" (DeVos 1975, 15) and "symbolic estate" (Lyman and Douglass 1973, 346) of Italian-American peoplehood. Above all, Italian-Americans were a "family people." Indeed, symbolic appropriation of the family is used to establish the legitimacy of Italian-American organizations.

The idea of the family as the center of Italian-American ethnicity is also intended for significant others. The Italian emphasis on family, especially in its peasant and immigrant manifestations (there is a concern, expressed within the group, that mainstream ethnic families have compromised many family traditions), is seen as an antidote to modern anomie (Covello 1967; Gambino 1974; Tomasi 1973). To this extent, "l'ordine della famiglia" may be the ethnic version of the "new conservatism" as a response to "the abandonment of values in modern society" (Hughey 1981).

Straight-line theory understands European ethnicity in terms of an attachment to the Old World, peasant culture (cf. Halle 1984, 270–71). Movement into the cultural mainstream and up the class ladder thus requires that ethnicity be "sacrificed" (Steinberg 1981, 257; Sandberg 1974, 74). Ethnicity, then, is for immigrants and, to a lesser extent, the working class in subsequent generations (see Enloe 1973; Sollors 1981). Straight-line theory has little appreciation, in particular, for the role of ethnicity and ethnic culture in facilitating upward mobility (Greeley 1976). It has also overlooked or downplayed the possibility that ethnicity can be meaningfully integrated within the mainstream and the middle class. The new Italian-American ethnicity, however, is situated within this society and in the context of mainstream values.

Italian-American ethnicity is also being reconciled with higher social standing. Straight-line theory tends to dismiss this as "fictional" and "dishonest," more "image making" (Aversa 1978, 51–54). In fact, Steinberg (1981, 62–63) sees a "crisis of authenticity" in a "new" ethnicity "tailored to middle class patterns" because it is "culturally thin." Ethnic groups typically re-create their cultural base (Barth 1969; Royce 1982), often engaging in "fictitious accounts" (Shibutani and Kwan 1965, 43) and "collective impression management" (Lyman and Douglass 1973). Refurbishing ethnic identity and style is not uncommon for ethnic groups that have improved their position in the social structure (Shibutani and Kwan 1965, 510–11; Horowitz 1975, 105; Lyman and Douglass 1973).

Although it is not rooted in the "actual and immediate background circumstances of Italian-Americans" (Aversa 1978, 51), "high" Italian culture is particularly appropriate as a framework for ethnic identity and style in the middle class. Appreciation of the arts, previously the property of a small elite within the Italian colony, has become more widespread through higher levels of education and affluence. Casa Italiana at Columbia University and the Institute of Italian Culture in New York City serve as repositories of high Italian culture for refined ethnic sensibilities. At the same time, the peasant and immigrant experiences may be appropriated as folk art, as with marionette theater and writers like Pietro DiDonato, or through historical scholarship. A firsthand connection with this heritage may be consummated by tourism; while there may be side trips to the family *paese*, the main itinerary is typically Rome, Florence, and Milan.

This middle-class version of Italian-American ethnicity is reflected in the glossy, coffee-table magazine *Attenzione*. Published since 1979, it proposes to "make hundreds of thousands of Italian-Americans prouder than ever of their heritage." It has special appeal, however, among the more affluent. Subscribers in 1980 had a median household income of $37,500; 80 percent owned their own homes. This profile invariably bears a relationship to the way ethnicity is presented. The entire publishing effort would seem to be based on an assumption that there is a demand for ethnicity among upwardly mobile Italian-Americans.

Attenzione gives higher-status Italian-Americans Renaissance art treasures, in four-color photographic layouts, and Carlo Levi's "Mezzogiorno" revisited. It also brings the "old country" into the present with a portrayal of a modern Italy of state-of-the-art automotive technology, fashion and home design, World Cup soccer, and ski resorts. There is a major focus on Italian food, which is not only a way to "keep the heritage" but, when raised to gourmet status, is evidence of a middle-class style as well. *Attenzione* provides a platform for attacking "negative" stereotypes, like the "Mafia myth" or the "Italian mama," which have to be cleared away if new ethnic images are to take hold. Finally, it shows Italian-Americans who have "made it" in terms of the dominant values of this society while staying ethnic in the process.

Attenzione may be viewed as middle-class advice literature. As such, it is a guide to consumption patterns as well as ethnic expression, instructing *arriviste* Italian-Americans in discretionary spending and leisure styles. Materialistic values reflected in advertisements for sumptuous ocean cruises, Alfa Romeo sports cars, and designer fashions constitute a break with the economy of scarcity that informed peasant and immigrant life. While the second generation has a reputation for "conspicuous consumption," *Attenzione* offers a "window into" consumer styles guided by middle- and upper-middle-class standards of taste. For the coffee-table set, affluence and leisure can be put in the service of ethnicity. There are parallels between *Attenzione* and *Ebony*, which has helped to bring ethnicity into the black middle class. There is also a similarity to *Southern Living*, which targets the "new middle class" in the "old South" (Reed 1982, 119).

Ethnic identity is "an interplay of the self-definition of members and the definition of other groups" (Horowitz 1975, 113). At the present time, there is evidence that Italian-Americans and the group's cultural referents are more favorably viewed by significant others. There has long been appreciation of high Italian culture among the elite. People of sophisticated taste have also expressed preferences for modern Italian design in clothing and home furnishings. Northern Italian cuisine is regarded as first-rate gourmet fare and served in "upscale" restaurants. More recently, humbler dietary items, previously symbols of poverty and cultural inferiority, have been reevaluated. It was a little-noticed event when the *New York Times* food critic announced that pasta was "in high fashion" (*New York Times*, 10 March 1982), although recipes for peasant dishes like "escarole with garlic" and "pasta e faggioli" are now frequently found in the paper's Living section.

Italian-Americans may be in a position to benefit from the positive evaluation of their heritage, although the larger society may be able to separate its feeling for one from its regard for the other and appropriate the heritage exclusive of Italian-Americans. The demand for elements of the Italian heritage among significant others also serves to keep it in focus for Italian-Americans; the new prestige may elict a greater attachment. While these developments indicate the assimilation of ethnic cultural items within the core culture, Italian-Americans may nevertheless claim a special, more authentic relationship.

At the same time, a new view of Italian-Americans is in evidence. The mass media have taken note of the group's mobility; and this should further improve the perception of its heritage. Significant middle-class others have expressed their approval of the Italian-American experience. The urban Italian neighborhood has attracted professionals, students, and artists as "a nice place to live" (Harris 1977). These areas are seen as embodying a sense of community and other traditional values that are in short supply, although gentrification and a rise in real estate values hasten their eclipse (Tricarico 1984). While none of this will keep Italian-Americans from moving to the suburbs, it may nevertheless have implications for an ethnic self-concept.

ETHNIC INTERESTS

Ethnicity entails feelings of attachment that are "elementary" (Francis 1947) and even "ineffable" (Lyman and Douglass 1973). But "primordial" considerations and the cultural referents that serve as the "epitome" of a group's "peoplehood" (Schermerhorn 1970,

12) may be harnessed for the rational, or purposive, pursuit of ends within segmental, "associative" relationships (Cohen 1981). Italian-American ethnicity still has significance on the level of "strategy" (Royce 1982) in the mainstream. In fact, there have been new developments in recent years.

Since the late 1960s, Italian-Americans have employed new ethnic strategies, perhaps the most notable being the appropriation of ideological themes identified with the "new pluralism"—the legitimacy and virtue of ethnicity as a communal and political strategy in post–melting pot America (Novak 1973; Weed 1971). With the eclipse of more traditional, *gemeinschaft* solidarities, ethnic strategy took on a more formal and associative character. There were a number of reasons for this shift. A principal one was the desire to obtain resources allocated by the welfare state to other organized groups, in particular, ethnic minorities. As traditional strategies waned, an emerging Italian-American stratum of activists and intelligentsia, armed with a pluralist ideology, raised ethnic issues within a new political agenda (cf. Nielsen 1985). Although regarded as an irrational "revival" in some quarters (Stein and Hill 1977), it may be better understood as signaling a new direction in the use of ethnicity as a strategy for realizing individual and group interests (Royce 1982; Glazer and Moynihan 1975).

Initial manifestations could be seen in community organizations that sought to preserve the residential and ethnic character of neighborhoods settled during the period of mass immigration (Vecoli 1985; Weed 1971). In New York City, the Congress of Italian-American Organizations (CIAO) pursued a share of federal community development funds. A CIAO report (1975) argued that there was a disadvantaged population in Italian-American areas of the city that had long been neglected by policy makers. Since "the melting pot never melted," Italian-Americans had to take care of their own. By 1978, the CIAO was administering $3 million a year in federal, state, and local antipoverty funds, primarily for senior citizens centers in Italian-American neighborhoods (*New York Times*, 5 July 1978). With the CIAO, Italian-Americans achieved an effective bureaucratic strategy, moving beyond the personal, "backroom" style of machine politics.

During the same time frame, the Little Italy Restoration Association (LIRA) was established in the Mulberry Street Italian neighborhood on the lower East Side. A "community development agency," LIRA sought to keep Italians in the area and attract those who had moved away; the latter's mobility and the expansion of Chinatown were seriously threatening the Italian character of the neighborhood. Backed by local ethnic business interests, LIRA prevailed upon the

New York City Planning Commission to issue proposals for the "risorgimento," or restoration, of the neighborhood, which was now officially designated "Little Italy" and accorded "special district" and "historic landmark" status. The risorgimento plan featured the construction of moderate-income housing, the upgrading of existing buildings, the expansion the community services, and street improvement. The city's planning professionals sought to enhance traditional Italian urban patterns like the *passegiatta*—an intensive use of the street, or "pedestrianization." An Italian-American Cultural Center was also proposed.

LIRA spawned similar efforts in other Italian-American neighborhoods. In Greenwich Village, young Italian-Americans formed a community organization that they proposed to call "Avanti" (Forward); they began referring to their neighborhood as "Little Italy West." A storefront was rented where staff members offered their services as mediators between residents and the complex urban services bureaucracies. In reference to developments in these neighborhoods, an Italian-American civic leader from Greenwich Village proclaimed in a LIRA pamphlet "a new feeling of togetherness that we must take advantage of in order to reaffirm in our minds and in the minds of others our unique identity as Italian-Americans." The "new pluralism" was revising the ambivalent, taken-for-granted ethnicity of the urban village.

Ultimately, a strategy based on preservation of the Italian neighborhood was undermined by the desire of Italian-Americans for more mainstream settings, including home ownership and the suburbs. To this extent, these efforts represent the last defense of enclave ethnicity (although not ethnicity as such) against the "forces" of assimilation and mobility. The fiscal crisis of cities like New York and the "new federalism" were also factors, depriving community development proposals of necessary funding. Thus, "Little Italy" has now effectively been absorbed by Chinatown, and the Italian Village, by the SoHo artists' community. But the restaurant economy has been revived and largely sustains the neighborhood as "a symbol of Italian life in New York City." Under the circumstances, Italian-Americans have apparently settled for a commercialized and symbolic "Little Italy."

In any event, preserving the Italian neighborhood and programs for "problem" constituencies like the elderly have not been the focus of ethnic "social action" (Keyes 1981) since the late 1970s. New interests have been articulated by groups that seek greater inclusion within mainstream institutions. Their organizations reflect more segmented, functionally specialized concerns, in contrast with "community" organizations, that transcend particular locales and may be national in scope. Indeed, the values, interests, and social organization in question are distinctly middle class.

The issue that has taken center stage is higher education. The National Italian-American Foundation (NIAF) regards education as the single most significant issue in its program and has established scholarships for Italian-American students and membership organizations. On the other hand, there is no mention of Italian-American communities or social services in its 1984 End of the Year Report. In New York City in 1978, a grant from the state funded the Italian-American Institute to Foster Higher Education. The institute, which has since affiliated itself with the City University (CUNY), provides educational services to an Italian-American student population that is seen as having distinctive ethnic cultural needs that have been ignored, and that continues to be stereotyped as anti-education and anti-intellectual.

Efforts on behalf of Italian-American students in New York City were actually an outgrowth of pressure by Italian-American educators and politicans to remedy the "slow and disproportionate" progress of Italian-Americans at the City University, a situation that was being worsened by the fact that "members of emerging ethnic groups are hired and promoted more rapidly than members of this older ethnic group." A report by the Association of Italian-American Faculty called for more Italian-American representation in faculty, administrative, and staff positions. Charges of "*de facto* discrimination" resulted in the granting of affirmative action status to Italian-Americans in the CUNY hiring process alongside racial minorities and women.

The CUNY case is perhaps evidence of an emerging stratum of Italian-American professionals who use ethnicity or ethnic issues to advance mainstream career interests. The Italian-American Historical Association provides a platform for scholars whose research may not be accorded equal distinction by mainstream professional societies. The National Organization of Italian-American Women (NOIAW) was founded in 1980 as a support system for Italian-American women in the professions and business; the organization specifically takes issue with media stereotypes of Italian American women (e.g., as submissive "mamas"), while looking to retain aspects of traditional roles as wives, mothers, and daughters. In 1984, the Italian-American Bar Association was established to serve as "a conduit of information for Italian-American lawyers nationwide" and generally "support an increase of Italian-Americans in the legal and political professions" (*Attenzione*, July/August 1984). The NIAF now compiles a data base of Italian-Americans in numerous fields and professions to facilitate "a formal networking of Americans of Italian heritage . . . for mutual benefit" (National Italian-American Foundation 1985).

For certain Italian-American professionals, then, ethnicity may be useful for gaining access to or consolidating status within various fields. Yancey et al. (1976) and Taylor (1979) point out that common occupational experiences can heighten the consciousness of ethnicity. Thus, fellow ethnics may also provide cultural and psychological support in uncharted territory. Ethnicity, however, is by no means an important resource for all occupational groups (di Leonardo 1984). Even when it is used, it has to be handled judiciously to avoid ethnic typing (i.e., submerging professional identities) and ethnic "mobility traps."

ETHNIC PERSISTENCE

Everywhere straight-line theory looks, it sees ethnic decline. The "loss of ethnic holding power" (Sandberg 1974, 74) is felt to be especially telling by the third generation and entry into the middle class (Crispino 1980, 9), although ethnicity tends to be accorded a "secondary importance" vis-à-vis social class among blue-collar workers (Halle 1984, 270; Gans 1962). Consequently, recent ethnic developments are dismissed as a "dying gasp" (Steinberg 1981, 51) or relegated to the "margins" (Alba 1985).

Contrary to straight-line theory, there are numerous factors that keep ethnicity from "fading" into insignificance for Italian-Americans:

1. Italian-Americans are still close to the immigrant experience, as 60 percent are members of the first and second generations (Alba 1985, 113). For the third generation, this means that one's family, if not one's self, is likely to be seen in ethnic terms, and a "lived" connection to ethnic culture persists even if this is mediated by second-generation parents. In the historic centers of Italian immigration, the concentration of Italian-Americans, the arrival of new immigrants, and the formation of new Italian neighborhoods furnish a demographic base for ethnicity. In these areas, ethnicity is a major social and ecological category. Individuals, including public figures, are to some extent ethnic actors, in part because significant others apply ethnic labels and appropriate ethnic symbols. The "new pluralism" amplified the importance of ethnicity throughout the society; it coincided with the maturity of a more assimilated and middle-class third generation that was "returning" to ethnicity, but only by embracing aspects of it in new ways.

2. Although there is a convergence of certain mainstream values and behaviors, this does not preclude the retention of ethnic patterns alongside or intertwined with the former. Thus, young, college-educated Italian-American women hold "an Old World view of the importance of maintaining ties with parents and in-laws while vigorously asserting the modern view of women" (Greeley 1976, 230). There may also be New World cultural contents that can preserve ethnic boundaries (Barth 1969). For example, urban Italian-Americans have been defined in terms of safe neighborhoods, well-kept homes, and, among males, a tough physical style (a major reason for the safe neighborhoods).

It should not be surprising that ethnic cultural traits show up in later generations. Like other cultural elements, they are transmitted by the family as part of the socialization of the young (Greeley 1976). Moreover, this may occur without a conscious connection to ethnicity and the ethnic heritage (Fandetti and Gelfand 1983, 112), although certain biographical events and wider social occurrences may activate ethnic consciousness. Behavioral and attitudinal traits should be seen not only in relation to an "English ancestry group" but in comparison with other ethnic groups. Greeley (1976) has pointed out widely differing tendencies for Irish and Italian Americans with regard to sex roles and political participation. Since the Irish and Italians have historically been reference groups for one another, this may be a more meaningful comparison (Vecoli 1969; Bayor 1978; Tricarico 1986).

Aside from actual differences in values and behavior, if people consider certain traits ethnic, then perhaps they are. These beliefs are formulated by ethnics for other group members as well as for outside consumption (Lyman and Douglass 1973). Outsiders formulate their own generalizations about ethnic characteristics, which may be quite at odds with empirical evidence, as with the tendency to exaggerate the solidarity of the Italian-American neighborhood (Harris 1977).

3. Ethnicity continues to be important because it is "in the family." Ethnic identity and culture are passed along by the family and frame the individual's relationship to the group and its members. Ethnicity is a medium for family interaction; family traditions are often ethnic traditions, and family events often reflect ethnic themes and generate ethnic feeling. Just as ethnicity provides a framework for experiencing the family, the family is the "emotional ground" (Douglass 1984) of Italian-American ethnicity. Its ethnic significance is not diluted by some extrafamilial, overarching institution, such as the Catholic church for Irish-Americans, whose ethnicity frequently has a significant religious dimension.

Rising rates of intermarriage may be expected to blur the family's connection to ethnicity and ethnic culture. Indeed, Alba (1985, 155) sees intermarriage as the major factor in the fading of ethnicity among Italian-Americans and other European immigrant groups (see also Gordon 1964). But the effects of intermarriage may not be as harsh as predicted. Alba (1985, 154) sees intermarriage submerging Italian-American ethnicity "since Italian-Americans represent a minority culture." This may not apply, however, if Italian-Americans do not marry WASPs (the "majority culture") but other ethnics. It may not apply in the case of WASPs, either, if being Italian-American constitutes a preferred and appropriate identity. Ethnic groups are not always minority groups. If Italians marry Irish-Americans, for example, their children may identify as "Italian-Irish." It is possible to belong to more than one ethnic group, just as one belongs to more than one kinship group (Keyes 1981, 6; Light 1981). The result would likely be a further compartmentalization of ethnicity. It is also possible for one ethnic identity and background to prevail over another.

The sparse research on Italian-Americans who marry outside the ethnic group indicates that ethnic influences are not unimportant. A Syracuse study (Johnson 1982) has reported that while "contact with relatives" was less than for homogeneous couples, it was greater than kinship interaction among Protestants; intermarrieds also saw more of Italian, compared with non-Italian, relatives. Italian-American men in a Maryland suburb, three-fourths of whom were married to non-Italians, stressed the importance of transmitting a sense of ethnic identity and an appreciation for the ethnic heritage to their children (Fandetti and Gelfand 1983).

4. Ethnicity has importance for the individual in modern society as a source of personal identity. It can satisfy the primordial needs of Italian-Americans who are not yet "emotionally grounded" in an "American ethnicity." With the eclipse of other symbolic universes, ethnic traditions and "feeling" can "break up the ordinariness of everyday life" (Goethals 1981, 128). As "one of the givens" (Keyes 1981, 5), ethnic identity is less uncertain than identities based on achievement (e.g., occupation or "fitness").

At the same time, mainstream Italian-Americans can have ethnicity "on demand." "Situational" ethnicity may be the only kind possible in the mainstream and, perhaps, the only kind the larger society will allow. Situational ethnicity may be likened to "mainline religion," which is less demanding and exclusive than the "new" conservative religious faiths (Marty 1985, 11–23; Roof and McKinney 1985). It is relevant for particular times and places, such as at family weddings or the meeting of an Italian-American organization. These gatherings furnish "backstage" opportunities for "ethnic signalling" and the cultivation of "cultural literacy" (Royce 1982, 187). Ethnicity may even be approached as a "cultural scene" (Irwin 1977) or a "lifestyle enclave" (Bellah et al. 1985) in which ethnic symbols are employed in the service of "expressive individualism." At this level, ethnicity is self-conscious and subjective (Tuan 1982, 35–36) and, perhaps, inauthentic in some respects; to this extent, ethnicity is affected by the general decline of traditional values and the self-conscious construction of identities and lifestyles, in some cases "known to be artificial," that are distinctive features of American society (Bensman and Vidich 1971, 122). Again, there is a parallel with "mainline," or institutional, religion in a modern "pluralistic" society, which "becomes a highly individualized, privatized matter" (Roof and McKinney 1985, 33).

Still, an identity based on ethnicity would seem to push the individual beyond situational concerns. A focus on ancestry and heritage also makes the ethnic group a "community of memory," a people "constituted by their past" (Bellah et al. 1985, 153). Without the "ancient hills of Abruzze" and Renaissance art treasures, *Attenzione* is just another lifestyle magazine (like *GQ*, the magazine for "today's man" in a "new world"). Ethnicity can furnish a primordial reference for the expressive self.

In the 1920s, Ware (1965, 168) observed that the affluent (and "Americanized") sought to "avoid being identified as Italians," a concern that was reflected in a desire to move to "a non-Italian" community. Presently, however, "new" identity frameworks may be more acceptable to middle-class Italian-Americans or, at least, not pose any major status dilemmas. Of course, earlier forms of identity and stereotypes have not been displaced, leaving some risks and trouble spots. This may explain why the second generation is more ambivalent than the third.

5. Differentials in wealth and income, occupational status, and educational attainment typically reinforce differences between ethnic groups. Thus, as Italian-Americans gain parity with "core Americans," an important basis for ethnic distinctions is weakened or removed (Alba 1985, 117–29). Italian-Americans and other European immigrant groups have made great strides in socioeconomic status. Still, "third generation ethnic populations" are not "indistinguishable from the core English group with regard to education, occupation, or per capita income" (Neidert and Farley 1985, 849). As a group, Italian-Americans are comparable to core Americans in income, although this does not mean that they are comparable at higher income levels. Sowell (1981, 120) points out, in addition, that Italian-Americans live in disproportionate numbers in cities where higher

incomes *and* higher living costs are common. Although younger members of the group are moving into managerial and professional occupations in increasing numbers, those born after 1945 still lag behind core Americans in occupational prestige (Alba 1985, 126; Neidert and Farley 1985, 846). Moreover, Italian-Americans lack visibility in the corporate elite (Alba and Moore 1982), notwithstanding Lee Iacocca, while remaining visible in low-prestige, blue-collar areas like sanitation and construction labor (although union workers in these fields are able to maintain a lower-middle-class standard of living). The mass media still largely project an image of Italian-Americans in "lunch-pail" jobs.

Although Italian-American men are now comparable to the English ancestry group in median years of school attended (Neidert and Farley 1985, 846), they are apparently not as successful in converting their education into prestigious jobs (Greeley 1976). This may be attributed to less-favored access to "recruitment networks" as a result of less-privileged circumstances (Alba and Moore 1982, 382). In particular, Italian-Americans are less likely to be found in the elite private colleges and professional schools (Martorella 1983). Discrimination may also be a factor (Italian-American Faculty Association of CUNY 1974). The greater disparities in educational and occupational attainments between women of English ancestry and Italian-American women (Alba 1985, 126) suggest that ethnic cultural considerations may also play a role (Greeley 1976).

Parity with the English ancestry group need not erase ethnic distinctiveness. Meaningful ethnic distinctions may be maintained relative to other ethnic groups. In New York City, for example, Italian-Americans may be more sensitive to the relative social standing of Irish and Jewish Americans on the one hand, and blacks and Puerto Ricans on the other (Bayor 1978). Notwithstanding statistical parity with an abstract WASP group, a sense of group position may be maintained within local and national arenas where scarce resources are being contested.

6. Ecological factors are also relevant for the persistence of ethnicity (Breton 1964). The size and density of the Italian-American population affects the salience of group identity and the viability of ethnic networks, including the likelihood of ethnic endogamy and the formation of ethnic organizations. Italian-American ethnicity has been institutionalized in the areas of mass Italian settlement like New York, Chicago, Boston, and Philadelphia (Gans 1962). In the case of New York, which was not atypical, although the Italian colonies in Manhattan withered, second settlements emerged in the outlying boroughs and the suburbs, residential areas that are predominantly

Italian-American and identified as such (the Bath Beach section of Brooklyn; Lodi, New Jersey; Howard Beach, Queens). It is even possible to discern third settlements, as with the influx of Italian-Americans into more suburban areas of Staten Island with the opening of the Verrazano Bridge in the 1960s (this was noted in the name given to the bridge on the CB radio: the "Guinea Gangplank"). At the same time, recent Italian immigrants have created thriving Italian communities in the boroughs, such as in the Bensonhurst section of Brooklyn, that can perhaps regenerate the ethnicity of Italian-Americans.

Italian-American ethnicity may not fade all that readily in a place like New York City where 18 percent of the population may be Italian-American (Italian-American Faculty Association of CUNY 1974) and there are other sizable ethnic blocs. The size and density of the Italian-American population sustains an institutional life that can support numerous and varied ethnic experiences.

7. Although Italian-Americans have been integrated into mainstream American life, the larger society continues to create situations that sustain and elicit manifestations of Italian-American ethnicity. Although systematic, blatant forms of prejudice and discrimination belong to the period before World War II (kept alive in collective memories and vented in the assertiveness of a decade ago), the historic pattern of denigration reserved for most immigrant groups is still evident. It is reflected in negative media stereotypes, ethnic jokes, and off-color remarks.

The media's keen interest in the "Mafia" fuels the notion that organized crime is exclusively an Italian-American product, evoking the most strenuous antidefamation efforts. Apart from media treatment and stereotypes, however, Italian-American crime syndicates create problems for organizations promoting Italian-American ethnicity. In fact, it is the most problematic issue for "collective impression management" (Lyman and Douglass 1973). One response is to deny it by defining it as a "media" problem. Referring to Mafia stereotypes "inflicted on himself and other Italian-Americans," Mario Cuomo most recently took the issue of bigotry against the group to a national level (*New York Times*, 17 December 1985). Cuomo pointed out that "Mafia" was "an Italian word and every time you say it, you suggest to people that organized crime is Italian." Cuomo's ethnic problem, however, raised a broader issue about the salience of Italian-American ethnicity in the larger society. This was evident in the assertion of a Democratic National Committee member from the Deep South, in response to a possible Cuomo bid for the Democratic presidential nomination in 1988, that "between Richmond and Houston, there are no Cuomos and damn few Marios" (*New York Times*, 19 January 1986). Cuomo complained that this reflected the general tendency of political analysts to view his political career in terms of "his ethnicity."

Although a *New York Times* (19 January 1986) editorial averred that the governor of New York "has become a bit touchy," within a week these issues surfaced again. In response to the murder of a plainclothes police officer, an organized crime task force searched thirty-one Italian-American social clubs throughout New York City. While the clubs are sometimes used by syndicate members (Tricarico 1984, 65–71), the response appeared to have been excessive. A member of a Greenwich Village V.F.W. club ransacked in a raid believed that the officials who ordered the action were "prejudiced because we're Italian-American."

8. Alongside situations that elicit a defensive ethnicity or disidentification, there is support in the larger society for an "upgraded" ethnicity. This stems from an appreciation of the ethnic heritage on the part of significant others; when Italian-American neighborhoods are gentrified, the bakeries, pasta stores, and other ethnic shops remain and, often, like Balducci's in Greenwich Village, are gentrified in the process. General approval enlarges the demand for aspects of the ethnic heritage and perhaps has revived Italian-American interest in customs and cultural items abandoned on the road to the mainstream, from olive oil and broccoli rape to street festivals and the Italian neighborhood. The enthusiasm of significant others corroborates the positive viewpoints originating from within the group. This is particularly important in light of entrenched feelings of ethnic inferiority.

Accompanying a transvaluation of Italian-American ethnicity is a measured ratification of ethnicity in general within American society. The mainstream has broadened, making it possible to have ethnicity and still be American. This choice between being "Italian or American" (Child 1943) is perhaps specific to the second generation and an earlier period. The federal government provided impetus for ethnic concerns when Congress passed the Ethnic Heritage Act in 1974, funding efforts to promote and display the culture and history of American ethnic groups. The political system of the late 1960s and 1970s rewarded ethnic organizations that claimed to represent ethnic constituencies with program grants.

A mainstream ethnicity has to meet certain conditions, however. It has to be subordinate to an American identity, which may partly explain the emphasis on ethnic "contributions" and "accomplishments." Lee Iacocca, for instance, is an important symbol because he is Italian-American and a superpatriot. His status is not disruptive of the consensus on core social values, unlike issues such as bilingual education. Moreover, mainstream ethnicity can not be invidious or chauvinistic. In mainstream America, everyone has a right to a respectable, generic ethnicity (You're ethnic, I'm ethnic). It is also an ethnicity that does not exclude nonethnics; *Attenzione* is also a magazine for "people who like what's Italian." It is a case of pluralism without hard edges.

9. Although identity and a "feeling" for the ethnic heritage may be the "primary way of being ethnic" (Gans 1979), ethnicity is still a basis for pursuing social interests in the mainstream (Glazer and Moynihan 1970; Gabriel and Savage 1976). In fact, this strategy appears to be particularly useful for advancing the career interests of middle-class Italian-Americans, although the needs of disadvantaged Italian-American constituencies may be invoked against it. Besides their practical advantages, ethnic networks may afford a milieu that is culturally and psychologically sensitive to ethnic mobility (Enloe 1973, 20). Voluntary associations may furnish an important ethnic link to individuals who are more estranged from traditional forms of ethnic solidarity. While membership in Italian-American organizations furnishes important benefits for the individual, they are perhaps more likely to supplement, rather than substitute for, mainstream affiliations. The social and economic position of Italian-Americans in this society would not seem to warrant an organization like the NAACP.

There is a vested interest in using ethnicity to secure market or career advantages. Little Italy merchants engineered a risorgimento to strengthen an ethnic economy threatened by the replacement of Italian-American with Chinese immigrants. The NIAF has initiated a "special project" with the Italian government to "make it easier for Italian-Americans to discover their roots and investigate their family history" (NIAF 1985). In addition, careers can be sustained as arbiters of the ethnic heritage and spokespersons for the "group interest." Italian-American professionals, for example, have offered "their expertise" to the mass media for the creation of more acceptable images of "our culture and concerns" (Giordano 1985).

There is, similarly, a vested interest in promoting ethnicity. Activists raise issues to be placed on an Italian-American political agenda. Academics focus attention on collective symbols that can resuscitate or sustain a "community of memory" (Bellah et al. 1985). Ethnicity is portrayed as a highly valued social resource, both as strategy and as ground for existential meaning.

Ethnicity in Another Light

Now well into a third generation, Italian-Americans may be taking their ethnicity into the middle class and mainstream of American life. This is occurring for reasons not appreciated by straight-line theory: straight-line theory overstates the extent to which ethnicity must be "sacrificed" to achieve upward mobility and, in particular, a middle-class status; straight-line theory employs a static sense of culture which gauges ethnicity by its resemblance to, literally, the world of the father, the immigrants; and the larger society appears to leave more room for ethnic identity and culture than straight-line theory allows.

It is likely that the majority of Italian-Americans, who are not far removed from immigrant circumstances, have never ceased being ethnic in important ways. In the late 1960s, new circumstances gave rise to new forms of ethnic expression and, thus, are an aspect of the ongoing transformation of Italian-American ethnicity. Proposing to make some corrections in straight-line theory, Gans (1979, 234–37) acknowledges "meaningful ethnic involvement" among "middle class adults of the third and fourth generation." But Gans's concept of "symbolic ethnicity" does not capture the full sweep of Italian-American ethnicity. Symbolic ethnicity involves a general "feeling" for the ethnic heritage, in particular, for elements that have been "abstracted" from the traditional cultural pattern, like dietary items or folk art (an "objects culture"), and transformed into "symbols." Identification with ethnic symbols, which becomes "the primary way of being ethnic," is compatible with "other, more urgent" dimensions of "the basic American middle class lifestyle." A symbolic ethnicity involves an element of intentionality, through which ethnicity can be cultivated, manipulated, or invoked (Royce 1982; Lyman and Douglass, 1973).

It also seems to entail a specific cognitive orientation involving an intent to acquire knowledge about ethnic phenomena. Italian-Americans have clearly evolved a symbolic ethnicity in this sense. Italian-Americans can "have ethnicity" as "a leisure-time pursuit" (Gans 1979) when ethnic identity is self-consciously constructed (Bensman and Vidich 1971; Tuan 1982). But Italian-Americans still appear to "live" ethnicity in everyday life, and not merely in peripheral settings and in taken-for-granted ways. This includes behaviors and values that can be traced back to traditional ethnic culture as well as cultural traits that have meaning in this society. Being ethnic in this sense may occasionally generate tensions vis-à-vis "the basic American middle class lifestyle." In addition, the concept of "symbolic ethnicity" does not reflect the strategic or instrumental use of ethnicity on the part of Italian-Americans in the mainstream. Interestingly, this appears to have the greatest relevance for Italian-Americans in middle-class occupations. Finally, it is important to note that ethnicity is not entirely "voluntary." Significant others apply ethnic labels and raise ethnic issues that influence a group's ethnicity, symbolic and otherwise, although impressions may be managed. Negative responses would seem to take ethnicity beyond symbolic manifestations.

Now that the dust of the "new pluralism" has settled, it would be a mistake to write off Italian-American ethnicity. For third-generation Italian-Americans, ethnicity will not be part of life "24 hours a day" (Sollors 1981). Nevertheless it may account for important aspects of behavior and group life. Moreover, new contents and symbols may emerge to sustain ethnic boundaries. Continuing research on Italian-Americans should focus on how the group is assimilating *and* how its ethnicity is being preserved and transformed in the process. Whether Italian-Americans will retain their ethnicity "in the end" (Alba 1985, 15) remains an empirical question. But Italian-American ethnicity is still a factor at present, and it may continue to have relevance if it can be adapted to mainstream, middle-class circumstances.

References

Alba, R. 1981. "The Twilight of Ethnicity among American Catholics of European Ancestry." *The Annals* 454 (March).

――――――. 1985. *Italian Americans*, Englewood Cliffs, N.J.: Prentice-Hall.

Alba, R., and G. Moore. 1982. "Ethnicity in the American Elite." *American Sociological Review* 47, no. 3 (June).

Aversa, A. 1978. "Italian Neo-Ethnicity: The Search for Self-Identity." *Journal of Ethnic Studies* 6, no. 2 (Summer).

Barbaro, F. 1974. "Ethnic Affirmation, Affirmative Action, and the Italian American." *Italian American* 1, no. 1 (Autumn).

Barth, F. 1969. *Ethnic Groups and Boundaries*. Boston: Little Brown.

Bayor, R. 1978. *Neighbors in Conflict*. Baltimore: Johns Hopkins University Press.

Bellah, R. et al. 1985. *Habits of the Heart*. Berkeley: University of California Press.

Bensman, J., and A. Vidich. 1970. *The New American Society*. Chicago: Quadrangle Books.

Breton, R. 1964. "Institutional Completeness of Ethnic Communities and the Personal Relations of Immigrants." *American Journal of Sociology* 70 (September).

Campisi, P. 1948. "Ethnic Family Patterns: The Italian Family in the United States." *American Journal of Sociology* 53 (May).

Child I. 1943. *Italian or American? The Second Generation in Conflict*. New York: Russell and Russell.

Cohen, A. 1981. "Variables in Ethnicity." In *Ethnic Change*, edited by C.F. Keyes. Seattle: University of Washington Press.

Congress of Italian-American Organizations. 1975. *A Portrait of the Italian American Community in New York City* 1 (January).

Covello, L. 1967. *The Social Background of the Italo-American Schoolchild*. Leiden, Netherlands: E. J. Brill.

Crispino, J. 1980. *The Assimilation of Ethnic Groups: The Italian Case*. New York: Center for Migration Studies.

DeVos, G. 1975. "Ethnic Pluralism: Conflict and Accommodation." In *Ethnic Identity: Cultural Continuities and Change*, edited by George DeVos and Lola Romanucci-Ross. Palo Alto, Calif.: Mayfield.

di Leonardo, M. 1984. *The Varieties of Ethnic Experience*. Ithaca: Cornell University Press.

Douglass, J. N. 1984. "The Emergence, Security, and Growth of the Sense of Self." In *The Existential Self in Society*, edited by J. A. Kotarba and A. Fontana. Chicago: University of Chicago Press.

Enloe, C. H. 1973. *Ethnic Conflict and Political Development*. Boston: Little Brown.

Etzioni, A. 1959. "The Ghetto: A Reevaluation." *Social Forces* 39 (March).

Fandetti, D., and R. Gelfand. 1983. "Middle Class White Ethnics in Suburbia: A Study of Italian-Americans." In *Culture, Ethnicity, and Identity*, edited by William McCready. New York: Academic Press.

Francis, E. K. 1947. "The Nature of the Ethnic Group." *American Journal of Sociology* 52, no. 5 (March).

Gabriel, R., and P. Savage. 1976. "The Urban Italian: Patterns of Political Accommodation to Local Regimes." In *The Urban Experience of Italian Americans*. New York: Center for Migration Studies.

Gans, H. 1962. *The Urban Villagers*. New York: Free Press.

———. 1979. "Symbolic Ethnicity: The Future of Ethnic Groups and Cultures in America." *Ethnic and Racial Studies* 2 (January).

Giordano, J. 1985. "Italian Americans and the Media: An Agenda for a More Positive Image." In *Italian Americans: New Perspectives in Italian Immigration and Ethnicity*, edited by L. F. Tomasi, 67–77. New York: Center for Migration Studies.

Glazer, N., and D. P. Moynihan. 1970. *Beyond the Melting Pot*. Cambridge: MIT, Press.

———, eds. 1975 *Ethnicity: Theory and Experience*. Cambridge: Harvard University Press.

Goethals, G. T. 1981. *The TV Ritual*. Boston: Beacon.

Gordon, M. 1964. *Assimilation in American Life*. New York: Oxford University Press.

Greeley, A. 1976. "The Ethnic Miracle." *Public Interest* 45. (Fall).

Halle, D. 1984. *The American Working Man*. Chicago: University of Chicago Press.

Harris, R. 1977. "A Nice Place to Live." *New Yorker*, April.

Horowitz, D. 1975. "Ethnic Identity." In *Ethnicity: Theory and Experience*, edited by N. Glazer and D. Moynihan. Cambridge: Harvard University Press.

Hughey, M. 1981. "The New Conservatism: Political Ideology and Class Structure in America." *Social Research* 49, no. 3 (Autumn).

Irwin, J. 1977. *Scenes*. Beverly Hills, Calif.: Sage.

Italian-American Faculty Association of the City University of New York. 1974. "Status of Italian-Americans in the City University of New York."

Johnson, C. L. 1982. "Sibling Solidarity: Its Origin and Functioning in Italian-American Families." *Journal of Marriage and Family* 44, no. 2.

Keyes, C. 1981. "The Dialectics of Ethnic Change." In *Ethnic Change*, edited by C. F. Keyes. Seattle: University of Washington Press.

Light, I. 1981. "Ethnic Succession." In *Ethnic Change*, edited by C. F. Keyes. Seattle: University of Washington Press.

Lyman, S., and W. Douglass. 1973. "Ethnicity: Structure of Impression Management." *Social Research* 40, no. 2 (Summer).

Martorella, R. 1983. "Italian Americans and the Medical Profession." Unpublished paper.

Marty, M. 1985. "Transpositions: American Religion in the 1980's." *The Annals* 480 (July).

Nagata, J. 1981. "In Defense of Ethnic Boundaries: The Changing Myths and Charters of Malay Identity." In *Ethnic Change*, edited by C. F. Keyes. Seattle: University of Washington Press.

National Italian-American Foundation (NIAF). 1985. "1984: End of the Year Report." Washington, D.C.

Neidert, L., and R. Farley. 1985. "Assimilation in the United States." *American Sociological Review* 50, no. 6 (December).

New York City Department of City Planning. 1974. *Little Italy Risorgimento: Proposals for the Restoration of a Historic Community.*

Nielsen, F. 1985. "Ethnic Solidarity in Modern Societies." *American Sociological Review* 50, no. 2 (April).

Novak, M. 1972. *The Rise of the Unmeltable Ethnics.* New York: Macmillan.

Park, R. E. 1950. *Race and Culture.* New York: Free Press.

Reed, J. S. 1982. "Grits and Gravy: The South's New Middle Class." In *One South*, edited by J. S. Reed. Baton Rouge: Louisiana State University Press.

Roof, W. C. and W. McKinney. 1985. "Denominational America and the New Religious Pluralism." *The Annals* 480 (July).

Royce, A. P. 1982. *Ethnic Identity: Strategies for Diversity*, Bloomington: Indiana University Press.

Sandberg, N. 1974. *Ethnic Identity and Assimilation: The Polish American Case.* New York: Praeger.

Schemerhorn, R. A. 1970. *Comparative Ethnic Relations.* New York: Random House.

Shibutani, T., and K. Kwan. 1965. *Ethnic Stratification: A Comparative Approach.* New York: Macmillan.

Shostak, A. 1973. "Ethnic Revivalism, Blue Collarites, and Bunker's Last Stand." In *The Rediscovery of Ethnicity*, edited by S. Teselle. New York: Harper and Row.

Sollors, W. 1981. "Theory of American Ethnicity, OR: ?S Ethnic/TI and American/TI, De or United (W) States S SI and Theor?" *American Quarterly* 33, no. 3.

Sowell, T. 1981. *Ethnic America.* New York: Basic Books.

Stein, H., and R. Hill. 1977. "The Limits of Ethnicity." *The American Scholar* (Spring).

Steinberg, S. 1981. *The Ethnic Myth.* New York: Atheneum.

Talyor, R. 1979. "Black Ethnicity and the Persistence of Ethnogensis." *American Journal of Sociology* 84, no. 6 (July).

Thomas, W. I., and F. Znaniecki. 1927 *The Polish Peasant in Europe and America.* New York: Alfred A. Knopf.

Tomasi, L. 1972. *The Italian American Family.* New York: Center for Migration Studies.

Tricarico, D. 1984. The *Italians of Greenwich Village*. New York: Center for Migration Studies.

———. 1986. "Influence of the Irish on Italian Communal Adaptation in Greenwich Village." *Journal of Ethnic Studies* 13, no. 4 (Winter).

Tuan, Y. 1982. *Segmented Worlds and Self*. Minneapolis: University of Minnesota Press.

Vecoli, R. 1969. "Prelates and Peasants: Italian Immigration and the Catholic Church." *Journal of Social History* 2 (Spring).

———. 1985. "The Search for an Italian American Identity: Continuity and Change." In *Italian Americans: New Perspectives in Italian Immigration and Ethnicity*, edited by L. Tomasi. New York: Center for Migration Studies.

Ware, C. 1965. *Greenwich Village, 1920–1930*. New York: Harper and Row.

Weed, P. 1971. *The White Ethnic Movement and Ethnic Politics*. New York: Macmillan.

Yancey, W., et al. 1976. "Emergent Ethnicity: A Review and Reformulation." *American Sociological Review* 41 (June).

3

Mixed Ethnic Identities among Immigrant Clergy from Multiethnic Hungary: The Slovak-Magyar Case, 1885–1903

BELA VASSADY, JR.

Historians and social scientists have observed the development of ethnic identity and national consciousness among immigrants after their arrival to the United States (Greene 1975; Bodnar 1973). These observers have demonstrated that once immigrants transcended their Old World regional orientation, they rapidly moved toward ethnic and national consciousness in their New World environment. While the veracity of this process of "ethnicization" (i.e., ethnic consciousness making [Greene 1975, 3]) will not be disputed here, the implied if not explicitly stated assumption that it developed in a linear progression will be questioned. With few exceptions (Harney 1981; Bodnar 1973; Morawska 1982), those who have described the process of ethnicization have either totally ignored evidence of mixed identities during the early stages of immigrant settlement or, because of the sparse and inconsistent nature of the evidence, at best have dismissed it with a few passing comments before moving on to the rise of ethnic and national consciousness. The present study will attempt to focus more fully on the operation of this complex, erratic, paradoxical phenomenon within immigrant communities from the heterogeneous ethnic regions of Austria-Hungary, with special emphasis on the shifting nature of ethnic identification among some of the Slovak clergy who served immigrants from northeastern Hungary during the period before and after the turn of the century (approximately the early 1880s to the early 1900s).

In her study of turn-of-the-century ethnic relations among Austro-Hungarian immigrants in Johnstown, Pennsylvania, Ewa Morawska (1982, 83) attributed the mixed identities she observed to the "continuation of the old country relationships transplanted to American soil." Overlapping geographical, cultural, and linguistic boundaries among contiguous ethnic groups in Hungary produced shared traditions, mixed identities, and, in the majority of cases, low or nonexistent levels of ethnic and national consciousness—all of which were transplanted to the immigrant communities founded by these groups in America. Such relationships were exhibited among the numerous Slavic minorities that emigrated from shared regions of southwestern Hungary, such as the Croatians, Slovenes, and Serbs; among the Slovaks and Carpatho-Rusins from northeastern Hungary; and among members of Slavic minority groups and the Magyar majority group from Hungary whenever the former close contact between these two groups occurred again in their new country. After briefly illustrating how some immigrant Slavic groups transplanted shared and mixed identities from Hungary to America, this essay will detail occurrences of the same phenomenon among some of the clergy who served the Slovak and Magyar immigrant communities whose members came from the multi-ethnic northeastern region of Hungary during the period under study.

Among the great majority of South Slav immigrants, who had come from common origins in the southwestern portion of Hungary, the establishment of cooperative immigrant institutions based on mixed identities was typical in the late-nineteenth and early-twentieth centuries ("Croats," 1980, 250; Petrovich and Halpern 1980, 916). The behavior of Slovenes and Croatians, who were closely related linguistically and ecclesiastically, fit this pattern (Buc 1960). The "borders between Croat and Slovene identity, which seem so firm now to scholars of ethnicity and then to nationalists," Robert Harney (1981, 16) has observed, "were capable of great elasticity." In their immigrant settlements the two groups lived closely together and often established common fraternal societies and Catholic parishes in which identities proved fluid and elastic. In a typical pattern observable in other mixed-group relationships, emerging ethnic consciousness intruded to separate them after the turn of the century (Prpic 1978, 72, 94, 101, 147, 149, 155, 161). In Steelton, Pennsylvania, Slovenes and Croatians divided over which of their languages should be used in their common church services, resulting in the establishment of separate churches (Bodnar 1973, 311; Bodnar 1977, 103, 115–16). Thus, in the alien industrial environment of America, separate and distinct ethnic communities eventually developed, but only after a period of erratic ethnic identity mixing. Indeed, in some cases a cross-ethnic pattern remains notable to this day. A significant number of Croatians still belong to St. Vitus, the first Slovene national parish established in

Cleveland, Ohio ("Croats," 1980, 253); a 1969 survey of these two ethnic groups found that intermarriage, one of the best indicators of cross-ethnic association, remained common among later generations of Slovenes and Croatians in America (Colakovic 1973, 156).

Serbians and Croatians who emigrated together from the southwestern portion of Hungary shared a common literary language, Serbo-Croatian, notwithstanding their use of different alphabets (Cyrillic for Serbs, Latin for Croats). Their close ethnic and linguistic Old World associations were maintained in some of the earliest mutual-aid societies, cooperatively established in locations as diverse as San Francisco, New Orleans, and Johnstown, Pennsylvania ("Croats," 1980, 250, 916; Morawska 1982, 84). But the fact that the East Orthodox Serbs did not share a common faith with their Roman Catholic Croatian cousins made the establishment of common parishes impossible. Since, like other Slavic immigrants, the Serbs and Croatians associated their respective churches with their respective ethnic identities, they were prevented from establishing the kind of longer-lasting mixed-identity relationships that were frequently exhibited by Croatian and Slovene immigrants of the same faith ("Croats," 1980, 251; Balch, 1969, 156, 418).

Mixed identities were likewise transplanted by the Carpatho-Rusin and Slovak immigrants who came from contiguous counties of northeastern Hungary where they had shared their lives. The strong admixture of the Slovak, Hungarian, and Ukrainian dialects found in the Carpatho-Rusin language attests to the close historical relations shared by these groups (Magocsi 1980, 206). In Johnstown, Pennsylvania, at the turn of the century, 25 to 30 percent of Slovak and Carpatho-Rusin immigrants were found to have intermarried. Local Rusin newspapers addressed both groups, their church and fraternal lodges had dual memberships, and their leadership overlapped "as a result of. . . social and cultural mixing and because of the often mixed identity of persons involved." In interviewing members of this border group, Morawska (1982, 84, 103) found many unable to name their ethnic group, identifying themselves instead by religion (Roman Catholic or Greek Catholic) or as "Slovak-Rusin." Likewise noting these blurred identites, Howard Stein (1980–81) and John Berta (1977) observed that many Rusins became "Slovakized" as a result of their shared institutions in the United States. Conversely, Mark Stolarik (1985, 49, 51–59) found that in Bethlehem, Pennsylvania, Greek Catholic Slovaks willingly submerged their ethnicity into Rusin identity because they preferred the traditional Slavonic rites of the Rusin-dominated Greek Catholic church to the Roman Catholic Latin liturgy. Especially among the Greek Catholic Slovaks and

Rusins, the strong commitment to faith over ethnicity is notable. To this day, many Slovaks and Rusins remain ethnically confused with each other (Petrovich and Halpern 1980, 932).

Scholars have demonstrated that in the process of building immigrant communities in the alien industrial, urban American environment, identity conflicts arose within the new social and especially new ecclesiastical institutions founded by these groups, which eventually aroused their ethnic consciousness and led to the breakdown of initial alliances and cooperation and the development of ethnic group separation (Greene 1975, 6–10; Bodnar 1973, 310–15). The experiences of the described immigrant groups from Hungary point to similar behavioral patterns. There were other influences, but common religious traditions and practices were the most uniform common thread in all of them, influencing both the initial establishment and practice of mixed identities and the parallel development of ethnic consciousness. While most of these mixed identities with their resultant cooperative and shared institutions did not survive (conflicts eventually arose over ethnic differences, especially the language to be used in shared churches), the confusion of ethnic identities and erratic mixing often endured for decades, in some cases into later generations.

The mixed identities that developed within the Slovak and Magyar communities in the New World environment appear to fall into a similar pattern. While linguistically unrelated to each other (Magyar is not a Slavic language; it is not even part of the Indo-European family of languages), a shared ecclesiastical tradition in Hungary, together with other geographical, cultural, and political cross-ethnic influences, frequently produced a blurring of identities within their immigrant communities. As with the other groups described above, mixed identities were especially evident in their early shared churches until the two groups moved toward separation, especially over the question of language usage, during the decades of "ethnicization." Because the Magyars were the rulers in Hungary, their relationship with other immigrants from Hungary, all of whom belonged to minority groups in the homeland, differed in some respects from that experienced by the other groups vis à vis each other. The awakening of anti-Magyar nationalism among the Slavs from Hungary and a strong sense of chauvinism among the Magyars produced efforts by 1903 on the part of the Hungarian government to influence the national loyalties of its immigrant subjects. As these efforts of the government became known, they proved to be counterproductive, as the resulting antagonistic anti-Magyar and pro-Magyar mass demonstrations moved the two immigrant groups strongly toward separation by 1903.

On the premise that by 1903 ethnic and national consciousness had percolated from the intelligentsia (especially the clergy) to a large segment of the rank-and-file, producing increasing mass separatism, the year 1903 has been selected as the cutoff date for this study.

The great majority of Slovak immigrants, and the relatively small number of their Magyar countrymen who followed or accompanied them during the last two decades of the nineteenth century, came from the ethnically mixed region of northeastern Hungary comprising the counties of Sáros, Zemplén, Abauj, Szepes, and Ung. Since this region lacked natural resources and was far from early industrial centers, internal migration of labor to the fertile Hungarian lowlands was a seasonal tradition among the highlanders. While mixed ethnically, the northeastern uplands were predominantly populated by Slovaks. The Magyar element was small, representing almost exclusively the landowning classes, most of whom were Magyarized Slovaks assimilated over the centuries. The towns and some of the larger villages contained a Magyar population, resulting partly from immigration of Magyar officials and workers and partly from Magyarization of Slovaks. Toward the southern plains the countryside was overwhelmingly Magyar, often consisting of Slovaks who had drifted south and had been Magyarized in a natural, spontaneous process over the centuries (Macartney 1937, 8, 34, 76–79).

Although the greatly increased rate of assimilation in the late nineteenth century was partially forced by a chauvinistic Hungarian state policy that insisted upon the Magyarization of all state institutions, it was also part of the spontaneous process of acculturation that naturally occurs in states experiencing modernization, urbanization, and middle-class mobility. Simply put, rewards and status went to those who assimilated, and the intelligentsia of the minority groups knew it. Since assimilation was necessary to gain entrance to the "gentlemanly" class, it inevitably attracted the Slovak educated elite to the Magyar middle-class lifestyle and mentality (Hanák 1978, 463–64). All secondary schools, seminaries, and the like were conducted in Magyar; most of the upper social and governmental echelons, as well as most of professional, business, and ecclesiastical life, at both the national and county levels, were either Magyar or Magyarized. Only at the local village level were ethnic character and language retained (Macartney 1937, 723–27). This process of assimilation took place over several generations, during which participants went through a transitional stage, characterized by bilingualism, dual identities, mixed families, and general acculturation with attachments to both groups (Hanák 1978, 419, 464). During the three decades before the First World War, approximately 30 percent of the increase in the

Magyar population (over 1 million) was derived from the assimilation of 300,000 Slovaks (Hanák 1978, 416, 419, 463–64).

As was the case with immigrants from other parts of Europe, the initial loyalties of the pioneers from northeastern Hungary were to their village, county, region of origin, church, and the people with whom they had shared their lives. Although Magyarization had not greatly affected isolated non-Magyar peasants in Hungary, their common homeland origins and experiences provided a common identity with Hungary, which, since most of them planned to return to their homes, they felt even more keenly in the isolation of America. As Puskás has noted, the common Hungarian language learned by many non-Magyars in Hungary and shared religious traditions initially produced mixed churches and proved to be especially cohesive forces in America:

> The common language (not always the mother tongue, but learned in Hungary) was such an important cohesive force that—especially in the beginning—it overruled ethnic and religious allegiances. . . . It was because of the initial mixing that the churches and parishes could become the main battlegrounds of ethnic and religious rivalry and conflict. (1982a, 257, 281–82)

Moreover, since in the northeastern counties of Hungary (whence most of the immigrants came during the 1880s and 1890s) the eastern Slovak (Sáros) dialect utilizing Magyar orthography was in common usage, the Slovaks who came from there tended to be more prone to Magyarization than those from other regions of Slovakia (Stolarik 1974, 134, 145). The common roots of the Slovak and Magyar peasant immigrants naturally led to common settlement patterns in America, reproducing relationships shared in the Old World that were often characterized by a remarkable lack of ethnic or national consciousness. The protean quality of ethnic identity among Slovaks in North America in the early twentieth century was well described by Harney: "He (the Slovak immigrant) could believe deeply in the existence of an independent Slovak people, or remember the Hapsburg monarchy nostalgically, or accept Masaryk's Czechoslovakia, or even believe . . . that Hungarians and Slovaks should share one (fraternal) society" (1981, 22).

New World alienation and insecurities, fed by commonly shared prejudices within the host society against "Hungarians" (a term used indiscriminately to refer to all immigrants from Hungary, regardless of ethnic affiliation), also help to explain early united action and shared identities. Nowhere was the perpetuation of this phenomenon more pronounced than in the shared churches that were founded soon after the arrival of Slovak and Magyar immigrants in the 1880s and early 1890s. Cooperative, mixed-ethnic (predominantly Slovak in constituency) churches, Catholic and Protestant alike, were established in Hazleton, Pennsylvania; Streator, Illinois; Cleveland, Ohio; New York City; Pittsburgh, Pennsylvania; Mt. Carmel, Pennsylvania; Passaic and Trenton, New Jersey; and other locations in the Northeast and Midwest. Frequently services were held in both the Magyar and Slovak tongue, and Hungarian names and flags often adorned the sanctuaries. Nationalistic and ethnically oriented divisions began to appear in the churches by the early 1890s and continued to accelerate thereafter, eventually propelling most of them to separation along national and ethnic lines by the early twentieth century.

Magyars and Slovaks coming from similar regional roots in Hungary often also exhibited shared identities in their early cooperative fraternal societies. During the 1880s, while these societies were still small, local, and uninfluenced by nationalistic pressures, and while the need for mutual support was strong due to the small number of immigrants, cooperation and expressions of loyalty to Hungary were especially evident. Unlike the churches, however, the fraternals did not have similar inherited common rituals to form a basis for mixed-ethnic practices. By the 1890s, moreover, agitation to convert many of these small local societies into nationalistically oriented chapters of emerging national societies placed many of them under great pressure to make decisions about their ethnic identities. Yet, even under these circumstances, Slovaks and Magyars frequently remained members of each other's societies, often without demonstrating visible concern for ethnic or nationalistic differences and agitation. In 1899, for example, a prominent Hungarian-American newspaper reported with great concern that almost as many Magyars were members of the three largest Slovak federations as of the comparable top three Magyar organizations (*Szabadsáq*, 9, 30 November 1899). Mixed-ethnic membership rules in Slovak and Magyar fraternals reflected the open sentiments about ethnic identity; many of them provided for admission of anyone who could speak the language of the organization, regardless of nationality (Harney 1981, 23). Similarly, Slovaks and Magyars frequently supported and attended social events sponsored by each other's ethnic societies and churches. It appears that despite the growing ethnic and national consciousness evinced within both the Magyar and Slovak communities, many on both sides remained passive to these pressures and maintained Old World loyalties and mixed identities.

Among every immigrant group, Slovaks and Magyars included, it

is the intelligentsia that interprets identities and ideologies and provides much of the early leadership for the ethnic community (Higham
1978). The Slovaks and Magyars quickly developed a small secular
leadership, composed mostly of businessmen and journalists, which
participated in playing this role. A small number of Protestant clergy
(especially Calvinist for the Magyars and Lutheran for the Slovaks)
also participated. Since most of the Slovak and Magyar immigrants
were Roman Catholic, however, and since religiosity was strongly felt
within both groups, from the outset it became evident that the Slovak
Catholic clergymen who dominated early mixed Slovak-Magyar
churches (until the end of the 1890s there was only one Magyar priest
serving Hungarian immigrants) were to be the key to defining ethnic
identities among the immigrants from Hungary. These immigrant
priests exhibited what Harney (1981, 15) has referred to as "that
wonderful chameleonic quality of clergy. . . who could move easily
from one central, east European identity to another for their flock."
Some of these Slovak clergymen suffered a severe identity crisis upon
their arrival in America and therefore exhibited ambiguous identities
as they moved toward ethnic consciousness. An assessment of their
role will comprise the main thrust of this essay.

In Hungary and in the American emigration, Slovak nationalists
referred pejoratively to Slovaks who had been assimilated (become
Magyarized) into Magyar culture and identified them as "Magyarones." This term first came into common usage in Hungary
during the 1840s when a Croatian political faction supporting the use
of Magyar as the official language in Croatia was labeled the
"Magyarone party" (Kann and Zdenek 1984, 265–66; Macartney
1968, 288, 294). By the mid-nineteenth century, the use of the term
had spread to describe members of other minority groups with pro-
Hungarian sympathies (Macartney 1968, 297). In the 1890s, the term
appeared in both the Magyar and Slovak immigrant press, clearly
referring to Magyarized Slovaks with strong pro-Hungarian sympathies. In his harsh indictment of the Magyarizing Hungarian system, Seton-Watson (1972, 210–11) described Magyarones as upwardly mobile "renegades" of Slovak extraction who became assimilated
for status and profit. May (1951, 375–77) and Macartney (1937, 87–
88) referred to "Magyarone Slovaks" who were opponents of the
Czech-Slovak connection and preferred the association and alignment
of Slovaks with Hungary. Kann (1977, 382) and Balch (1969, 111)
observed that since Magyarones were recent converts desirous of
acceptance as full-fledged Magyar nationalists, they frequently became fanatical laborers for the Magyar cause. In the immigrant
context, Stolarik (1972, 157) defined Magyarones as those Slovak

clergymen who worked for the assimilation of the Slovaks by the Hungarians and opposed all manifestations of Slovak nationalism.

While all of these definitions are accurate descriptions, they over-simplify the complex, enigmatic nature of the Magyarone personality. The assimilation process was fraught with frustration and mental anguish for those who participated in it. Since Magyars and Mag-yarones considered the Magyar language to be a manifestation of "patriotic sentiment" and of "higher social position," and since social privileges, jobs, schooling, membership in the church hierarchy, own-ership of large amounts of land, and the peerage were all controlled by Magyars and Magyarones in northern Hungary, Magyarized Slovaks frequently confronted strong antipathy from the Slovak lower classes that they dominated. Moreover, the necessity of forsaking their own ethnic heritage to win high position caused underlying frustration and resentment among the Magyarized upper classes as well as among those whom they exploited. Finally, Magyarized Slovaks resented the fact that, regardless of their level of loyalty, they normally remained excluded from the higher posts in government service and from the upper aristocracy, and were frequently looked down upon with con-tempt as "pushy upstarts" by the Magyar upper classes (Glettler 1980, 393; Seton-Watson 1972, 211).

When they departed for America, many of these individuals were at various levels of assimilation, bilingual and dual in their loyalties. While for the upwardly mobile in Hungary there had been little choice other than Magyarization, in America a variety of choices offered them potential routes to success: they could profess to be Magyar, pro-Magyar Slovak (i.e., Magyarone), or Slovak in identity, depending on personal objectives or ambitions. During the 1890s and early 1900s, many shifted back and forth in identity for a variety of reasons, greatly frustrating and irritating both their Slovak and Magyar compatriots.

The mixed identities and the resultant switching of loyalties were mostly exhibited by a segment of the Slovak clergy who came from Hungary during the period under study. In the United States, as in Hungary, most of the Slovak intelligentsia were Catholic priests. Since, until near the end of the 1890s, the very small Magyar com-munity in the United States was provided with only one Magyar priest, most of the Roman Catholic Magyars worshiped with their Slovak co-religionists in Slovak immigrant churches. And, until the end of the decade, the Slovak priests who served these mixed-ethnic churches were generally perceived by the Magyar community as sup-porters of Hungary and the Hungarian cause (*Szabadsáq* 1, 6, 25 June 1894; 6 June, 20 October 1898). It was during this period of ethnicization that identity shifting took place, with much of it naturally focusing on the language and/or languages to be used in church services. Notwithstanding the erratic development of ethnic self-awareness during this period, as the Slovak and Magyar immigrant communities struggled with their new-found ethnic institutions in the American environment, a pattern of Slovakization eventually developed among the Slovak clergy.

By the beginning of the twentieth century, two groups or "schools" of Slovak priests had emerged. One of the groups tended to include Slovak and Czech priests from the western or central counties of northern Hungary. Some were educated in Prague, and others, in the United States; most were Slovak nationalists who supported the codified central Slovak dialect as the literary language for all Slovaks. Because many were frustrated, alienated individuals who had run into trouble with the Hungarian authorities and had found it expedient to leave Hungary, they planned to remain in the United States (Glettler 1980, 396). Since they comprised by far the large majority of the clergy available to serve Slovak immigrants, they dominated the Slovak churches in America. The second group was composed of priests mostly associated with the Diocese of Kassa, which was located in Abauj-Torna County and served the more Magyarized northeastern region of Hungary. The majority of these priests were loyalist Magyarones who insisted on continuing to use both the Magyar language and the northeastern Slovak dialect in their church services, as had been their custom back home. Since this group operated within the Magyar ecclesiastical system in Hungary, its members had little incentive for emigrating, and they never comprised more than a small minority of the Slovak clergy working in America (Glettler 1980, 124, 133, 396). Yet, because before the turn of the century the greater portion of the immigrants from Hungary came from the northeastern counties, and since these immigrants naturally preferred clergymen who understood their dialect and liturgical traditions, northeastern Slovak clergymen, whether as opponents or proponents of Slovak or Magyar nationalism, played an influential role in the development of ethnic consciousness within their mixed-immigrant communities before the First World War.

The two Slovak priests to arrive first in the United States, during the mid-1880s, Jozef Kossalko and Ignác Jaškovič, were loyalist Kassa priests who supported mixed-ethnic congregations with bilingual (Magyar and eastern Slovak) services. After serving one of the earliest Slovak churches in America (Hazleton, Pennsylvania) and espousing pro-Magyar sentiments, Jaškovič founded and edited in Hazleton a Catholic eastern Slovak newspaper (*Katolícke Noviny*, 1889–1891) that, although short-lived, later became the basis for a Hungarian newspaper founded by Jaškovič and a Hungarian immigrant intellectual named Mogyorossy (Glettler 1980, 80). In the 1890s, *Szabadsáq*, a rival Hungarian newspaper published in Cleveland, described Jaškovič as a Slovak priest in Hazleton who had been turned into a Magyar priest and criticized this tendency toward "changing nationality" (*Szabadsáq*, 21 July 1891, 9 February 1893, 20 August 1896, 15 July 1897).

Kossalko's career likewise demonstrated the paradoxical identities that emerged in some members of this group. In 1889, Kossalko, too, founded a Catholic newspaper (*Zásztava*) that used the eastern Slovak (Sáros) dialect, in opposition to a secular Slovak nationalist newspaper edited in Pittsburgh by the Slovak nationalist leader, Peter Rovnianek. Rovnianek and his supporters thereafter perpetually accused Kossalko of being an ardent Magyarone, and, indeed, the priest's abrasive pro-Magyar sentiments occasionally led his Slovak churches to force his transfer and at times even proved embarrassing to his Hungarian sympathizers (Berta 1977, 56; *Szabadsáq*, 9 February 1983). Yet, despite his apparent pro-Magyarism, during the early 1890s when Kossalko cooperated in the founding of the First Catholic Slovak Union and its newspaper, *Jednota*, the Austro-Hungarian consul in Pittsburgh accused him of competing with Rovnianek and other secular leaders for "Panslav" (Slovak nationalist) leadership in the Slovak community (Glettler 1980, 283). Similarly, while in 1901 he was contributing loyalist articles to one of the Hungarian government subsidized newspapers published in the eastern Slovak dialect, he was simultaneously suspected by an Austro-Hungarian consul of working "in secret" to obtain a Pan-Slavic replacement for his mixed-ethnic congregation in Bridgeport, Connecticut (Glettler 1980, 85–86; OL, K 26-1903-XX-228, pp. 256, 382). This type of paradox was repeated in 1902 when, while Kossalko's name appeared on the top of the Hungarian government's recall list for suspicion of surreptitious Slovak nationalist activities, he was being praised by Tihamér Kohányi, the Hungarian nationalist editor of *Szabadsáq*, for his tough loyalism (OL, K26-1903-XX-228, p. 381). When in 1909 Kossalko finally returned to Hungary in retirement, the Hungarian government declared him "absolutely loyal" (Glettler 1980, 86–87). Clearly, then, even Kossalko, perhaps the leading Magyarone priest in America, exhibited contradictory behavior as he ostensibly shifted identities on several occasions. Like most of his colleagues, Kossalko had many objectives. He fought secularism and Czechophile tendencies and also sought personal financial gain and status, and he was not averse to exploiting shifting allegiances to achieve his goals.

The dilemmas faced by Slovak priests who operated with mixed identities within the new economic and political pressures of America were also well demonstrated by the experience of Ján Poľakovič, the priest who served a mixed-ethnic congregation founded in New York City in the early 1890s.[1] Under tremendous pressure from a Slovak nationalist faction within his church, at one point Poľakovič reportedly claimed to be a "Hungarian patriot" wishing "to escape the panslavs" and offered his priestly services to a group of Magyars who were organizing a church in Indiana. In the mid-1890s, however, a drawn-out controversy over whether the plaque on his recently erected New York church should be inscribed in eastern Slovak or literary Slovak apparently convinced Poľakovič to switch to the nationalist side (*Szabadság*, 16 June, 15, 29 August, 12 September, 3 October 1985). Following the typical pattern in such cases, the factions in the congregation formed two separate churches (Culen 1972, 102–103). During the 1890s there were numerous similar controversies in early mixed churches in New York, New Jersey, Pennsylvania, Ohio, and Connecticut, usually over the question of whether Magyar, eastern Slovak, or literary Slovak should be used in services. Where eastern Slovak was in use, Magyar services were generally also preferred. Where supporters of Slovak nationalism came into the majority, however, only literary Slovak was condoned, leading to confrontations and eventual splits. In all of these cases, the clergy in charge were caught in the middle, often vacillating at first and, when necessary, shifting identities to fit the situation.

The 1890s marked the arrival of three eastern Slovak pro-Magyar priests from the Diocese of Kassa who were to become the loyal confidants of the Hungarian government. They were Ferenc Dénes, Béla Kazinczy, and Imre Haitinger. All three insisted on conducting bilingual eastern Slovak and Magyar services in their mixed congregations. Dénes served the New York City Slovak church, which used the eastern Slovak dialect and was pro-Magyar in loyalties. By 1901 he was operating as an agent of the Hungarian government by placing Magyarized priests sent from Hungary and reporting his observations to the Austro-Hungarian consul in New York. In 1901 the New York consul commended Dénes' "unbroken loyalty" despite the many attacks made upon him by his nationalist Slovak colleagues. In the same year the Hungarian government began subsidizing his Catholic eastern Slovak dialect newspaper, *Šlebodni Orel*, in an effort to appeal to eastern Slovak regionalism and pro-Hungarian loyalism and to offset the nationalistic influence of other Slovak newspapers, most of which were by then published in literary Slovak (OL, K26-1903-XVI-71, pp. 129, 208; Glettler 1980, 89–91). During the years

1904 to 1906, however, as the failure of his newspaper became apparent, Dénes reportedly became indifferent and despondent, and further
subsidies to his newspaper were provided only because it was feared
he might "switch" to the Slovak nationalist side, providing a "victory
to the panslavs." Indeed, when in 1906 the subsidies finally did stop,
Dénes sold his newspaper presses to a nationalist Slovak newspaper in
New York (*Slovák v Amerike*) and publicized his previous role as an
agent of the Hungarian government, thereby also shifting his loyalties
to suit the occasion (Glettler 1980, 90–95).

Imre Haitinger served a large pro-Magyar northeastern Slovak
congregation in Passaic, New Jersey. Together with Dénes he reported to the Austro-Hungarian consul in New York and helped place
and supervise loyal Magyarized priests. Like Kossalko, Dénes, and
others, he demonstrated a contradictory, flexible ethnic identity.
Thus, while in 1904 the consul reported him to be an ardent Hungarian patriot, he was simultaneously campaigning for and getting
elected to an important committee of the First Catholic Slovak Union,
an organization that nationalist Hungarian immigrants and the
Hungarian government perceived to have Pan-Slavic sympathies
(Glettler 1980, 303). Like Kossalko, Haitinger was clearly exhibiting
an ability to shift his ethnic loyalties to fit his objectives. Béla Kazinczy, an ardent loyalist who served a pro-Magyar eastern Slovak congregation in Braddock, Pennsylvania, likewise reported to the consul
and placed priests in the Pittsburgh region. Despite a long record of
pro-Hungarian behavior, by 1903 he joined the First Catholic Slovak
Union, supporting it in its battles against Rovnianek's secular
nationalist movement. Like the others, he came under suspicion for
supporting the Hungarian cause only for "material motives" and personal prestige (Glettler 1980, 301–304). Apparently, Hungarian and
Slovak observers alike had difficulty accepting the fact that under the
circumstances, the shifting of ethnic identity more often reflected
practical opportunism and community politics than ideologically
motivated nationalism.

In 1901 the Austro-Hungarian consul in Pittsburgh reported that of
forty-two existing Slovak congregations only seven remained under
"patriotic" (pro-Magyar) Slovak priests. One year later, another
consul listed ten loyalists out of a total of forty-nine priests (OL, K26-
1903-xx-228, pp. 13–14, 298–99, 314–15). These statistics clearly
demonstrated that despite the paradoxical shifting of ethnic identity
exhibited by some of the Slovak priests in America, a growing movement toward Slovak ethnic consciousness continued to manifest itself
within the clerical leadership. This development was one of several
reasons why in 1902 the Hungarian government instituted its

so-called American Action program to maintain homeland loyalties among its immigrants. Based on continued reports from Magyarone priests in America that the majority of eastern Slovak immigrants preferred eastern Slovak priests if they were available, the program included a plan to send only loyal (eastern Slovak, Kassa-trained) priests to America and, where possible, to urge American bishops to recall those clergy who had become Slovak nationalists (Glettler 1980, 122–125). Although eastern Slovak recruits continued to be difficult to find, a small handful of carefully selected loyalist priests were duly sent to the United States during this period, including László Neurwirth, Gyula Szabó, and Pál Virágh. Despite the careful screening process used to select these men, their actions were to follow the familiar mixed-identities pattern exhibited by their predecessors.

All three had been motivated to emigrate by frustration over their lack of success back home. All were familiar to their Kassa colleagues in the United States and were sponsored and supported by them. Upon their arrival, Dénes sought to influence the local bishop to remove Czech priests serving mixed eastern Slovak and Magyar congregations in New York and New Jersey in order to place the new arrivals. At first all three worked closely with the Magyarone loyalist group and supported Dénes' New York–based newspaper, *Šlebodni Orel*. They soon came under nationalist pressure, however, and began to shift their loyalties. They joined the First Catholic Slovak Union and sold their shares in *Šlebodni Orel*. After exhibiting contradictory behavior, eventually all announced themselves to be Slovak nationalists, accepted the Slovak literary language, and denounced the eastern Slovak dialect (Glettler 1980, 134–36; OL, K26-1903-xx-228, pp. 381–87). Neurwirth, of Magyar origin, even founded a scholarship fund to support the education of Slovak students in Prague University. Szabó, in contrast, by 1906 was reportedly again exhibiting loyalist behavior and was under consideration as Dénes's replacement to edit *Šlebodni Orel* (Glettler 1980, 135–36).

On the surface, the above summary would imply that loyalists evolved from Magyarone sympathies to Slovak nationalism due to pressures from Slovak nationalists. Indeed, Neurwirth's response when asked why he had switched loyalties seemed to bear this out (OL, K26-1903-xx-228, p. 384). But a letter Virágh sent to a friend in Sáros County in Hungary during this period in 1902 revealed that the dilemma of the switching priests was much more complex than that. Virágh described his deep disappointment with conditions he found in America: priests had low status; they were ordered about by their parishioners; they lived in poverty unless they learned to be "good beggars"; and they were forced to use their congregations against each other to wrest lucrative parish posts from one another. He confirmed the growing anti-Magyar agitation within the Slovak community and complained that anyone attempting to mediate between the two factions was either accused of being a "Pan-Slav" or a "fanatical Magyar." Interestingly, however, he said much about the typical shifting nature of Magyarone behavior when he claimed that his decision to join the Slovak nationalists was only a pretense, and that he was actually spying with the intention of reporting his findings to the Hungarian government. He probably revealed his real motives when in closing he requested the "anonymous support" of the Hungarian government and asked for a parish upon his return to Hungary (OL, K26-1903-xx-228, pp. 505–11).

Virágh's letter illustrates the tremendous mental anguish faced by these marginal individuals, these men in transition. The transplanted priests felt homelessness, isolation, and disintegration in their alien environment. Learned Magyarized behavior was not easily relinquished, however, especially since most of these priests planned to return home or were subject to recall. Only those who made a permanent break with the homeland could take a clear stand on their ethnicity and national sympathies. Since the Kassa group did not fit into this category, its members were more prone to switching identities than any other group. Yet, even those Slovak clerics who had been well on their way to Magyarization in Hungary eventually awoke to national consciousness as a result of the conflicts that arose within their immigrant communities over ethnic identity issues. When they did, some occasionally compensated for their past frustrations with the Magyarized system and their alienation from their own ethnic group by responding with extreme Slovak nationalism. For the large majority, however, practical reasons were probably more influential in determining their actions than ideological ones. As upwardly mobile individuals they responded in the United States as they had in Hungary, by switching to the identity that offered the greatest rewards. Because the absence of subsidized state churches in the United States left the clergy insecure and exposed to their parishioner's whims, initially it was not always clear which identity was most favorable for them to assume. This ambiguity produced much of the vacillation and shifting of identities that occurred among them during the early years (Puskás 1982b, 200–204; Puskás 1982a, 70–73).

Financial, ideological, and political influences, as well as progressive ethnic community development, were not the only factors pushing these Slovak priests toward national and ethnic consciousness by the turn of the century. Another important element was the huge increase in the rate of immigration from Hungary of Slovaks, but especially of Magyars, after the turn of the century. From a practical point of view, the Slovaks and Magyars (especially the Magyars, since they were a small minority to this point) had been frequently compelled to cooperate in order to build viable immigrant organizations in the early years. But as this need diminished with the continued large influx of Slovaks and greatly increasing numbers of Magyar immigrants after the turn of the century, the two groups moved toward building separate social and ecclesiastical organizations along ethnic lines.

This evolution of attitudes is clearly seen in the Magyar immigrant press as represented by the Cleveland-based newspaper *Szabadsáq* during the 1890s. Until the late 1890s references in *Szabadsáq* to the activities of Slovak priests usually were positive in tone, as efforts were made to retain a symbiotic relationship between the two ethnic groups from Hungary. Since the clergy often served mixed congregations, *Szabadsáq* referred to them as loyal patriots of Hungary, attacking only those it identified as Pan-Slavists (mostly secular nationalists) and "switching" Magyarones. During the 1880s and 1890s the majority of the Slovak priests were reluctant to get involved in nationalist agitation. They preferred to stay out of politics and concentrate on their ecclesiastical duties, including offering mixed services where needed and opposing the secular Slovak nationalist movement. Their Magyar and Slovak peasant-rooted parishioners were usually more concerned about having priests who understood their language, customs, and ecclesiastical traditions than they were about ethnic or national consciousness (OL, K26 1903-XX-228, pp. 101–103).

When in 1899 Tihamér Koháнyi, the influential Magyar nationalist editor of *Szabadsáq*, accused politically neutral Slovak clergymen of Pan-Slavism and criticized Károly Böhm (the only prominent Magyar priest serving in the United States until the late 1890s) for serving Magyars and Slovaks alike without concern for nationality issues, Koháнyi was signaling a change in *Szabadsáq*'s editorial policy. This change probably reflected the influx of new Magyar immigrants and Magyar priests and, with them, the potential for founding Magyar Catholic churches, which in turn pressured more of the clergy on both sides toward nationalist sympathies (*Szabadsáq*, 5 October, 9 November 1899; 5 April 1900; 18 July 1901; Puskás 1982b, 256). *Szabadsáq*'s 1899 attack on Böhm resulted from the latter's attempt to effect the transfer of a Slovak priest named Brunkala to a Magyar church then being organized. In response to Böhm's contention that Brunkala was a "good Magyar," the editor of *Szabadsáq* insisted that the Slovak priest was a Pan-Slavist who, because his Slovak congregation had rejected him, had "metamorphosed into a Magyar priest"

(*Szabadság*, 21 September 1899). This incident demonstrated that opposition to mixed identities came from both Slovak and Magyar nationalists and again illustrated the important role that Magyarized Slovak clergymen played in the development of ethnic consciousness during this period. Moreover, in 1899 *Szabadság* first accused the Slovak and Rusin Catholic and Greek Catholic unions (both of which had many Magyar members) of dropping their loyalties to the homeland and permitting "Panslav undercurrents" and "good business" to turn them into nationalist organizations (*Szabadság*, 9, 30 November 1899; 14 June 1900). When the clergy among the leaders of both organizations vehemently denied these charges and professed their continued loyalty to the homeland (*Szabadság*, 9, 30 November, 5 April 1900), they demonstrated the reluctance with which the movement toward total separation was accomplished.

By the turn of the century, however, the arrival of increasing numbers of Magyar and Slovak immigrants progressively pushed the two groups toward a hostile mood, destroying pre-existing mixed-identity relations between them in the United States. The economic, social, and political incentives for supporting Slovak nationalism soon outdistanced any benefits Magyarization provided for the Slovak clergy and other Slovak intelligentsia. From the point of view of the Hungarian immigrant community, the benefits derived from Magyarone priests who served mixed congregations diminished with the arrival of Magyar priests; moreover, also from the Hungarian point of view, the switching of identities frequently practiced by these clergy made them especially dangerous, because when they shifted to Slovak nationalism their influence among their eastern Slovak parishioners was that much greater. Thus the clergy came under increasing presure from both sides to drop their mixed-identity roles. At the same time the growing impact of political events in Hungary also produced intensified rivalries. This was especially true after the Hungarian government, in 1902–3, instituted its "American Action" program in its attempt to perpetuate loyalties to the homeland among ethnic groups that had emigrated from Hungary. As the details of this program, such as the 1902 decision that only loyalist priests would be permitted to leave Hungary, became known among Dual Monarchy minority group immigrants residing in the United States, it proved to be very counterproductive, as it fueled anti-Hungarian agitation. This growing ethnic and national consciousness on the part of both groups was reflected in the advent of mutually antagonistic mass immigrant demonstrations in the United States that for the first time incorporated rank-and-file participation on a large scale. In 1902, the Hungarian immigrants made efforts to symbolize their growing numbers and influence, as well as their patriotic zeal, by receiving from Hungary with great fanfare a "sacred" Hungarian flag with the inscription "Be steadfastly loyal to your country, Hungarian" and by erecting, with equal fanfare, a statue of their revolutionary hero, Louis Kossuth. Perceived by Slovaks and other Slavs from Hungary as deliberate provocations, both of these acts stimulated numerous mass deomonstrations and a great amount of debate within the ethnic and American press (Kende 1927, 164–69, 178–79). Consequently, these increased tensions and conflicts worked to solidify each of the two immigrant communities, so that most of their mutually established institutions, already in the process of separating along ethnic lines, were pushed further in that direction.

To conclude, from the 1880s, when immigrants from northeastern Hungary first began to arrive in America, until at least 1903, when mass nationalist agitation began on both the Magyar and Slovak sides (but in many cases not until after the outbreak of World War I), ethnic self-identification was often blurred and shifted back and forth. As Monika Glettler (1980, 398–400) has shown, a portion of the Slovak intelligentsia identified with the Hungarian homeland, were aware of a common history, and aimed for peaceful symbiosis of the national minorities and the majority group. Some Magyarized and Slovak individuals (in Hungary and in the United States) alternatively confessed to belonging to one or the other nationality, depending on the economic situation, personal interest, or political pressures. Some were more regularly and closely associated with the Magyars or Magyarones, others with the Pan-Slavists or national Slovaks, but many were perceived or at least suspected of switching allegiances and/or identities at various times (Glettler describes nineteen such cases). These individuals belonged to what Glettler has called the "floating nationality" element—close to both ethnic groups but also in conflict with both. Most of them eventually moved to ethnic and national consciousness, but only after passing through a transitional intermediate stage, characterized by a cultural no man's land of mixed identities.

This small group of switching clergy, insecure and undecided about its own ethnic identity, played an influential part in the development of ethnic consciousness within both the Slovak and Magyar immigrant communities. Initially, these transitional men of mixed allegiances were mediators, supporting harmony, cooperation, and alliances between the two ethnic groups. The period of mixed identities lasted for at least two decades, and in some cases for a good bit longer; however, the conflict generated by the flexible self-identification practiced by some of the clergy was itself an important catalyst in shaping ethnic consciousness, as their activities became increasingly suspect and stimulated nationalist attacks from both sides. The two-decade debate over mixed identities played a part in propelling the two ethnic groups toward separation by the turn of the century.

Note

1. The dual identities under which many of these northeastern Slovak priests operated was illustrated by the dual names they were known by, depending upon which community—Magyar or Slovak— they were serving. In the official Hungarian and Austrian sources and in the Hungarian-American press, the names of Magyarized Slovaks were usually rendered in their Hungarian version, while in the Slovak-American press they usually appeared in Slovak. Since in Hungary Magyarized names were considered status symbols because they were the most obvious evidence of assimilation (Magyarization), the Magyarized Slovaks who were recruited by the Hungarian church (and government) to serve in the United States naturally arrived using Magyarized names. However, after their arrival, all had to choose between Magyarized and Slovak versions of their names depending upon which identity they eventually selected as their own. The varied ways in which their names appear in the sources illustrate this point. For example, the Slovak priest, Ján Poľakovič, appears in Hungarian sources as János Pollykovits; likewise, the Slovak Jaškovič appears as Jaskovits.

References

Balch, E. 1969. *Our Slavic Fellow Citizens.* New York: Arno Press.

Berta, J. 1977. *Slovaks in New York City.* M.A. thesis, Florida State University, Gainesville.

Bodnar, J. 1973. *The Ethnic Experience in Pennsylvania.* Lewisburg, Pa.: Bucknell University Press.

—————. 1977. *Immigration and Industrialization: Ethnicity in an American Mill Town, 1870–1940.* Pittsburgh, Pa.: University of Pittsburgh Press.

Buc, B. 1960. *Slovak Nationalism.* Middletown, Pa.: Slovak League of America.

Colakovic, B. 1973. *Yugoslav Migrations to America.* San Francisco: R. and E. Associates.

"Croats." 1980. In *Harvard Encyclopedia of American Ethnic Groups,* edited by Stephan Thernstrom. Cambridge: Harvard University Press.

Culen, K. 1972. "The Cult of S. S. Cyril and Methodius Amongst the Slovaks in the United States and Canada." *Slovakia* 22.

Glettler, M. 1980. Pittsburgh-Wien-Budapest; Program und Praxis der Nationalitätenpolitik bei der Auswanderung der ungarischen Slowaken nach Amerika um 1900. Vienna: Verlag der Österreichischen Akademie der Wissenschaften.

Greene, V. 1975. *For God and Country: The Rise of Polish and Lithuanian Ethnic Consciousness in America, 1860–1910*. Madison: Historical Society of Wisconsin.

Hanák, P., and F. Mucsi. 1978. *Magyarorszag Története, 1890–1918*. Budapest: Akademiai Kiado.

Harney, R. 1981. "Unique Features of Fraternal Records." In Immigration History Research Center, *Records of Ethnic Fraternal Benefit Associations in the United States: Essays and Inventories*. St. Paul, Minn.

Higham, J., ed. 1978. *Ethnic Leadership in America*. Baltimore: Johns Hopkins University Press.

Kann, R. 1977. *A History of the Hapsburg Empire, 1526–1918*. Berkeley and Los Angeles: University of California Press.

Kann, R., and D. Zdenek. 1984. *The Peoples of the Eastern Hapsburg Lands, 1526–1918*. Seattle: University of Washington Press.

Kende, G. 1927. *Magvarok Amerikában*. Vol. 2. Cleveland, Ohio: A Szabadsag Kiadasa.

Macartney, C. 1937. *Hungary and Her Successors*. New York: Oxford University Press.

―――――. 1968. *The Hapsburg Empire, 1790–1918*. London: Weidenfeld and Nicholson.

Magocsi, P. R. 1980. "Carpatho-Rusins." In *Harvard Encyclopedia of American Ethnic Groups*, edited by Stephan Thernstrom. Cambridge: Harvard University Press.

May, A. 1951. *The Hapsburg Monarchy, 1867–1914*. Cambridge: Harvard University Press.

Morawska, E. 1982. "The Internal Status Hierarchy in the East European Immigrant Communities of Johnstown, Pa., 1890–1930's." *Journal of Social History* 16 (Fall).

OL Országos Levéltár (Hungarian National Archives) Miniszterelnökségi Levéltár (Prime Ministry Archives). 1903. Microfilmed in Budapest, Hungary. Available in the Immigration History Research Center of the University of Minnesota, St. Paul.

Petrovich, M., and J. Halpern. 1980. "Serbs." In *Harvard Enclycopedia of American Ethnic Groups*, edited by Stephan Thernstrom. Cambridge: Harvard University Press.

Prpic, G. 1978. *South Slavic Immigration in America*. Boston: Twayne Publications.

Puskás, J. 1982a. *Kivándorló Magyarok az Eqyesült Államokban, 1880–1940*. Budapest: Akadémia: Kiadó.

―――――. 1982b. *From Hungary to the United States (1880–1914)*. Budapest: Akadémia: Kiadó.

Seton-Watson, R. 1972. *Racial Problems in Hungary*. New York: Howard Fertig.

Stein, H. 1980–81. "An Ethnic History of Slovak American Religious and Fraternal Associations." *Slovakia* 29.

Stolarik, M. 1972. "Lay Initiative in America-Slovak Parishes: 1880–1930." *American Catholic Historical Society of Philadelpia Record* 83 (September–December).

―――――. 1974. "Immigration and Urbanization: The Slovak Experience, 1870–1918." Ph.D. diss. University of Minnesota, Minneapolis.

―――――. 1985. *Growing Up on the South Side: Three Generations of Slovaks in Bethlehem, Pa., 1880–1976*. Lewisburg, Pa.: Bucknell University Press.

Szabadsáq. Major Hungarian-American newspaper published in Cleveland, Ohio, from 1892 to the present.

4

The Attenuated Ethnicity of Contemporary Finnish-Americans

PETER KIVISTO

In an intriguing though not entirely convincing argument, Sollors (1986, 221) contends that the impetus to emphasize generational analyses in ethnic studies derives primarily from their ability to delineate a "moral map." In other words, such analyses are not so much concerned with the development of a precise classificatory scheme as they are with constructing a redemption history, one in which the second generation is typically seen as falling from grace while it is the moral imperative of the third generation to effect a return to and rejuvenation of the *Gemeinschaft* world compromised by their parents. From this perspective, one can view the writing of figures such as Greeley (1971) and Novak (1972) as essentially "community-building jeremiads," with, one might add, articles such as Howe's "Limits of Ethnicity" (1977) constituting, in effect, moral rejoinders.

Nonetheless, since it is only possible to adjudicate issues of persistence and change in temporal perspective, and since it is clear that different ethnic generations have markedly different experiences in America, it is necessary to ground research in generational terms. Indeed, Sollors himself makes use of the work of scholars who have sought to address issues related to the future of ethnic groups and ethnic identity in just such a perspective. In particular, he refers to the work of Nahirny and Fishman (1965) and Gans (1979). This work is important insofar as it serves to challenge the claim that an ethnic revival occurred in the 1960s and 1970s among European-origin groups, a claim that explicitly or implicitly is undergirded by Hansen's (1938) "law of third generation return." Nahirny and Fishman dispute Hansen by suggesting that the generations experience their ethnicity differently: for the first, it is a concrete, unreflective, lived experience, while for subsequent generations it becomes more abstract, idealized, reflective, and ultimately optional. According to them, both the second and third generations are conscious of their ethnic identity, and the differences between these generations and between them and the immigrant generation involve not simply the degree of identification with the group but the nature of the identification with "ethnicity." And, they go on to note, ethnic identification is, at best, a "murkey concept" (1965, 312).

It is precisely that murky concept that Gans (1979) takes up in his seminal piece on "symbolic ethnicity." The thrust of the article is that there has been no ethnic revival, but instead American ethnic groups have experienced a steady process of "straight-line assimilation." The insititutional and communal component of ethnic groups continues to erode, and ethnic cultures similarly recede in salience. Gans writes "that in this generation, people are less and less interested in their ethnic cultures and organizations—both sacred and secular, and are instead more concerned with maintaining their ethnic identity" (1979, 7). This identity becomes voluntary rather than ascriptive and is woven into an image of self that is composed of multiple identities. This new, symbolic ethnicity does not entail the constraints on behavior that the older mode of ethnic identification did, but neither does it provide a basis for a preservation and/or re-creation of ethnic organizations or institutions. It is primarily motivated "by a nostaglic allegiance to the culture of the immigrant generation, or that of the old country; a love for or pride in a tradition that can be felt without having to be incorporated in everyday behavior" (Gans 1979, 9; see also Alba 1985). While symbolic ethnicity may linger for generations, it bespeaks the significant attenuation of ethnicity that assimilationists all along have predicted.

Smith (1981, p. xiii) would appear to challenge this because he sees the ethnic revival as a worldwide phenomenon that is not of momentary interest. Instead, it constitutes a long-term renaissance that is a response to the disenchantment of the world brought about by the alienating consciousness of modernity. In other words, it is a modern form of a secular theodicy that is designed to "heal the rift" generated by the anomic conditions produced by industrial civilization. In general, however, he concurs with Gans that conditions in the United States differ considerably from those in other parts of the world, including Western Europe. This is particularly the case for white ethnics. Like Gans, he suggests that for a genuine revival to occur, ethnics would have to be propelled by political and economic interests to mobilize and organize. While Gans does not think this is very likely, Smith suggests one possible scenario: academic overproduction will send an unemployed intelligentsia back to the ethnic community where it will constitute a new leadership that will make demands for incorporation into the mainstream on behalf of the ethnic group itself (Smith 1981, 159; see Tricarico in this volume for an illustration of this). But the likelihood of unemployed or underemployed academics returning to ethnic communities (which, in any event, may no longer be viable communities) appears quite a remote possibility. Furthermore, he does not differ appreciably from Gans in his assessment that white neo-ethnicity in the United States is essentially conservative and nostalgic.

While the concept of symbolic ethnicity has been used increasingly in discussions of larger European-origin groups, it has not, to my knowledge, been applied systematically in discussions of smaller groups. This essay will concentrate on one such group, the Finns, who, according to the 1980 census, constitute a mere .33 percent of the nation's population. While Finns, like many eastern and southern European ethnic groups, evidenced a resurgence of interest in ethnic identity during the past two decades, its significance during the recent past and its implications for the future are unclear. This is especially the case for Finns because scholarship has tended to focus almost exclusively on the ethnic community prior to midcentury. This essay is, therefore, a prolegomenon to future research and will begin to analyze that period beginning when the third generation came of age. It seeks to provide a description of the particular contours of change in the institutional framework of the ethnic community, in geographical mobility patterns and their impact, and in the value patterns of Finnish-Americans.

As ethnicity takes an increasingly attenuated form, its salience remains a puzzle to unravel, and thus, at present, circumspection is required in addressing the following questions: (1) Are observers witnessing a gradual dissipation, continuity over time, a resurgence of interest, or a transfiguration of ethnicity? (2) What are the chances of entirely new ethnic institutions being forged? and (3) Can ethnic identity persist, and if so, in what form if institutional supports are lacking?

Institutional Erosion

At its zenith the Finnish-American community developed four major types of ethnic institutions wherever there were significant population concentrations: (1) fraternal organizations or *Landsmannschaften*, with temperance societies being the most important; (2) consumer co-operatives; (3) radical political organizations; and (4) churches (primarily Lutheran). By the 1930s, however, and at an accelerated pace in the postwar period, far-reaching changes in the institutional structure occurred, resulting in a steady erosion of members from the first three institutions and the progressive "Americanization" of ethnic churches.

The fate of temperance societies was actually sealed before the time period under consideration. Karni (1981, 163) notes that they were primarily a nineteenth-century phenomenon, although there was some growth prior to the passage of the Eighteenth Amendment. The societies had been severely weakened early in their lives in many locales where they had been the focus of intra-ethnic conflict waged by radical and church Finns. In many cases, radicals succeeded in their efforts to take control of them, transforming them into explicitly political organizations (although radicals, like their religious counterparts, were inclined to support abstinence from alcohol). But ethnic strife alone cannot account for the demise of these organizations. Ultimately, their fate was the same as that of organizations forged by native-born participants in the Prohibition movement, such as the Woman's Christian Temperance Union. The repeal of the Eighteenth Amendment signaled the end of what sociologist Joseph Gusfield (1955) has referred to as a "symbolic crusade." The movement, which had been sponsored by the dominant Protestant middle class of rural and small-town America, was undermined by the changing mores adopted by the new, urban professional middle class, mores that included the acceptance of social drinking. Temperance advocates both within and without the ethnic community were increasingly perceived as old-fashioned and parochial. By the middle of the 1940s, many societies had closed their doors for good, while others lingered on in the postwar era without the benefit of new recruits (Karni 1981, 167).

The history of consumer cooperatives differs in some key respects. Co-ops were more closely aligned with radical Finns than with the religious sector of the ethnic community. Initially arising as a stopgap measure during strike actions when the business community often denied credit to workers, they became lucrative enterprises that provided many cooperators with a countercultural model of a future socialist commonwealth. The Finnish cooperators were both admired and mistrusted by the larger cooperative movement and by various social reformers. Intra-ethnic strife had an adverse effect on cooperatives, though in this case the conflict pitted the extreme Left against the moderate Left. In the early 1930s the latter succeeded in driving Communists from their ranks—symbolically reflected in the replacement of the "Red Star" logo, with its hammer and sickle, by an apolitical pair of pine trees (Kivisto 1984, 169–72).

In the postwar period the distinctly Finnish character of the cooperatives began to decline. Not only did second- and third-generation Finns often lack a familiarity with the Finnish language, but non-Finns became an increasingly prominent part of the membership. Thus, a survey conducted in 1952 revealed that whereas the board composition of cooperatives when they were founded was 93 percent Finnish, with foreign-born Finns constituting 88 percent of the membership, by 1952 the foreign-born had declined to 22 percent while the non-Finnish representation had risen to 29 percent. Furthermore, changes occurred regarding the language used to conduct meetings. In 1952, 81 percent of board meetings were conducted in English, and 49 percent of membership meetings relied solely on English (only 13 percent of membership meetings were entirely conducted in Finnish, and these were all in small, rural establishments) (Jokinen 1975, 11–12). By 1956, Donald Lehtinen, the director of membership services for the Central Cooperative Wholesale, would write that "the melting pot of the U.S. works here as well as elsewhere" (general memo to members, Central Cooperative Wholesale Collection, Immigration History Research Center).

Although cooperatives were, in many locales, thriving business concerns well into the 1950s—operating cooperative stores, oil associations, buying clubs, creameries, boarding houses, savings banks, a coffee roasting plant, a bakery, and a feed and flour terminal—a recurrent complaint of older members was that the younger generation did not fully understand the principles of cooperation. While they saw themselves as allies of the labor movement and as promoters of "economic democracy," they were concerned that such views were not shared by the younger, more Americanized membership. Indeed, the two weekly publishing ventures of the Central Cooperative Wholesale, the English-language *Cooperative Builder* and the Finnish *Co-op Weekly* reflected this tension between the generations. While the former concentrated on portraying cooperatives as viable business concerns, it downplayed over time the anticapitalist character of cooperative ideology. In contrast, the Finnish publication sought to appear to a readership that was very much concerned with such ideological features of the cooperative movement.

As the Finnish cooperatives forged closer links with the larger national organizations, this transition to an emphasis on business issues accelerated. National organizations had earlier been suspicious of the political character of the Finnish cooperatives, and their willingness to bring Finns into the fold reflects the profound changes taking place in these ethnic organizations. Just as the change in logo in the wake of the struggle over communism symbolically reflected a significant shift, so, too, a change to the name "Mutual Service and Cooperatives" was followed subsequently by a decision to drop the word "cooperative" from the name altogether. The rationale for this change was explained by a former general manager of the organization: "The change was made to identify the name of the companies immediately and more simply. It was found that to people not familiar with cooperatives, the word 'co-op' often raised a question and agents now and then found that their sales of insurance depended more upon their ability to explain the cooperative idea than upon their competence as insurance men" (Douthit 1973, 68). In short, the organizational charisma of the earlier epoch had eroded, with cooperatives opting for a modern, pragmatic rational, calculating business approach.

They did so, however, against serious competition posed by the advent of the corporate supermarket chain. These chains, due to their high sales volumes, were able to undercut cooperative prices and therefore captured a significant percentage of the former cooperative market. In addition, the supermarket chains' more generous attitude regarding credit reflected changing mores to which the cooperatives had not adequately responded. As a result, beginning in the late 1950s an increasing number of cooperative stores were closed, while enterprises that were deemed competitive were modernized and stores were encouraged to emulate the tactics of their competitors. Despite such efforts, the number of such enterprises has steadily declined.

For radical political organizations, the post–World War II era marked a precipitous downward trend in the level of support they were able to elicit from the ethnic community. Although a number of factors conspired to undermine the efficacy of these organizations, four can be singled out as being particularly significant (Kivisto 1983). First, internecine political strife, especially the battle over the Bolshevization of the CPUSA, took a heavy toll and reflected an inability on the part of large sectors of the Left to come to terms with the unique features of American social and political life. The demand for the elimination of ethnically based organizations and their replacement by work-place-oriented cells caused a great deal of bitterness and conflict within the Finnish organizations. It resulted in a loss of members that was not compensated for by the growth of the CP due to the depression. Second, the rapid and contradictory shifts in the Communist party's official lines regarding domestic and foreign politics reflected not an attempt to grapple with the creation of a truly indigenous political Left but a growing subservience to Moscow. According to Klehr (1984), the shifts in position were primarily at the behest of the Kremlin, and it, quite simply, was not in tune with the particularities of the American situation. The consequence was a fracturing of radical unity that was never overcome. Compounding this was the flight of perhaps as many as six thousand North American Finns (many of them coming from the ranks of the most dedicated party cadre) to Soviet Karelia during the early 1930s (Kero 1983, 1975).

Related to these changes was the emergence of new options for leftists within the mainstream of American political culture, due largely to the birth of the New Deal and the creation of the CIO. The major beneficiary of the growing dissatisfaction with the extreme Left was the left wing of the Democratic party, which was linked to the labor movement principally through its relationship with the newly created CIO. This new union organization differed from its most obvious predecessor, the IWW, insofar as it proved successful in its attempts to, in Irving Bernstein's (1960, 77) words, breach "the bastions of the mass production industries." Furthermore, the CIO repudiated syndicalism and proceeded to organize with a "confident reliance on liberal government." The consequence of this shift was, according to Bert Cochran (1977, 332), an increase in labor solidarity, but at the same time a muting of anticapitalist radicalism.

Third, working-class radicalism was unprepared for a shift in the class structure of American capitalism caused by the expansion of public-sector bureaucracies and the increased demand for scientific and technical expertise in economic institutions, with the simultaneous decline in labor-intensive industries as a direct consequence of automation (Noble 1977; Bensman and Vidich 1970; Mills 1956). The result was an increase in the size of the professional white-collar middle class. The opportunities for upward mobility afforded by the transformations at this historical juncture cracked the protective shell of the working-class subculture, and notions of individual advancement began to supplant a belief in the desirability of collective (class-based) improvements in life chances.

Finally, the anticommunism of the McCarthy era was felt in its rather virulent repression of the weakened remnants of immigrant radicalism. In the case of William Heikkila, his forced deportation and subsequent return to the United States became a source of embarrassment for the U.S. Naturalization and Immigration Service because of the mass media's rather general condemnation of the government's flagrant violation of due process (Cook 1982). Nonetheless, the service persisted in its attempts to deport him until his death in 1960. In other instances, former radicals were imprisoned, deported, or, in some cases, such as that of Taisto Elo, left the country voluntarily. Elo's was a rather typical case; whatever his political attachments two or three decades earlier, he was not a member of any leftist organization in the 1950s, but, on the contrary, expressed the rather unrevolutionary "hope that Americanism wins over McCarranism (Kenneth Enkel Papers).

For a few thousand Finns, however, a somewhat modified ethnic radicalism has managed to persist through a tenacious preservation of organizations and newspapers reflecting the social democratic, Wobblie, and Communist camps. They maintained their allegiance to the Left for decades after its halcyon days. Their institutions exist without the infusion of new recruits, and most of the remnant appear aware that their days are numbered. *Industrialisti*, once the official newspaper of the IWW, finally ceased to publish in 1975. The Communist Työmies Society continues to operate, publishing a newspaper—*Työmies-Eteenpäin*—that was the result of a merger of the two largest Finnish Communist papers. Its readership is steadily declining in numbers. Furthermore, its inability to find a Finnish-American editor has forced it to rely on support from Finnish journalism schools. The social democrats, having split with the Socialist party in 1936 because of presumed Communist tendencies within the ranks of the latter, created and have maintained various locals of the Finnish-American League for Democrary. Their newspaper, *Raivaaja*, continues to be printed, though for a dwindling readership. In all three instances, the remaining first- and second-generation radicals are participants in institutions of nostalgia.

Religious Finns in the postmigration milieu tended to affiliate with Lutheran churches, though some, in part due to a deeply rooted anticlericism, chose to join other established Protestant denominations in which the role of the laity was more pronounced (this was most prevalent on the East Coast, where Finns often opted for either Congregationalism or Methodism). Among Lutherans, unity proved to be impossible as various antagonistic strains developed, the differences often based on conflicting views about the appropriateness of establishing an arm of the Finnish state church in America. Thus, soon after the establishment in 1890 of the Finnish Evangelical Lutheran Church in America, or Suomi Synod, it was challenged by a variety of sectarian groups that referred to themselves as Apostolic Lutherans, or Laestadians, as well as by the more denominational church body founded in 1898, the Finnish American National Church (Kivisto 1984, 77–79; Ollila 1963).

The recent histories of Apostolic Lutherans and those affiliated with either the Suomi Synod or the National Church diverge, predicated on the otherwordly sectarianism of the former in contrast with the denominational character of the latter two. The Apostolic Lutherans have been divided into several antagonistic groups whose boundaries have been subject to dramatic fissures and fusions. In 1947 Uurus Saarnivaara (82–89) identified five major groups: (1) the Apostolic Lutheran Church, the largest assembly, contained approximately 14,000 members; (2) the Heidemanians, named after a charismatic founder, had 6,000 to 7,000 members who were exponents of "extreme evangelism"; (3) the Evangelicals, or Pullarites, had about 3,000 members; (4) the Firstborn, the first group to use the English language in religious services, counted 2,000 adherents; and (5) the New Awakenists, a very small sect, included about 200 followers. Since that time, the fortunes of various groups have evidenced both growth and decline, with a number of new bodies that explicitly define themselves as Laestadian having emerged in recent years. Some groups are composed largely of aging members, while others have managed to attract younger members from either inside or outside the particular sect.

Common to the various dissenting groups of Apostolics is an otherwordly orientation often tinged with apocalyptic themes, manifesting itself in a deep-rooted hostility to rationalistic humanism and modernity, to "this crooked and prevarious generation who are seeking only for pleasure in the world, in this bright and brilliant time when there is so much glory, but it is nothing but tinsel" (Apostolic Lutheran Church 1927, 29). In practice, however, the response to the world has been ambivalent, with many bitter struggles waged over such issues as dancing, women's makeup, the purchase of television sets, and a host of related concerns. The recent history of these groups is far too complicated to comment upon further here, and indeed, the lack of reliable information concerning changes that have occurred during the past four decades makes even speculation difficult.

One thing is clear: to the extent that these sect members have managed to retain their distinct religious identities, an unintended consequence has been the reinforcement of ethnic identity. Moreover, in several pockets of the United States, including Washington State, northern Minnesota, and especially the Upper Peninsula of Michigan, ethnic islands have been created. One recently constructed Laestadian church in Michigan has not merely a large membership but a young membership, and one that is growing, due primarily to the sect's hostility to birth control. While members are encouraged to socialize only with the other sect members, there are indications that this is a group undergoing change. This is by no means a church of the dispossessed, its members mainly coming from the working class; the parking lot on a Sunday morning is filled with cars and pickup trucks of recent vintage. Furthermore, numerous compromises have been made with the larger society as manifestations of an immersion in, rather than an avoidance of, consumer culture—the world of tinsel. If second-generation elderly women continue to opt for simple, black dresses and a covering for their heads, younger women are just as likely to come to Sunday services with fashionably styled hair, makeup, and designer jeans. In short, the sect has paid a price in its efforts to attract the younger generation. What that will mean for the future of the group's distinctive religious orientation and, parenthetically, for its ability to remain an ethnic island, is open to question.

In contrast with this distinct minority of the ethnic group, a rather different transformation has occurred in the Suomi Synod and, in parallel fashion, in the National Lutheran Church. From the 1920s, the issue of Americanization was a topic that produced considerable internal strife in both bodies. In the case of the National Church, links with the Gospel Association of Finland were not adequate to provide a sufficient number of trained clergy. Unable to sustain its own seminary, the church body developed ties with the German Missouri Synod, and seminarians began to be sent to the larger body's Concordia Seminary in St. Louis (Nopola 1958, 25). The somewhat larger Suomi Synod created its own college and seminary, but discussions about the long-term fate of a distinctly ethnic church became a storm of controversy with the publication of Suomi College president John Wargelin's (1924) thesis in which he suggested that an inexorable process was at play that spelled the inevitable deracination of the Finnish heritage. Synod members were asked to distinguish two heritages, the ethnic and the religious, and they were informed that the latter was more important than the former.

Whether the laity was convinced by this argument is unclear. Nonetheless, distinctly ethnic features of the churches progressively eroded. The introduction of English into the churches got underway in the 1920s and accelerated appreciably in the following two decades. The changes often occurred in the Sunday schools first, as children unfamiliar with Finnish could not avail themselves of the heretofore standard texts employed: Luther's *Katekismus* and J. K. Nikander's *Raamataa Historia*. As a result, despite an aversion to doing so, the Synod's publishing firm, the Book Concern, succumbed to increased pressures to publish English-language materials. The introduction of English into Sunday services followed this trend at a varied pace. While some congregations had completely substituted English for Finnish by the early 1940s, others only began to haltingly implement English services alongside those in Finnish in the late 1950s.

Another trend suggests a desire to de-emphasize the ethnic character of churches. Many congregations decided to change their name, eliminating reference to their Finnish origin. Thus, a not uncommon tranformation was to recast the Finnish Evangelical Lutheran Church as the First Evangelical Lutheran Church.

Linked to these Americanizing trends was the commencement of discussions aimed at merger with other ethnic Lutheran bodies. Though the issue had been broached as early as 1930, a serious initiative did not began until 1948. Synod leaders argued that their "ultimate destiny is not to remain an isolated church body but to become eventually an organic part of wider American Lutheranism" (Suomi Synod 1962, 31). Despite resistance from some quarters, on 1 January 1963 the Synod leadership accomplished that goal by joining with Danish, Swedish, and German Lutherans to form the Lutheran Church in America. A second merger with the American Lutheran Church (heavy represented by Norwegians) and the American Evangelical Lutheran Church took place in 1988. In similar fashion, the considerably smaller National Church fused with the Lutheran Church, Missouri Synod, in 1964.

The Retreat of Finnish and the Expansion of Exogamous Marriages

The significance of language maintenance, or, in Joshua Fishman's (1966) phrase, "language loyalty," in terms of the preservation of ethnic identity is not a particularly well understood phenomenon. Conversely, the impact of the decline of usage of the ancestral language on members of the third generation and beyond is also not easily interpreted. What is clear is that Finns, like most of their European immigrant counterparts, witnessed dramatic declines in Finnish-language proficiency from 1940 onward. Furthermore, there was no concerted campaign from any quarter of the ethnic community to stem this development, which was viewed by many ethnic leaders as regrettable but inevitable, given the demands of the host society to use English not only in public but in private life.

The decline in language maintenance was slower for Finns than for many other groups, due in part to the difficulties many Finns had in learning English. The fact that Finnish is not an Indo-European language made the acquisition of English-language skills unusually difficult. In addition, because Finns were more rural-based than many of the other new immigrants, and in many instances created relatively isolated rural communities that constituted language islands (e.g., enclaves such as Tapiola, Pelkie, and Nisula in Michigan's Upper Peninsula), the pace of change was somewhat retarded. As Lowrey

Nelson's (1948) analysis of 1940 census data indicates, however, even in rural regions a dramatic change was occurring among Finns by the fourth decade of the century. In urban centers, the changes began even earlier and were well advanced by the outbreak of World War II. Kolehmainen's (1937a, 887) study of the Conneaut, Ohio, area revealed "the slow and orderly retreat of Finnish before the dominant language."

Marked changes could be seen between the first and second generations. While the former maintained their firm command of Finnish, they were unable to achieve enough skill in English to permit them to feel comfortable with it as a second tongue. Their children, on the other hand, became proficient in English usage due to their experience in public schools, while simultaneously becoming increasingly uneasy about their familiarity with Finnish. In this context, the "Finnicisation of English" served as a mode of mediation between the two generations in a period of transition. Kolehmanien's (1937b, 66) conclusion concerning the fate of Finnish in America has proven to be essentially accurate. "As a whole, the second generation has proved to be an unreliable guardian of the language, and to their children, Finnish will be an alien tongue." Efforts in the 1960s and 1970s to encourage language study among Finns were sporadic and met with little success. As a consequence, there are only four remaining Finnish-language newspapers, and Pilli (1986, 33) reports that their combined subscriptions total only two thousand.

Related to language maintenance is the issue of intermarriage, for when exogamous marriages increase, language maintenance generally decreases. Analyzing rates of Finnish intermarriage and obtaining comparisons with other ethnic groups has proven difficult, however, due to the lack of adequate data. In terms of national-level data, the U.S. Census Bureau's decision to exclude any questions about European ethnic ancestry for several decades prior to 1980 creates a serious lacuna for researchers. Furthermore, when a decision was made to include a question about ethnic ancestry for the 1980 census, the manner in which the question was posed makes it necessary to treat the results circumspectly. Respondents were given the option of listing from one to three ethnic-origin groups. Among the Finnish group, over one-half were of mixed ancestry (U.S. Bureau of the Census 1983). But the relatively large segment that cited only Finnish ancestry must be viewed carefully before concluding that this segment is the product of endogamous marriage patterns. Given the way the question was posed, individuals of mixed ancestry did not have to cite all of their ancestral groups; in other words, they could list only one ethnic group, perhaps the one they most closely identify with due to last name or other factors. Consequently, while the data would appear to suggest that for about 40 percent of the Finnish-American populace endogamous marriages have continued to be the norm, this figure is undoubtedly inflated. At this point, there is not sufficient information to reach definitive conclusions about the intermarriage rate for Finns.

At the community level, only a few studies have been conducted to date, and they are several decades old. In Nelson's (1943) study of Minnesota's rural Wright County, Finns, along with Germans and Swedes (the three largest ethnic groups in the county), had relatively high rates of endogamy during the 1940s. Since Nelson's data point to religion as a major factor in reinforcing endogamy, the fact that Wright County had a large concentration of Apostolic Lutherans would suggest that a higher rate of endogamy characterized this region in comparison with other areas of Finnish settlement. Indeed, Kolehmainen's (1936) community study of urbanized Finns during the late 1930s discovered that over 57 percent of the marriages of native-born Finns were to non-Finns. He saw this trend as part of a larger rebellion against Finnish customs and traditions. Since Finns have lacked significant institutional or ideological defenses against exogamous marriages, it is not surprising that the impressionistic evidence available suggests that the rate of intermarriage during the decades since these studies were conducted has been ever upward.

Geographical Mobility

The geographical destinations of immigrant Finns resulted in a rather distinctive settlement pattern—pattern that continues to be of significance. Unlike earlier-arriving Scandinavians, who had a genuine opportunity to obtain farmland, Finns were propelled by an industrializing economy into the ranks of the proletariat. While this meant that they initially found themselves in urban America, due in large part to the fact that they worked in primary extractive industries, they tended to settle in smaller cities. They were thus found in larger numbers in Duluth rather than Minneapolis, in the iron and copper mining communities in Michigan's Upper Peninsula rather than Detroit, in the Oregon coastal town of Astoria rather than Portland, in Worcester rather than Boston, and in Ashtabula rather than Cleveland. New York City, where Finns located in the Red Hook section of Brooklyn and in Harlem, constitutes the only major exception to this pattern. Finns were heavily represented in the relatively sparsely populated regions of the upper Midwest, with over half of the immigrant generation locating in Michigan, Minnesota, or Wisconsin.

A consequence of this settlement pattern was that Finns frequently comprised one of the largest if not the largest group in the community, something that would not have occurred for what was a rather small ethnic group nationally if it had settled in large cities. This situation made it possible for Finns to exert a significant amount of influence in the sociopolitical lives of the communities where they resided. It also made possible the construction of a viable ethnic community.

As early as the second generation, however, there is evidence of a drift to larger cities. Virtanen (1977), for example, has documented that the development of the automotive industry in Detroit served as a magnet to attract workers out of the mining communities (especially from the copper mining regions of the Keewenaw Peninsula of Michigan, which had been economically devastated by the precipitous drop in international copper prices). Their arrival coincided with the change Zunz (1982) depicts as a movement from ethnic divisions to one characterized by an admixture of ethnic and class factors. In the Finnish case, the second generation did re-establish an ethnic enclave, though, according to Loukinen (1981, 121), it differed insofar as the tensions between radical and conservative Finns were largely mitigated by a desire to be with other Finns as a means of avoiding the potentially alienating character of a rapidly growing urban center. Loukinen (1981, 111) characterizes the twelve-block Woodrow Wilson area as an "urban village." Although perhaps not as dramatically as in the Detroit case, given the fact that its growth rate between 1910 and 1940 was more than two and a half times the national average (Virtanen 1977, 73), similar movements of Finns from smaller towns and cities to nearby major urban hubs occurred between 1920 and 1940. In most instances modified ethnic communities were created, replete with churches, mutual aid societies, social clubs, restaurants, and taverns.

In terms of regional distribution, the 1980 census (U.S. Bureau of the Census 1983, 16–20) indicates that Finns remain heavily concentrated in the upper Midwest, since 39.3 percent of the 615,872 people who reported Finnish as either their single ancestry or as part of a multiple ancestry resided in Michigan, Minnesota, and Wisconsin. A total of 60,459 were reported in California; 39,496, in Washington; and 33,583, in Massachusetts. Other well-represented states included, in descending order of importance, New York, Oregon, Illinois, Ohio, and Florida.

Since 1950, as the third generation came of age, the changes already underway were expanded and intensified in several ways. The move to major cities continued apace. Particularly significant in this regard was the movement of college-educated middle-class professionals into the bureaucracies of corporate America, and, coincidentally, into such large metropolitan centers as New York, Boston, Chicago, Minneapolis and St. Paul, Detroit, Portland, Seattle, and San Francisco. Unlike the second generation, they did not settle in ethnic neighborhoods but generally opted for the suburbs. Indeed, locales such as the Woodrow Wilson area began to disappear in the 1950s and 1960s as the second generation also headed for the suburbs, or, when retirement came, for the Sun Belt.

One of the reasons that Florida appears among the states containing larger Finnish populations is that a thriving ethnic community has been created by retirees in the Lake Worth–Lantana area, north of Boca Raton. While Finns, like other groups, were drawn to Florida before World War II, it was not until after 1945 that the exodus, abetted in part by the financial stability provided by social security and by union pension plans, began to attract significant numbers of Finns. As Copeland (1981, 128) observes, many of these people "moved to Florida gradually" insofar as they frequently chose initially to live there only during the winter months, returning to their homes in the Northeast or the Midwest during the warmer parts of the year.

There is a sufficient concentration of Finns in a relatively small setting to have an impact. Churches and social halls serve this clientele, and local businesses, both those owned by Finns and those owned by non-Finns, seek to cater to this market. An enterprising rest home in the area publishes a "Puhelinluettelo" (i.e., a telephone directory of the Finnish-speaking population in the area). In interviews with a small number of residents, several stated that they have experienced a resurgence of interest in their ethnic heritage and in some cases have had to attempt to resuscitate a rather weak command of the Finnish language (and this despite the fact that those who choose to reside in a distinctly Finnish environment are a group more inclined that others to identify strongly with the ethnic community). This community has been assisted in preserving a distinctive ethnic identity by the decision on the part of a small number of Finnish businessmen to establish homes in the area, motivated in part by a desire to avoid Finland's high taxes. Nonetheless, whether this community persists will depend, ultimately, on whether retirees from subsequent generations choose to settle in such communities, preserving them as ethnic islands. Given the tenuous ties of the third generation and beyond to the cultural heritage of the Old World, already quite removed from the second, the prospects do not look particularly sanguine.

Small numbers combined with residential dispersal have led to the virtual disappearance of distinctly ethnic enterprises and organizations in most cities. Indeed, these have also experienced progressive erosion in areas such as the Mesabi Range of Minnesota and the Upper Peninsula of Michigan. In the case of the latter, a rather interesting, though unstudied, phenomenon is taking place that raises questions related to the variable character of ethnicity. In a region with a large Finnish-ancestry population, and with large numbers of other Scandinavian groups as well as Polish, Italian, French, and Cornish ethnics, a form of regional identity may be in the making that is, in effect, a composite of the various groups that make up the region. The region has tended to see itself as removed from Michigan's lower peninsula: on the one hand residents uphold the virtues of small-town America against the evils of urban life; on the other, they describe a sense of disenfranchisement from political and economic power. At various points in the past quarter of a century small numbers of the disgruntled have speculated about the possibility of becoming either a separate state or a new nation. While there is absolutely no possibility of mobilizing citizens to push for such dramatic changes, and, indeed, the proposals are frequently made with tongue in cheek, they do reflect a feeling of alienation from the larger society and a desire to maintain a sense of separateness. A regional dialect serves as a marker of identity when residents travel "downstate." Recently, when the state's tourist bureau began a campaign to promote the state, it widely circulated red bumper stickers with the slogan: "Say yes to Michigan!" Almost immediately, green bumper stickers began to appear on automobiles in the Upper Peninsula: "Say ya to da U.P., eh!"

Especially as the mining industry in the region continues to progressively decline, the possibility exists that the region may become increasingly similar in key respects to Appalachia. One indication of a growing sense of regionalism can be seen in the increased use during the past decade of the self-identification term *Yupper*; its use is embraced by some residents of the region and decried by others. While it is certainly too soon to predict what the outcome of this behavior might be, one intriguing approach to understanding the phenomenon is to treat it as a manifestation of "emergent ethnicity" (see Marger and Obermiller 1983 for an attempt to treat residents of Appalachia in this way). If such an identity is construed either as ethnic identity or as a surrogate or parallel to ethnic identity, the question must be posed: What would such an identity, if it developed (it is, at best, at an incipient state of development), do to the viability of a distinctly Finnish-American identification in the area?

While much remains to explore concerning these issues, what this suggests is that it is probable that regional variations will play a differential role in the future shaping of ethnic identity. Except for the unique case of the Florida retirement enclave, however, in neither the regional centers of immigrant settlement nor in major cities is there any indication of any impetus to preserve old ethnic institutions or to forge new ones.

Cultural Shifts

The preceding analysis of changes in the ethnic community relating to institutions, language, marriage, and geographical location lends credence to Gans's (1979) claim that ethnicity for the third generation and beyond increasingly becomes a matter of symbolic identification with one's ancestors. Two additional questions remain, however: Can cultural values surivive without such institutional supports, as Greeley (1971) claims, and, if so, can they continue to shape behavior? If, as Swidler (1986) has recently argued, cultures are "tool kits" of symbols, values, and world views, then to what extent do contemporary Finnish-Americans make use of tools derived from their ethnic background rather than tools supplied by the dominant culture?

The precise manner in which inherited cultural systems shape the personality traits of ethnic group members is a complex issue in any event, but for Finns analysis is additionally problematic due to the bifurcated community that in some key respects may have resulted in very different value systems. For religious Finns, for example, the Lutheran heritage demanded a deferential attitude toward authority that, when linked to the tradition's ambiguous doctrine of the two kingdoms, produced a marked conservatism (cf. Christen 1983 on Norwegian-Americans). In contrast, the impact of secularization on radical Finns encouraged skeptical thinking that provided the basis for a general willingness to challenge established authority. These two sectors of the community exhibited rather different attitudes toward tradition and toward the future. Explicating these and a wide range of issues, such as attitudes about individualism, cooperation, and family ties, among others is necessary if one is to comprehend the shifts that have occurred in recent years.

Unfortunately, relatively little research has been conducted on the value system of Finns in America. Nonetheless, a few community studies provide some useful data. First, Schoefer's (1975) study of Finns in northern California up to 1960 depicts radical Finns as becoming acculturated to mainstream political life primarily by finding a place in the left wing of the Democratic party. Their earlier belief in the revolutionary potential of the working class dissipated, though a muted critical stance toward the power structure and capitalism

remained. Although his evidence is very limited, he views religious
Finns as very similar to mainstream Protestants; for example, a desire
for the church to play an active role in such social issues as the civil
rights movement had emerged by the 1960s, thereby distinguishing
the present generation's view of social ethics from the more conservative views of its immigrant forebears. For both groups, the Finntown
was rapidly disappearing, and with it the heretofore strong emphasis
on communally oriented rather than individually oriented action,
thereby signaling a decline of what William Hoglund (1980) has
termed the "associative spirit" of the immigrant generation.

These findings are, to a large extent, reinforced in David Hayes's
(1958) study of Lanesville, Massachusetts. Hayes stresses the disappearance of the earlier divisions in the ethnic community as both
sectors attained lower-middle-class status. He argues that, in the process of moving up the social ladder, they have adopted the values of
the American middle class. Capturing the quiescent period of the
Eisenhower administration, with its political conservatism and its
promotion of a civic religion, he notes a marked move to the political
right among all Finns. With a decline in negative stereotypes (cf.
Owen et al.; 1981), Finns were able to manipulate the more positive
images held by the host society and integrate them into the large value
pantheon of the American middle class.

A third study, both analytically rigorous and empirically rich, is
that conducted by Harry Rickard Doby (1960, 23). His research on
the rural community of Waino, Wisconsin, concluded that the "rapid
and abrupt change" from a relatively isolated folk community to a
modern one immersed in mass society occurred without any appreci-
able degree of social disorganization. He observed, for example, that
by the 1950s traditional festivals had ceased, and the third generation
eschewed distinctively Finnish foods and clothing. Third-generation
families were smaller than those of the first and second generation,
suggesting to him a greater emphasis on individualism and atomized
family units. Related to this is the fact that mutual aid in the form of
shared labor had become rare.

The overwhelmingly radical political proclivities of the community's founders were not shared by the third generation. The aversion
of young people to "isms" was apparent when the Marxist-Leninist
Sunday School was closed due to lack of interest. Waino was, in this
respect, a microcosm of Finnish-American radicalism. Unlike that
other ethnic group with significant radical proclivities, Jews, Finns
did not produce a third generation of "red diaper" babies. The third
generation had a substantially different assessment of religion and
capitalism, viewing both in an essentially positive light. Similarly,

there were marked generational differences over such issues as the function of education, work roles, alcohol consumption, social justice (Doby describes the third generation as "inarticulate"), the orientation toward the burgeoning consumer culture, and premarital sex (Doby 1960, 111–14).

These studies bolster the claim that Finns "have not reproduced their cultural legacy intact from the Old World" (Hoglund 1980, 370). Furthermore, studies that have sought to indicate the preservation of a distinctive Finnish-American culture fail to provide sufficient evidence to conclude that such a culture is being transmitted generationally. Olin-Fahle's (1983, 3) anthropological study of Finntown in New York City, for example, attempted to indicate how Finns "manipulated some values, norms, symbols, and ceremonials from their traditional culture and established new rules to keep them distinct from other groups." Examining *sisu* (perseverance, endurance, fortitude), *talkoohenki* (spirit of cooperation for the common good), and sauna, she illustrates how these material and ideal artifacts of a transplanted culture served to carve out a distinct group identity by highlighting the boundaries between the in-group and out-groups. In contrast with the previously noted studies, the emphasis here is on cultural persistence, not on assimilation. But given the fact that her subjects are an aging and diminishing population, it is not possible to extrapolate these findings to describe the larger community. What Olin-Fahle fails to explain is the conflict between these values and the values of the dominant culture, a conflict in which a consumption-oriented value scheme would serve to undermine *sisu* while a spirit of possessive individualism similarly undercuts *talkoohenki*. In the case of material culture, saunas are at least as much a mark of mass society (what health club or Holiday Inn would be without one?) as they are a marker of ethnic identity.

Similarly, Loukinen's (1979, 24) research on the maintenance of culture in rural hamlets is ultimately unconvincing in its claim that the social networks embedded in the structure of the communities have preserved the "distinctiveness of a Finnish-American meaning system." In his study of visiting patterns, for example, he looks at such factors as frequency of visits, sex role constraints, the rituals involved in discourse, and the obligations of reciprocity that visits to neighbors generate. But by failing to examine this material comparatively, he does not provide evidence that what is happening among Finnish-Americans differs from events occurring within other ethnic groups. Indeed, whether there is anything distinctively ethnic about this is open to question.

Conclusion

The preponderance of evidence discussed in the preceding pages suggests two things. First, it lends support to Hoglund's (1980, 370) statement that "by the late 1970s, in fact, it could not be claimed that the lives of most Finnish Americans still revolved around the preservation of their ethnicity." Second, in terms of the visible manifestations of a resurgence of interest in ethnicity for a part of the community, heavily represented by members of the educated middle class, this interest is overwhelmingly symbolic in nature. Ethnic identification has not entailed a concomitant interest in reviving ethnic institutions or in living among fellow ethnics. Nor has it entailed the articulation of political demands on behalf of Finnish-America.

Instead, a significantly attenuated ethnicity persists that is chiefly based on the desire of some Finnish-Americans to feel ethnic. Thus, the myth of St. Uhro, a conscious analogue to St. Patrick, emerged in Minnesota (not Finland) three decades ago, its chief function being to provide a marker of identity in a context from which the original signs of ethnicity have all but disappeared. While Finnish-Americans are increasingly removed from the political and cultural life of Finland, their sense of attachment to the homeland and to the immigrant generation is maintained by establishing familiarity with the *Kalevala*, Finland's national epic, and with the music of Sibelius, the architecture of the Saarinens, handicrafts, and folklore. In short, the display of ethnicity increasingly occurs not in lived experience but in museum-like compartments.

References

Alba, R. 1985. *Italian Americans: Into the Twilight of Ethnicity*. Englewood Cliffs, N.J.: Prentice-Hall.

Apostolic Lutheran Church of America. 1927. *Pöytäkirja*. Thompson, Minn.

Bensman, J., and A. Vidich. 1970. *The New American Society*. Chicago: Quadrangle.

Bernstein, I. 1960. "Union Growth and Structured Cycles." In *Labor and Trade Unionism*, edited by Walter Galenson and Seymour Martin Lipset. New York: John Wiley.

Central Cooperative Wholesale. Collected Papers. Immigration History Research Center, University of Minnesota, St. Paul.

Christen, J. 1983. *Value Systems and Personality in a Western Civilization*. Columbus: Ohio State University Press.

Cochran, B. 1977. *Labor and Communism*. Princeton: Princeton University Press.

Cook, B. 1982. "Perpetual Antagonists, Perennial Adversaries: William Heikkila and the United States Immigration and Naturalization Service, 1947–1960." Unpublished paper, University of Minnesota, Minneapolis.

Copeland, W. 1981. "Early Finnish-American Settlements in Florida." In *The Finnish Diaspora, II,* edited by Michael Karni. Toronto: Multicultural History Society of Ontario.

Doby, H. R. 1960. *A Study of Social Change and Social Disorganization in a Finnish Rural Community.* Ph.D. diss., University of California, Berkeley.

Douthit, D. 1973. *Mutual and Cooperative.* Minneapolis, Minn. Cooperative Printing Association.

Enkel, K. Collected Papers. Immigration History Research Center, University of Minnesota, St. Paul.

Fishman, J., ed. 1966. *Language Loyalty in the United States.* The Hague: Mouton.

Gans, H. 1979. "Symbolic Ethnicity: The Future of Ethnic Groups and Cultures in America." *Ethnic and Racial Studies* 2, no. 1.

Gleason, P. 1983. "Identifying Identity: A Semantic History." *The Journal of American History* 69, no. 4 (March).

Greeley, A. 1971. *Why Can't They Be Like Us?* New York: E. P. Dutton.

Gusfield, J. 1955. "Social Structure and Moral Reform: A Study of the Woman's Christian Temperance Union." *American Journal of Sociology* 61, no. 3.

Hansen, M. L. 1938. *The Problem of the Third Generation Immigrant.* Rock Island, Ill.: Augustana Historical Society.

Hayes, D. 1958. *The Role of the Finnish Immigrant in the History of Lanesville, Massachusetts, 1870–1957.* Honors thesis, Harvard University, Cambridge.

Hoglund, A. W. 1980. "Finns." In *Harvard Encyclopedia of American Ethnic Groups,* edited by Stephan Thernstrom. Cambridge: Harvard University Press.

Howe, I. 1977. "The Limits of Ethnicity." *The New Republic,* 25 June.

Jokinen, W. 1975. "The Finnish Cooperative Movement." Institute of General History Publication no. 7. Turku, Finland: University of Turku.

Karni, M. 1981. "Finnish Temperance and Its Clash with Emerging Socialism in Minnesota." In *The Finnish Diaspora, II,* edited by Michael Karni. Toronto: Multicultural History Society of Ontario.

Kero, R. 1975. "Emigration of Finns from North America to Soviet Karelia in the Early 1930s". In *The Finnish Experience in the Western Great Lakes Region,* edited by Michael Karni et al. Turku, Finland: Institute for Migration.

————. 1983. *Neuvosto-Karjalaa Rakentamassa.* Helsinki: Suomen Historiallinen Seura.

Kivisto, P. 1983. "The Decline of the Finnish-American Left, 1925–1945." *International Migration Review* 17, no. 1 (Spring).

————. 1984. *Immigrant Socialists in the United States.* Cranbury, N.J.: Fairleigh Dickinson University Press.

Klehr, H. 1984. *The Heyday of American Communism.* New York: Basic Books.

Kolehmainen, J. 1936. "A Study of Marriage in a Finnish Community." *American Journal of Sociology* 42, no. 3.

————. 1937a. "The Retreat of Finnish." *American Sociological Review* 2, no. 4.

————. 1937b. "The Finnicisation of English in America." *American Sociological Review* 2, no. 1.

Loukinen, M. 1979. "The Maintenance of Ethnic Culture in Finnish American Rural Communities." *Finnish Americana* 2.

————. 1981. "Second Generation Finnish-American Migration from the Northwoods to Detroit, 1920–1950." In *The Finnish Diaspora, II*, edited by Michael Karni. Toronto: Multicultural History Society of Ontario.

Marger, M., and P. Obermiller. 1983. "Urban Appalachians and Canadian Maritime Migrants: A Comparative Study of Emergent Ethnicity." *International Journal of Comparative Sociology* 24 nos. 3–4.

Mills, C. W. 1956. *White Collar*. New York: Oxford University Press.

Nahirny, V., and J. Fishman. 1965. "American Immigrant Groups: Ethnic Identification and the Problem of Generations." *Sociological Review* 13.

Nelson, L. 1943. "Intermarriage among Nationality Groups in a Rural Area of Minnesota." *American Sociological Review* 8, no. 5.

————. 1948. "Speaking of Tongues." *American Journal of Sociology* 54, no. 3.

Noble, D. 1977. *America by Design*. New York: Alfred A. Knopf.

Nopola, J. E. 1958. *Our Threescore Years: A Brief History of the National Evangelical Lutheran Church*. Ironwood, Mich.: National Publishing Co.

Novak, M. 1972. *The Rise of the Unmeltable Ethnics*. New York: Macmillan.

Olin-Fahle, A. 1983. *Finnhill: Persistence of Ethnicity in Urban America*. Ph.D. diss., New York University, New York.

Ollila, D. 1963. *The Formative Period of the Finnish Evangelical Lutheran Church in America or Suomi Synod*. Ph.D. diss., Boston University, Boston.

Owen, C., et al. 1981. "A Half-Century of Social Distance Research: National Replication of the Bogardus' Studies." *Sociology and Social Research* 66, no. 1.

Pilli, A. 1986. "The Art of Frugality: Prospects for Publishing North American Finnish Newspapers." *Finnish Americana* 7.

Saarnivaara, U. 1947. *The History of the Laestadian or Apostolic-Lutheran Movement in America*. Ironwood, Mich.: National Publishing Co.

Schofer, J. 1975. *Urban and Rural Finnish Communities in California, 1860–1960*. San Francisco: R. and E. Research Associates.

Smith, A. 1981. *The Ethnic Revival*. Cambridge: Cambridge University Press.

Sollors, W. 1986. *Beyond Ethnicity*. New York: Oxford University Press.

Suomi Synod. 1962. *Yearbook*. Hancock, Mich.: Finnish Lutheran Book Concern.

Swidler, A. 1986. "Culture in Action." *American Sociological Review* 51, no. 2.

U.S. Bureau of the Census. 1983. *Ancestry of the Population by States: 1980*. Washington, D.C.: GPO.

Virtanen, K. 1977. "The Influence of the Automotive Industry on the Ethnic Picture of Detroit, 1900–1940." Institute of General History Publication no. 9. Turku, Finland: University of Turku.

Wargelin, J. 1924. *The Americanization of the Finns*. Hancock, Mich. Finnish Lutheran Book Concern.

Zunz, O. 1982. *The Changing Face of Inequality*. Chicago: University of Chicago Press.

5

Class, Ethnicity, and the New Deal: The Croatian Fraternal Union in the 1930s

PETER RACHLEFF

The Great Depression is recognized as a central period in twentieth-century American history. Numerous historians have explored the depression for the origins of the welfare state, Keynesian economics, the interest group coalitions that make up the Democratic party, and industrial unionism, among other institutions and various social movements and ideologies. Some of these historians have also noted the participation of ethnic groups in these developments. But few have specifically considered the impact of the depression upon the evolution of any ethnic group.

Taking such a focus, however, can provoke new insights, not only into the history of the given ethnic group, but also into the depression experience more generally. Ethnic communities and organizations participated in the new political coalitions of the period, influenced foreign policy, helped build the new industrial unions, and were, in turn, changed by their new experiences. The interaction between the developments within an ethnic group and the broader events of the Great Depression offers a fertile field to the historian.

I do not intend to claim any special typicality for the Croatian-American experience (cf. Prpic 1971, 1978; Chmelar 1973; Zivich 1977; Gazi 1956; Govorchin 1961; Eterovich 1969). I am not at all sure that it can serve as a useful microcosm of the American ethnic experience. The following essay is intended, rather, to stimulate similar research into the experiences of other ethnic groups and the interaction between groups. As such research bears fruit, it will become possible to make some useful comparisons, leading in turn to the construction of some meaningful generalizations.

This essay will focus on the Croatian Fraternal Union, also known as Zajednica (unity), during the Great Depression. The CFU was

the critical source of unity among Croatian-Americans. It brought
together the diverse elements of the Croatian diaspora: Dalmatian
sailors in San Pedro and New Orleans; Licani, Bosnians, and Herce-
govinians among coal, iron, and copper miners in Pennsylvania,
Michigan, Minnesota, Montana, and Colorado; former peasants and
soldiers, now steelworkers and meatpackers in the industrial cities of
Pittsburgh, Cleveland, Buffalo, Chicago, and Gary. Village loyalties,
regional dialects, and provincial identities were submerged within the
CFU's slogan, "One for All—All for One," and its symbol of two
hands grasped in fraternity (Bandinovac 1939; Stipanovich 1980;
Croation Fraternal Union 1926).

The CFU also provided a bridge to the old country, even as it
assisted its members in adapting to their new lives in America. Delegates to the first national convention in 1894 pledged "to encourage
the members to be true sons of their nation and to become good
citizens of the United States." The CFU promoted knowledge of the
Croatian homeland and respect for its heritage. In the early twentieth century, for example, it launched a nationwide campaign to
teach Americans (and some Croatians in the United States) not to
"call the Croatians strange names such as Austrian, Hungarian, etc.,
but give them their proper name, Croatians" (Prpic 1971, 126). The
CFU also organized English classes, encouraged its members to become U.S. citizens, and provided the insurance so desperately needed
by workers toiling in America's most dangerous industries.

At times, the CFU wove these threads together and blended the old
and the new in creative, syncretic ways. By World War I, Croatian
immigrants used America as a model for their homeland. They
envisioned a "United States of Yugoslavia," in which Croatia,
Serbia, Hercegovina, Bosnia, Dalmatia, Macedonia, Montenegro, and
Slovenia would enjoy a status comparable to that of Pennsylvania,
Illinois, or Minnesota in the United States. Cultural autonomy, political federalism, democracy, and economic unity were to be combined
and then infused with the values and hopes of a centuries-old peasant
romanticism. This new system would be so constructed "that every-
body may understand what it means to be a free man, in a free country, and how to respect and use this liberty" (CFU 1926, 46; Lukas
1955; Palmieri 1919; Spalatin 1976).

In April 1921, delegates to the Second National Croatian Convention in Pittsburgh organized the Croatian Republican League of the
United States. The league's constitution drew heavily on American
notions of "rights," even quoting Woodrow Wilson on "the right of
those who submit to authority to have a voice in their own government." It called for "a national policy based upon the People's will,

with equal right and equal opportunity for every citizen" (Mirth 1979, 132–35).

This sort of syncretic process—revivifying ties to Croatia, facilitating adjustment to America, and blending the two together—had a dynamic quality. All elements of the relationship, both internally and in relation to one another, changed over time. These changes reflected changes in the composition of the Croatian community as it evolved from predominantly single men in the early twentieth century into young, growing families in the 1910s and 1920s, and then into a community in which the generation born and raised in America became a prominent force in the 1930s and 1940s (Colkovic and Colkovic 1973; Bodnar 1976; Brentar 1971). They also reflected changes in the American economy, in American culture, and in the political fortunes of Croatia (Rachleff 1985, 1986).

At the heart of Croatian-American communities, or "colonies," as they were called, was the CFU. It maintained the history and culture of the Old Country, eased the adjustment to the demands of life in America, maintained Croatian-American unity, and provided insurance. No institution, not even the Catholic Church, compared with the CFU in significance. The activists who built the CFU held a firm commitment to religious ecumenicalism. Unlike many other ethnic fraternal orders, the CFU did not require membership in any church as a condition for participation. Free thinkers and secularists of all stripes were welcome. This position was challenged on more than one occasion by Catholic clerics and their supporters, but to no avail. In 1921, a rival organization, the Croatian Catholic Union, was created (Croatian Catholic Union 1935; Mladineo 1937; Cerrezin 1929). It was virtually identical to the CFU, except for the requirement of a letter from one's parish priest as the ticket for admission. The number of CCU members would never surpass even 10 percent of the CFU's membership. In 1947, the CFU convention overwhelmingly rejected a resolution to require church membership. Its traditional ecumenicalism was reaffirmed.

CFU activists maintained an equally tenacious commitment to a sense of belonging to an interethnic working class. The first set of bylaws adopted by the new CFU in 1926 gave the society's newspaper, *Zajedničar*, the responsibility to "publish accurate accounts of the struggles of union labor for its rights and especially reports of strikes of workingmen's organizations." Strikers, moreover, could apply to the "Culture and Enlightenment Fund" for support. "A justified struggle and demands of the workingmen for the accomplishment of their rights shall also be supported." Consequently, Croatian workers played important roles in several American labor organizations: the United

Mine Workers in the 1890s; the Industrial Workers of the World from the early twentieth century to World War I; the National Miners Union and the Trade Union Unity League in the late 1920s and early 1930s; and the CIO in the mid and late 1930s (Cizmic 1983; Barrett et al. 1981; Rasporich 1978; Ward 1904; Berman 1963; Friedlander 1972; Stipanovich 1978).

By the late 1920s, the CFU included more than sixty thousand adult and thirty thousand child members, organized in more than nine hundred local lodges. In an effort to attract and maintain the allegiance of the second generation, many lodges had established "junior nests," and some were beginning to organize "English-speaking lodges." All members received *Zajedničar*, the weekly fraternal newspaper, which kept them informed about American and Yugoslav events, as well as fraternal activities. Basic policy was set democratically by a convention of hundreds of delegates who assembled every three years. More than ever, the CFU was the heart of Croatian-American communities (Galey 1977, 43; Stipanovich 1978, 171; Prpic 1971, 271).

Thoughts of the depression and the problems it posed for American families and communities are usually framed in economic terms. But the CFU faced three interrelated dilemmas in the 1930s: one was economic—how to help its members survive the hard times, and how to survive itself; the second was cultural—how to win the interest and maintain the commitment of the second generation, the immigrants' children, to their parents' organization; and the third crisis was political—how, in the context of international politics, to protect Croatia from the Fascist onslaught while also helping to emancipate the homeland from the Serbian monarchy that had ruled Yugoslavia since 1918. National and local activists and rank-and-file lodge members from colonies around the country struggled together to resolve these crises. Their responses creatively blended traditional values and practices with new experiences, realities, and opportunities.

The CFU and the Labor Movement

The financial base of the Croatian Fraternal Union came from the dues of its more than sixty thousand adult members. Layoffs, cutbacks, and wage cuts reduced the income of most CFU members during the depression. In the wake of these conditions, the English editor of *Zajedničar* reported to the 1935 CFU convention: "We find today an army of destitute men and women, shorn of their life's savings, jobless and penniless, with nothing to look forward to in the twilight of their life except the stark reality of want and privation."

In response to appeals from local lodges, the CFU Supreme Board announced in December 1930 that unemployed members could draw on their insurance policies in order to keep up their dues. By late in the winter of 1933, an estimated twenty thousand men and women— nearly one-third of the adult membership—were doing so. Clearly, this was no solution, since it salvaged the individual's membership by imperiling the organization's overall solvency. *Zajedničar* (10 December 1930) urged CFU members to expand their own charitable activities, to act upon the traditional mutuality that had marked the *zadruga* (extended family) and the village: "In this period of depression, every true member of the CFU should be like a great rock in the weary land, under whose shelter the way-worn traveller—the unemployed member—may rest from his journey and find a helping hand in these, the dark days of unemployment." But soon, both individuals and communities found themselves unable to help. Many of the unemployed clamored for the opportunity to draw upon their insurance policies for the immediate income they desperately needed.

Over the course of the early 1930s, the CFU's national leadership reached the limits of its ability to help members survive the hard times. No amount of manipulation of dues and expenditures, or special fund-raising efforts, could produce the required money. In the fall of 1932, it became necessary to cut all sick benefits in half. Deficits continued to grow. CFU activists looked outside their own organization's limited resources. "It needs no argument to prove," contended one activist group in late 1931, "that if anything is to be done to help the unemployed and the needy, it must be done by strong government action and assistance. Charity and voluntary contributions will not suffice" ("Hard Times," 1931, 36; Prpic 1971, 284–91).

In March 1933, the very month of Franklin D. Roosevelt's inauguration, the CFU began to adopt a more aggressive political stance. *Zajedničar* (27 March) called on its readers to protest the McLeod-Norris bill, which would have allowed cities to scale down their debt to municipal bondholders. Like most fraternal orders, the CFU and its local lodges had invested heavily in municipal bonds. *Zajedničar* noted that organized participation in American politics might be a new experience for many CFU members, but it was very necessary. In the summer of 1933, *Zajedničar* (7 June) campaigned for restrictive legislation in the areas of child labor and sweatshops. Over the next five years, the CFU and its organ, *Zajedničar* (e.g., 29 May, 11 December 1935; 4 March, 6 May, 11 November 1936), championed one New Deal measure after another. The CFU saw this legislation as necessary to correct some of the more profound inequities in the private economy, provide a material base for all, and restore the economy to an even keel.

Alongside New Deal legislation, the CFU saw industrial unionism as central to resolving the economic crises facing its members and threatening its treasury. The CFU convention in the summer of 1932 decried "the very unfavorable situation existing among the working class in the present industrial depression, the reduction of wages and extension of working hours." A resolution placed the convention on record as "favoring the formation of militant labor unions, so that they may compel their employers to offer better working conditions and greater earnings" (*Zajedničar*, 13 July 1932).

The CFU urged members to join unions in their industries, to honor picket lines, and to support strikers. Individual lodges were encouraged to pay out strike benefits and to expel strikebreakers and company police. Many lodges were used as meeting places by organizing committees, and some became directly involved in strikes. *Zajedničar* (7 June 1933, 20 June 1934) educated its readers about working conditions in the clothing, textile, and steel industries, the inadequacies of the National Recovery Act ("National Run Around"), and the workers' struggles to unionize these industries. *Zajedničar* (29 May 1935) also presented theoretical justifications for unionism— that better earnings and working conditions would improve the health of Croatian workers, that higher wages would make it easier to afford CFU dues, and that increased income would promote increased demand, which would, in turn, stimulate production and employment.

Through 1935, however, all of this sentiment remained little more than theory. Actual successes were few. And the overall economic condition of Croatian-American workers and the CFU remained critical. On the eve of the CFU's 1935 convention, Michael Horvath, editor of the English section of *Zajedničar* (10 June 1935), grimly assessed "our opportunities," writing that "the evils of unemployment continue to be with us."

With the launching of the CIO organizing drive in late 1935, the dynamics in the Croatian-American colonies began to change. In January 1936, the CFU announced an organizing drive of its own. The drive focused on the second generation, primarily via the vehicle of English-speaking lodges. It received its greatest response in industrial cities like Steelton, Aliquippa, and Lackawanna, where the Croatian-American colonies were already in ferment from the union organizing drive in the steel industry. By October 1936, more than ten thousand new members had joined the established lodges, the English-speaking lodges, and the junior nests of the CFU (*Zajedničar*, 4 December 1935; 8, 22 January, 19 February, 4 March, 1 April, 6 May, 8, 22 July 1936).

Thousands of Croatian-Americans participated in the Steel Workers Organizing Committee (SWOC) drive. *Zajedničar* (20, 27 May, 17 June 1936) regularly gave front-page space to news from the organizing drive. Bylined columns and editorials hailed its successes. Letters from lodges bore witness to the intensity of the feelings let loose. "The poor working man," wrote one columnist, "realizes today, better than ever before, that only through efficient organization can he cope with the might of money. . . . The day of victory—let's admit—is not yet so near, but it is coming, and coming fast." In September, the CFU Supreme Board formally endorsed the SWOC campaign (Friedlander 1972, 37). It released a statement to "call upon its members who work in the steel industry to join that union, and it also calls upon all other members and lodges to help them in their organizing." The board pledged "moral and, if possible, financial support. . . so as to accomplish a complete organization of steel workers into one large union as soon as possible." The CFU president John D. Butkovich chaired a "Fraternal Orders Committee," organized by SWOC to better mobilize rank-and-file lodge members (Croatian Fraternal Union 1947, 26–27).

Croatian-American workers also joined in the great political campaign to re-elect Franklin D. Roosevelt. This took on the character of a popular referendum on the New Deal, the rise of industrial unions, and other related economic and social changes. As one *Zajedničar* (14 October 1936) columnist put it, the issues were "increased wages, shorter work week, the right to organize into unions, the elimination of the sweat shop and child labor, and all such things to aid the working man and woman." Croatian-Americans were enthusiastic, active participants in this campaign. Among the sixty thousand supporters who turned out to cheer FDR at Pittsburgh's Forbes Field on 1 October were Croatians "by the baker's dozens," reported one CFU activist.

As the CIO organizing drive spread to other industries, Croatian-American workers joined in. Despite the continuing economic depression, despite widespread unemployment, an air of optimism swept the colonies, not just of Croatians, but of most ethnic groups. In a year-end editorial entitled "The Old and the New," *Zajedničar* (30 December 1936) gave voice to these feelings. "We shudder at the thought that many thousands of men and women will continue to walk the streets, to seek food, shelter, and clothing," the editor warned. "Among these thousands will be many of our kind and kin."

Enthusiasm continued to grow. *Zajedničar* introduced a new, front-page column in January 1937 entitled "News of the Workers' Movement." Strikes, organizing drives, and the political struggle for unemployment insurance and social security took up more and more space in the paper. The CFU slogan *U Slogi Je Moć* (In unity there is strength) seemed to have taken on new meaning with the advent of the CIO. Reports from local lodges expressed the explosion of rank-and-file energies. "Casting off the cloak of oppression and submission he has worn for the past half century," wrote one correspondent, "the Man of Steel has finally awoke and come into his own (13 January 1937).

In March 1937, the Supreme Board of the CFU reaffirmed the order's commitment to "the great labor movement in America, whose goal is the general organization of workers in large American industries for the purpose of providing better working conditions and decent wages." This movement, they noted, was about even more than working conditions and wages. It was "the key to their[the workers'] better future and to the assurance of their rights, which belong to them as humans and creators of all the wealth and progress of this country." The Supreme Board called upon all CFU members to offer, "on every occasion and with all their energies, their moral and, if possible, financial support to that movement" (Croatian Fraternal Union 1947, 28–29).

The CFU launched another organizing drive of its own, again aimed primarily at the second generation. The organization set as a target the expansion of the CFU to 100,000 members. New tactics were to be used, especially in relation to sports, music, and other elements of American mass culture. There was also to be a more direct linkage to the ongoing CIO drives. In city after city, stages were shared by CIO and CFU organizers, who encouraged their audiences to join both organizations. *Zajedničar* (6 January, 10 February 1937) urged lodge members to help unionize the H. J. Heinz plant on Pittsburgh's North Side and the Westinghouse plant in east Pittsburgh. The response to such appeals was enthusiastic. "In all the history of America's labor movement," *Zajedničar* noted on 12 May 1937, "no organization has had such a tremendous following among the working people in this country as the Committee for Industrial Organization."

Over the next several years, the CFU continued to contribute to the CIO drives in the steel, auto, electrical products, meat packing, and food processing industries. Thousands of Croatian-American workers joined, and some were elected leaders of local unions. They experienced new on-the-job security, higher wages, and better benefits. They were also able to count on unemployment insurance and social security. In the short run, at least, this strengthened their commitment to the CFU, the CIO, and to the New Deal and its political vehicle, the Democratic party. But this is not all there was to the story. The CFU's efforts to resolve its cultural and political crises reinforced the economic roots of these developments.

The CFU and American Culture

By 1930, the second generation, the American-born children of the immigrants, began to outnumber the first generation. Many of them had grown up during the pro-Americanization years of the 1920s. They were American citizens; they spoke English; they enjoyed American music, sports, and movies. And many of them were not attracted to the Croatian Fraternal Union. This portended a serious actuarial crisis. No insurance organization could survive an aging membership and a diminished influx of new, young, healthy members—especially in the midst of a prolonged depression (Prpic 1971, 271–80; Barrett et al. 1981, 43–6; Schereck 1957, 84–95; Stipanovich 1980).

CFU leaders on both the national and local levels moved to establish "English-speaking lodges" for the new generation. Not only would business be conducted in English, but these lodges would be permitted to use American sports (bowling, baseball, basketball, football, hockey) and cultural entertainments appropriate for American-born teens and young adults (dances, weenie roasts, beach parties, and the like).

Committing the CFU to the project of organizing English-speaking lodges was not so easy, however. Neither was actually organizing these lodges. There was resistance from two groups: those among the immigrant generation who did not want to accommodate the American culture, and those among the second generation who had no interest in the "old fashioned" ways of their elders. "Our younger people have been born and bred in a wholly different atmosphere," CFU president John D. Butkovich remarked. "Their daily life, their habits, differ considerably from the habits of our older people in days gone by." There seemed to be little empathy across generational lines. The youth rejected the "dry routine" of lodge activities. The immigrants were displeased that "the younger generation is concerned primarily with entertainment and joyful surroundings" (Horvath 1932, 63).

But CFU activists were determined to bridge this gap. They would embark on a two-sided process: on the one hand, the older generation would learn to tolerate their children's attraction to much of American culture; on the other hand, the second generation would learn the history, language, and culture of their parents' homeland. Out of this process, unity would be preserved, as well as continuing loyalty to Croatia.

The debate started, in the late 1920s, over structural changes in the CFU. Should there be separate English-speaking lodges (or ESLs) independent of the immediate supervision of the lodges established by the immigrant generation? Should *Zajedničar* include an English-language section, under the direction of its own editor? This debate was fought out at both the local and national levels, even within households in Croatian colonies. Though the advocates of change won the argument, and, therefore, control over the institutions they wanted to transform, they continued to face opposition from some members of the first generation. While it became increasingly rare for this opposition to openly voice its dissatisfaction, noncooperation at the local level remained a nagging problem in many colonies throughout the 1930s (Preveden 1947, 19).

In 1929, the CFU convention voted to establish English-speaking lodges and to initiate a two-page English section in *Zajedničar*. Michael J. Horvath was selected editor. Over the next decade, he would be the leading voice for modifying the CFU's relationship to American culture. The new development got off to a fast start. Forty ESLs were organized in a year. The 1932 CFU convention reaffirmed the organization's new cultural strategy and voted to expand the English section of *Zajedničar* to four pages ("Hard Times," 1931, 32).

The economic difficulties posed by the depression plagued this new development. "Youth Movement and Depression Arrive Simultaneously," proclaimed a *Zajedničar* headline. On 27 March 1933, the English section of the paper was trimmed to three pages for financial reasons. Overall membership in the CFU plummeted for four consecutive years, falling to less than fifty thousand adults by 1934. Younger members were particularly hard hit by unemployment. Since few had belonged to the CFU long enough to build up substantial reserves, they had little to draw upon to keep up their dues payments. On 4 December 1935, a Pennsylvania activist published a report in *Zajedničar* titled "Trials of an English Speaking Lodge: Economic Conditions Prevent Progress." "After four months of endeavoring to increase the membership of Croatian Youth Lodge 806," he admitted, "we have finally come to the conclusion that this is a task of the most difficult nature. Lack of adequate income to support one's self and family is the basic reason for this difficulty." CFU activists put great effort into the cultural strategy of reaching the second generation. Beyond the structural changes already discussed, this strategy meant the promotion of specific cultural activities. The three key areas were sports, social activities between the sexes, and the renewal of an interest in the language, culture, and history of Croatia. The second generation found the traditional gymnastics of their parents boring in comparison with American team sports like football, basketball, and baseball. They rejected "the restraint of the old stereotyped gymnastics and the dull and heavy setting up exercises which merely develop automatons," noted one observer (*Zajedničar*, 23 October 1929). When the CFU and particularly the English-speaking lodges sought to organize teams in American sports and to encourage members of high school and college age to participate in their school teams, they faced the opposition of some of the immigrant generation.

CFU activists softened the potential clash by promoting the organization of Croatian teams that would play only Croatian teams from other cities. This competition would then have as a byproduct an increase in the communication among different colonies. Organizers also sought to mute competitiveness and promote the "ethics of true fraternal sportsmanship." Baseball, basketball, and football teams were common elements of English-speaking lodges. English editor Horvath credited sports with "the addition of new members in many of our lodges . . . and the prevention of many suspensions" (*Zajedničar*, 4 February 1931). The benefits of sports activity became more and more obvious. CFU activists also found that sports could provide a new bridge between the generations. In the mid-1930s, bowling became an absolute rage. Members of senior lodges also took up the sport, and soon there were hugely successful regional tournaments, uniting immigrants and Croatian-Americans in new ways. And Croatian-American college athletes began to win recognition for themselves and for their communities (*Zajedničar*, 25 December 1935).

It helped a great deal that the first two all-American football players—Starcevich and Basrak—were members in good standing of English-speaking lodges. Their names, *Zajedničar* (20 January 1937) noted, were "on the lips of every Croatian boy and girl in the country." *Zajedničar* (7 July 1937) readers sent in their own all-Croatian teams or their suggestions for all-American recognition for a specific Croatian-American athlete. In 1940, *Zajedničar* (10 January, 3 April) actually picked its own all-Croatian football team. The strength of the first generation had been handed down to the second, but to be used in new ways, argued some. "In the U.S., the men of Lika took precedence over others in all occupations requiring unusual strength and endurance," argued the *Jugoslavia Kalendar* in 1939. Now, it was the children of the Licani who made the best football players. What had threatened to be a source of intergenerational discord in the early years of the depression had become a new source of unity.

Although CFU activists were largely successful at infusing organized sports with such traditional values as cooperation, fraternalism, and community, they could not ward off the cultural changes reflected in and promoted by these new activities. "The modern and practical trend in health education is free play," argued a *Zajedničar* (4 July 1982) columnist. The purpose of American sports was to teach "initiative through competition, fair play, and sportsmanship." Here, again, was the two-sided process of cultural change: reinforcement of the traditional went hand in hand with accommodation to the new.

While organized sports appealed primarily to the boys and young men of the second generation, the development of new social activities promoted the CFU's English-speaking lodges among both sexes. "Dances, picnics, socials, parties, and the like not only are inducements for getting new acquaintances and new applicants for our lodges, but are also great tonics for keeping those already members in the societies" (*Zajedničar*, 7 January 1931). Most potential ESL members were single, and new social activities allowed them to meet the opposite sex without the sort of parental interference typical of the first generation's experience. Even though they remained largely within the Croatian community, this second generation was incorporating American dating and socializing practices.

As with organized sports, the promoters of new social activities faced the opposition of the immigrant generation. ESL participation in "jazzmania" and sponsorship of dances provoked criticism from traditionalists in the community. The junior nests were under the regular direction of the senior lodges, but the English-speaking lodges were managed by their own members. This seemed like a dangerous breakdown in community control over its younger generation (*Zajedničar*, 11 February 1931).

Nevertheless, new social activities proliferated. "The opinion of a few dissenters certainly will not dampen the ardor of our youth." Letters to *Zajedničar* (23 January 1935) reported on masquerades, Halloween parties, beach parties, weenie roasts, Valentine parties, dances, plays, and the like. Some lodges sponsored radio shows. On 4 December 1935, *Zajedničar* profiled Cleveland's "American Croatian Pioneers," one of the most successful ESLs in the order. They consistently attracted a thousand or more participants to such events as an annual "anniversary dance," a "spring frolic," a "blue hour dance," a "baseball dance," an "Easter dance," and a "fall dance." A record of attendance at lodge meetings was necessary in order to be admitted to these socials. The lodge also sponsored baseball and basketball teams. Not all ESLs were this active or this large, but they all developed new, American-oriented social activities in the 1930s. The CFU, on a national level, promoted these developments, especially through the English section of *Zajedničar*.

English-speaking lodges were not on a headlong rush to assimilation, however. In both their organized sports and their new social activities, they maintained elements of traditional culture: cooperation, fraternalism, and marriage within their own community. From Kenosha, Wisconsin, came this report on an ESL's "beach party," complete with wieners and marshmallows roasted over an open fire:

"After we were all too stuffed to move, we'd sit around the fire and sing all the old Croatian and English songs." The letter writer added, almost as an afterthought: "'Sfunny how we ESLers like our Croatian songs the best." There were even more explicit ways in which these CFU lodges preserved and transmitted Croatian language, history, and culture. Over the course of the 1930s, ESLs functioned as vehicles through which the American-born generation could be socialized into Croatian-American life and culture (*Zajedničar*, 1 July 1936).

In colony after colony, ESLs offered Croatian language classes. Local CFU activists not only expressed concern about "the boys and girls of today whose only misfortune is that they lack sufficient knowledge of their mother tonuge," but they organized schools and classes to teach it to them. There was also considerable attention paid to teaching Croatian history, geography, and culture to "the average younger CFU members, whose knowledge of conditions 'over there' is somewhat limited" (*Zajedničar*, 15 December 1928). The 1932 CFU convention voted to promote the publication of Croatian historical essays in the English section of *Zajedničar*. Such articles soon became regular features of the newspaper. From the local to the national level, the CFU's new English-speaking lodges promoted the preservation of Croatian language and culture every bit as much as they engendered accommodation to American culture.

Many lodges organized activities through which the second generation not only learned about the traditional culture but actively participated in it. *Zajedničar* and individual CFU lodges sponsored essay contests in which younger members were given themes such as "Impressions of Jugoslavia" and "Why Should Every Child of Croatian Parentage Be in the Croatian Fraternal Union?" Croatian folk songs like "Oj te vilo, vilo velebita" remained popular. Traditional games, like "Igraj Kolo," and dances were also common. Even an element of mass culture, the movie, was used to spread identification with Croatia. Milwaukee's ESL showed *Domovina*, which took the viewer "through Croatia, Slavonija, Dalmatia, Bosnia, and Hercegovina, showing peasants at work and play." Lodges frequently produced plays, in Croatian and about Croatian subjects, in which second-generation members participated.

No social activity promoted traditional culture among the second generation more than the tamburica orchestras that became very popular in the 1930s. By late 1937, Matt Gouze, author of a regular *Zajedničar* column entitled "On Tamburica Interest" and director of the Duquesne University "Tamburitzans," estimated that there were 335 tamburica orchestras in the United States, and that most of the performers were members of the second generation (Baldrica 1978).

The popularity of Gouze's column reflected the interest in this traditional instrument manifested by the younger generation.

The celebration of holidays provided a way to accommodate American culture, preserve traditional culture, and blend the two. Thanksgiving and Christmas were of special interest to Croatian-Americans. A *Zajedničar* (25 November 1936) columnist urged his readers to observe Thanksgiving with thoughts of their own experience more than those of the Pilgrims, Plymouth Rock, and the *Mayflower*. Christmas was portrayed as the very embodiment of fraternalism and community mutuality, especially in the context of the depression (*Zajedničar*, 16 December 1936).

During the 1930s, CFU activists actually created a new holiday—"Croatian Day"—that blended traditional and American culture in a way that reflected the emerging identity of the second generation. This was a midsummer holiday, with no fixed date, usually held at an amusement park. It provided an opportunity for Croatian-American youths to go on rides, swim, dance, and hear Croatian music and even a few speeches. Croatian Day was an opportunity for Croatian-American youths to meet others outside their own colonies. It was also their affirmation of American culture and a proud assertion of their specific heritage, even as they participated in that larger culture. From the start, ESLs were the organizers and promoters of Croatian Day in colony after colony. The first of these holidays was celebrated in Pittsburgh's Kennywood Park in 1932. By the next year, most large colonies had organized their own celebrations, and, by the later thirties, virtually all the colonies marked Croatian Day. A local lodge activist wrote to *Zajedničar* (13 July 1932): "A day such as we are planning will bring pleasant old memories to those of our people who left their homesteads many years ago, and for others a realization that there is something noble and honorable in giving thought to the country of one's origin."

The CFU also promoted the notion of Croatian-Americans as one ethnic group among many, and of the desirability of interethnic solidarity. Regardless of changing political circumstances in Yugoslavia, the CFU consistently advocated south Slavic unity in America. By the thirties, its categories had broadened to include all ethnic groups. The CFU, at both the national and the local levels, participated in organizations like the Slavic Non-Partisan League of Allegheny County (Pennsylvania), the Jugoslav Fraternal Federation, the American Jugoslav Association of Minnesota, the National Fraternal Congress, the American Youth Congress, the All-American Slavic Congress, the Common Council for American Unity, various labor organizations, and such events as the Festival of Nations in St. Paul, National

Fraternal Day, union organizing drives, strikes, and the like. The Common Council for American Unity best expressed these sentiments when it announced that it "will stand squarely for an America which accepts all its citizens, whatever their national or racial backgrounds, as equals. It will attack and try to dissipate the whole atmosphere of prejudice which diminishes the mutual respect, understanding, and unity which should exist among the American people (*Zajedničar*, 4 July 1928).

CFU activists wove these many threads—sports, English-speaking lodges, "Americanized" social activities, traditional Croatian cultural events, holidays, and an evolving ethnic consciousness—into a series of effective, youth-oriented, organizing drives in the mid and late 1930s. These were the most successful membership campaigns in the CFU's history. Between January and July 1936, 10,600 new members were attracted, more than two-thirds of whom joined ESLs or junior nests. Another drive was launched on 1 February 1937, and yet another, a forty-fifth anniversary "Jubilee Campaign," in 1939. Thousands more joined. The financial situation of the CFU regained stability. By March 1939, it was so good that the Supreme Board voted to waive four monthly assessments for all lodge members. Evolving a new approach to members of the second generation through American culture, and then teaching them Croatian culture, had been a great success.

Yugoslav Politics and the CFU

CFU activists faced a third challenge during the Great Depression—how best to assist the movement for a democratic, autonomous Croatia, freed from both monarchy and fascism. Ever since the beginning of the decay of the Austro-Hungarian Empire in the 1870s, Croatia had experienced economic disruption and insecurity. Two popular responses had emerged: on the one hand, a mass emigration to America, which took on Exodus proportions by 1905–1914; on the other, a variety of political movements that aimed to shape the configuration of a new Croatia. These two responses were interrelated: political frustration or fear of imprisonment motivated many emigrants; political movements often sent organizers to the American colonies in search of financial support; Croatian immigrants read the publications of "old country" organizations; ethnic newspapers regularly featured "old country" happenings; and immigrants and their children built organizations to influence American foreign policy toward their homeland.

The outbreak of World War I in Bosnia sounded the death knell of the Austro-Hungarian Empire (Jelavich 1967; Krizman 1967; Trouton 1952). Two issues dominated political debate within the Croatian colonies in New York, Pittsburgh, Cleveland, St. Louis, Gary, Chicago, and smaller industrial cities: (1) What should be the geographical and cultural contours of the new state (Rothenberg 1966)? Should it be based on Croatian autonomy or south Slavic unity (Kraja 1979)? And (2) What should be the political character of the new state? Should it be a democrary or a monarchy (Palmieri 1919; Mirth 1979; Dragnich 1983)? How widely should citizenship and the franchise be made available (Gazi 1962–63; Tomasic 1962–63)? These questions were posed in the ethnic press, in mass public meetings and on lecture tours, and in hundreds of local fraternal lodge meetings (Mihanovich 1936; Prpic 1978; Tomasevich 1955).

Out of this debate in the colonies, a consensus emerged. On the one hand, it reflected the deep traditions of Pan-Slavism and peasant populism, and, on the other, it revealed the influence of years spent in America. Croatian immigrants articulated a vision of a "United States of Yugoslavia," grounded in the principles of democracy, political federalism, and cultural autonomy. This position was articulated in March 1915 at a "national congress" of 563 Croatian, Serbian, and Slovenian immigrant delegates in Chicago. Unity was further enhanced by German-American attacks on members of all three groups in city after city (Palmieri 1919, 356–59; Krokar 1984; Billich 1931).

At this very time, the Radić brothers, Ante and Stjepan, were agitating for the same program among the Croatian peasantry. Their Peasant party called for a Pan-Slavic union with thoroughly democratic features. It also promoted a vigorous social and economic program for the purpose of bringing justice and dignity to peasants and landless wage-laborers (Raditch 1928–29, 95; Orr 1936, Adamic 1943).

Reality proved far different, however, from both what the Croatian Peasant party and the American émigrés desired. In part through President Wilson's own direct involvement, the "Kingdom of Serbs, Croats, and Slovenes" was established, and a Serb was installed on the throne. The new government jailed Stjepan Radić for the next eleven months. He would spend much of the next decade fending off governmental repression, until he was finally assassinated in 1928 (Pandžić 1954, 37).

Over the course of the 1920s, the Radić brothers and their associates built the Croatian Peasant party into a powerful force. In December 1920, they changed the party's name to the Croatian Republican Peasant party, to stress the character of their opposition to the Serbian monarchy that ruled over them. Stjepan Radić led teams of organizers into villages, while Ante edited their lively newspaper (Maček 1960). During the early 1920s, the party participated in elections but boycotted the Duma, which it saw as powerless against the king. As the organizers and newspapers reached village after village, the popular movement grew. At the same time, Stjepan Radić, the head of the party, sought international help. He visited London, Vienna, and Moscow, where he met with Lenin and affiliated the Croatian Republican Peasant party with the "Peasant International." Organizers were also sent to America, where they traveled from colony to colony , speaking in fraternal halls and distributing newspapers—and collecting money to help the growing movement at home (Dragnich 1983, 34–49; Gazi 1956, 13).

To their dismay, however, these organizers found that interest in the Croatian colonies for old country politics was on the wane. First the war and then the new restrictive immigration legislation had slowed the flow of new arrivals to a mere trickle. There were progressively fewer in each colony with firsthand experience and intense commitments. The second generation was growing to adulthood. They spoke English, played American sports, listened and danced to American music. Like all immigrant communities, the Croatian colonies were subjected to intensive "Americanization" campaigns in the 1920s. In this environment, it was difficult to sustain an enthusiasm for old country politics (Prpic 1971, 99).

But this was soon to change. Interest in Yugoslavia surged forward in 1928 when Stjepan Radić was assassinated in the Duma and King Alexander instituted martial law. A cry of anger and oaths of renewed commitment rang out from colony after colony. In August 1928, delegates from all over the United States met in New York City and organized the Croatian Circle, or the Hrvatsko Kolo. They resolved: "We promoise you, O Mother Croatia, we promise you from this distant land, to help you carry the unbearable cross to Golgotha, and will help you doing it to the day of your resurrection" (Dragnich 1983, 50). Kolo organizers appealed to Croatian immigrants and their children to be *more* "American," since "according to the best traditions of American citizenship, a good American means, in the first place, a man or woman with a backbone, not a jellyfish!" They set as their goal the opposition of everything that promoted "inferiority complexes" among Croatian-American youths, through teaching Croatian history, language, and culture, and through helping to make their homeland a source of pride. Like earlier activist organizations, the Kolo worked through mass membership Croatian organizations like the CFU ("Hard Times," 1931, 37).

The onset of the Great Depression thus found Croatian colonies

undergoing a renaissance of interest in their homeland's politics.
When hard times engulfed their communities, Croatian immigrants
and their American-born children sought strategies that would improve both their own situation and that of their homeland. The Kolo
issued a call for an All Croatian Congress "to promote and protect the
interest of our immigrants here and also help our brothers in Croatia"
("Hard Times," 1931, 37). In order to help their "brothers in
Croatia," activists realized that they had to get their communities and
organizations more involved in the American political process. They
also needed to reach beyond the influence and resources of the Croatian colonies, especially to other ethnic groups and their organizations.

Political activity grew. CFU activists called for unemployment insurance, protections for municipal bondholders, and federal programs
that would stimulate economic growth, as well as support for the
political emancipation of Croatia. At the local level, they entered the
political process in numerous ways, from joining Slavic Non-Partisan
leagues to participating in Democratic party ward organizations. By
the time of FDR's re-election in 1936, Croatians had become an
integral part of the New Deal Coalition.

In the aftermath of Radić's assassination, the interest of Croatian-
Americans in their homeland had increased significantly. *Zajedničar*
regularly devoted large sections of its front page to news from
Yugoslavia in particular, and, a few years later, to the rise of the Fascist menace across Europe. Local CFU lodges sponsored lectures and
discussions on European politics. Local branches of the Croatian Republican Peasant party were organized in colonies all over the United
States. The Kolo and the Croatian National Council circulated peti-
tions, held plebiscites, and sent memoranda to presidents Hoover and
Roosevelt and to the League of Nations. "We appeal to the whole
civilized world," resolved the June 1930 Kolo convention, "but especially to our fellow citizens to take an interest." Some months later,
Radić's son-in-law was arrested when he arrived in New York for a
speaking tour of the colonies. Protest was widespread (Kraja 1979,
152–57). Years later, Louis Adamic touched the hearts of tens of
thousands when he published *The Native's Return* (1943), an account of
his 1932 pilgrimage to Yugoslavia. The CFU itself bought thousands
of copies and made them available to members.

The dramatic character of the situation in Yugoslavia further
gripped Croatian-Americans' interest. Conflict between Croatian
peasants and the Serbian monarchy was rapidly subsumed within the
great power conflict shaking Europe. Mussolini moved toward the
Dalmatian coast. His promises of "liberation" from the Serbians

struck some responsive chords, both in Croatia and in the colonies. Ante Pavelić left the Peasant party; attacked its leader, Vladko Maček; organized the Uštaša, according to the Mussolini model; and allied with the Italian Fascist. Pavelić even took to calling himself "Duce." The Uštaša launched a terroristic campaign, very different from the Radićs' approach to popular politics. It initiated an unsuccessful uprising in Lika and masterminded the assassination of King Alexander in 1934 (Clissold 1979, 3–4).

The Uštaša sent organizers and fund-raisers to the American colonies. It also promoted the spread of a new Croatian-American organization, the Hrvatski Domobran (Home Defenders). Its goal was to organize political pressure within the United States and to raise support in the colonies for the Uštaša. Domobran members wore blue shirts and modeled themselves after Mussolini's Fascist legions. They claimed that their new strategy for Croatian independence made sense in terms of the rapidly changing European situation (Prpic 1971, 284).

But Croatian-Americans largely rejected this approach. Labor activists, CFU local leaders, Communists, Democratic party organizers, and even some priests openly challenged the Domobran. They contended that fascism was contrary to the thinking of "American citizens" and the political traditions of the Croatian peasant movement. Other organizations within the colonies specifically rejected the Uštaša and the Domobran. The Kolo announced at its spring 1935 convention: "Much as we want independence for the mother country, we must not look to Italy for help." In the summer of 1935, the CFU convention turned down all motions of support for the Fascists (Kraja 1979, 197; Prpic 1971, 284).

In the winter of 1936, news reached the colonies of widespread hunger and suffering in Croatia. As if the continuing political turmoil were not enough, a severe drought in the summer of 1935 had left peasants unprepared for winter. Despite their own financial problems, the CFU Supreme Board sent $5,000 in immediate aid. Local lodges followed suit and took up their own collections. "While our people in this country find themselves in most unfortunate circumstances," the board noted, "this appeal of the hunger stricken populace in Croatia shall not go unanswered" (*Zajedničar*, 12 February 1936). All the money was sent directly to Vladko Maček, Stjepan Radić's successor as head of the Croatian Republican Peasant party and an outspoken opponent of Pavelic and the Uštaša.

CFU involvement in Yugoslav affairs went beyond humanitarian aid for the hungry and homeless. In July 1936, the Supreme Board cabled a protest to the government of Yugoslavia, decrying the practice of "terror" against "political prisoners." *Zajedničar* (8 July, 12 August, 30 December 1936) kept its readers well informed about the worsening political situation. CFU leaders discussed sending President John Butkovich on a fact-finding mission to the old country. They also discussed sending delegates to the founding convention of the "American League Against War and Fascism." Meanwhile, the CFU and its lodges were swept up in a membership drive, the CIO's steel and auto organizing campaigns, and Roosevelt's re-election campaign.

In the summer of 1937, Butkovich led a delegation of CFU members to Yugoslavia. Croatian-Americans eagerly followed their exploits, especially when it was announced that the group was being expelled and sent back to the United States (*Zajedničar*, 8 September 1937). Butkovich went on a nationwide speaking tour upon his return. Lodges were full of life from the organizing drives and were eager to hear from him.

Over the next four years, Croatian-Americans continued to concern themselves with conditions and events in their homeland, even as they extended their participation in industrial unions, local Democratic political organizations, Pan-Slavic congresses, and Americanized and ethnic cultural affairs. Croatian Day celebrations were organized in industrial cities all over the country. These events included amusement park outings, baseball games, picnics, tamburica music, kolo dancing, traditional foods, and more than a few speeches. Mirko Chalupa explained why his lodge was holding its first Croatian Day in July 1938: "In these critical times, when there is a general turmoil in the world, it is well for us to give thought to our people across the sea, and to consider their welfare as well as our own" (*Zajedničar*, 8 June 1938).

These concerns helped cement Croatian-Americans' relationships with other Slavic members of industrial unions and political coalitions. Whether Croatian, Slovenian, or Serbian, they followed the fortunes of the CIO and the New Deal. They supported FDR's program, from the Wagner Act to unemployment insurance and social security. And they increasingly explored and expressed their shared interests in new organizations like the All-American Slavic Congress. There could be no greater confirmation of these evolving attitudes and of their American character than the entry of the United States into World War II. Then, the very government that had served as a model for Croatian immigrant aspirations for their homeland, and that, in the Great Depression, had responded to popular appeals to create unemployment insurance, social security, and jobs programs, as well as legislation to facilitate union organization, would enter the life-or-death battle on the side of the "oppressed," the "underdog,"against the Fascists. The political, cultural, and economic developments of the 1930s seemed to become fused under fire during World War II. In September 1940, the Supreme Board of the CFU passed an extensive resolution on the European political situation and the board's perceptions of both its own role and that of the American government in this developing crisis. It encouraged all local lodges to consider the resolutions themselves and, if they agreed, endorse them and pass them along to their local and state governmental officials. The formulations encapsulated decades of political and cultural evolution in the Croatian colonies: "Be it resolved, that at meetings of our membership, that freedom of speech, press, and religion be stressed and respected; that attention be called to the rights and privileges of all in their honest and rightful pursuit of the American way of life" (St. Paul *Daily Reporter*, 10 September 1940).

Interest in Yugoslav politics thus reinforced the CFU's involvement in the American labor movement and New Deal politics. This involvement was further underpinned by the CFU's increased participation in American culture, particularly through the English-speaking lodges, and by the CFU's reaffirmation of traditional culture, such as tamburica music. Together, these developments helped the CFU weather the storms that buffeted it in the depression years.

Conclusion

The Great Depression certainly meant hard times for the CFU and its tens of thousands of members. Yet, the difficulties it posed provoked creative responses. Through these responses, the CFU emerged at the end of the 1930s stronger than it had been before the depression. CFU activists blended traditional values, experiences, and outlooks with American cultural, economic, and political developments to breathe new life into their fraternal organization. Industrial unions, political coalitions, English-speaking lodges, competitive team sports, Americanized social activities, tamburica music, new holidays, and interethnic activities made up the patchwork quilt of the Croatian-American experience in the Great Depression every bit as much as unemployment and privation. A dynamic, syncretic process welled up within the Croatian colonies, institutionalized in the CFU, and helped carry them through the hard times.

Another point must be made. The CFU did not simply survive the Great Depression through these new undertakings. It transformed itself, and the Croatian-American community of which it was the heart, through these activities. The community as a whole greatly increased its participation not only in its own collective affairs but also in broader-based movements and institutions. Croatian colonies also opened up more to the trends of American music, sports, socializing patterns, and the like. Yet colony residents also drew closer to their homeland through increased involvement in its political affairs and through the second generation's increased knowledge of and identification with Croatian language, history, and culture. The sum total of these changes was not a simple balance sheet, but a complex dynamic.

These changes would continue after the depression. The patriotism of World War II, the impact of new, anti-Communist immigrants after the war, McCarthyism, the cold war, the surge of a consumerist mass culture, suburbanization, and the rise of a third generation would continue to change Croatian-American communities. The CFU, at the heart of those communities, would continue to change, too. But they were all determined to remain both Croatian and American, no matter how great the changes. And so they remain today.

References

Adamic, L. 1939. *Two Way Passage*. New York: Harper and Brothers.

————. 1943. *The Native's Return*. New York: Harper and Brothers.

Badinovac, J. 1939. "The Croatians as Pioneers in the Field of Fraternalism." *The American Slav* (September).

Balch, E. 1910. *Our Slavic Fellow Citizens*. New York: Charities Publishing.

Baldrica, J. 1978. *Tamburitza Music, History, and Origin on the Iron Range of Minnesota*. M.A. thesis, University of Minnesota, Minneapolis.

Barrett, J., et al. 1981. *Steve Nelson: American Radical*. Pittsburgh: University of Pittsburgh Press.

Berend, I., and G. Ranki. 1974. *Economic Developments in East Central Europe in the Nineteenth and Twentieth Centuries*. New York: Columbia University Press.

Berman, H. 1963. "Education for Work and Solidarity: The Immigrant Miners and Radicalism on the Mesabi Range." Unpublished paper, University of Minnesota.

Billich, M. 1931. "The Croatian Question." *Croatian Review* 1 no. 1 (April).

Bodnar, J. 1976. "Materialism and Morality: Slavic-American Immigrants and Education." *Journal of Ethnic Studies* 3 no. 4.

Brentar, J. 1971. *The Social and Economic Adjustment of the Croatian Displaced Persons in Cleveland, Compared with that of the Earlier Croatian Immigrants*. San Francisco: R. and E. Associates.

Cerrezin, M. 1929. *Case of the Rev. Milan S. Hranilovich: Was His Expulsion from the CCU of the USA Legal?* Cleveland: Cerrezin.

Cesarich, G. 1955. "Yugoslavia Was Created against the Will of the Croatian People." In *The Croatian Nation in its Struggle for Freedom*, edited by Antun Bonifacic and Clement Mihanovich. Chicago: Croatia Publishing Co.

Chmelar, J. 1973. "The Austrian Emigration, 1900–1914." *Perspectives in American History* 7.

Cizmic, I. 1983. "Yugoslav Immigrants in the U.S. Labor Movement, 1880–1920." In *American Labor and Immigration History*, edited by Dirk Hoerder. Urbana: University of Illinois Press.

Claghorn, K. 1904. "Slavs, Magyars, and Some Others in the New Immigration." In *Charities* 4, no. 2.

Clissold, S. 1979. *Croat Separatism, Nationalism, Dissidence, and Terrorism.* London: Institute for the Study of Conflict.

Colkovic, B., and M. Colkovic. 1973. *Yugoslav Migrations to America.* San Francisco: R. and E. Associates.

Croatian Catholic Union of the USA. 1935. *Historijsko Statiscki*, Cleveland: Croatian Catholic Union.

Croatian Fraternal Union (CFU). 1926. *Constitution and By-Laws of the Croatian Fraternal Union of America.* Chicago: Croatian Fraternal Union.

————. 1947. *A Brief Historical Review 1894–1947.* Pittsburgh, Pa.: Croatian Fraternal Union.

Dragnich, A. 1983. *The First Yugoslavia: Search for a Viable Political System.* Stanford, Calif.: Hoover Institute.

Eterovich, A. 1969. *Yugoslav Migrations to the U.S.* Salt Lake City, Utah: Mormon Church.

Friedlander, P. 1972. "Labor and Society in the 1930s: The Slavic Immigrants and SWOC." Unpublished paper, Wayne State University, Detroit.

Galey, M. 1977. "Ethnicity, Fraternalism, Social and Mental Health." *Ethnicity* 4.

Gazi, S. 1956. *Croatian Immigration to Allegheny County, 1882–1914.* Pittsburgh, Pa.: Zajedničar.

Goverchin, G. 1961. *Americans from Yugoslavia.* Gainesville: University of Florida Press.

"Hard Times." 1931. *Croatian Review* 1, no. 2.

Horvath, M. J. 1932. "Report of M. J. Horvath, English Editor of Zajednicar." *Izvjesca: Glavnik Odbornika, Odborai Casnika HBZ.* Gary, Ind.

Jelavich, C. 1967. "The Croatian Problem in the Habsburg Empire in the Nineteenth Century." *Austrian History Yearbook* 3, no. 2.

Kosinski, L., ed. 1974. *Demographic Developments in Eastern Europe.* New York: Praeger.

Kovacevic, M. 1903. *In Memory of the 1000th Anniversary of the Croatian King Tomislav's Coronation.* Allegheny, Pa.: n.p.

Kraja, J. 1979. "The Croatian Circle, 1928–1946: Chronology and Reminscences." *Journal of Croatian Studies* 20.

Krizman, B. 1967. "The Croatians in the Habsburg Monarchy in the Nineteenth Century." *Austrian History Yearbook* 3, no. 2.

Krokar, J. 1984. "The 1915 Yugoslav Immigrant Conference and the Chicago Croatian Community." Unpublished paper, De Paul University, Chicago.

Lukas, P. 1955. "A Geopolitical Analysis of Croatian Territory." In *The Croatian Nation in Its Struggle for Freedom*, edited by Antun Bonifacic and Clement Mihanovich. Chicago: Croatia Publishing Co.

Maček, V. 1960. *In the Struggle for Freedom.* New York: Praeger.

Mamatey, V. 1957. *The United States and East Central Europe, 1914–1918.* Princeton: Princeton University Press.

Mestrovic, I. 1955. "The Yugoslav Committee in London and the Declaration of Corfu." In *The Croatian Nation in Its Struggle for Freedom*, edited by Antun Bonifacic and Clement Mihanovich. Chicago: Croatian Publishing Co.

Mihanovich, C. 1936. *Americanization of the Croats in St. Louis.* St. Louis: St. Louis University Press.

Mirth, K., ed. 1979. "The Constitution of the Croatian Republican Peasant League of the United States." *Journal of Croatian Studies* 20.

Mladineo, I. 1937. *Narodni Adresar.* New York: Mladineo.

Movern, J. 1927. *United States of America: Information about Federal, State, and Local Government.* N.p.: American Jugoslav Association of Minnesota.

Orr, D. 1936. *Portrait of a People: Croatia Today.* New York: Funk and Wagnalls.

Palmieri, A. 1919. "The Growth of Croatian Nationalism." *The Catholic World* 109 (June).

Pandžić, S. 1954. *A Review of Croatian History.* Chicago: Croatia Publishing.

Preveden, F. 1947. *Povijest Hrvata: Na Engleskum Jczika.* Washington, D.C.: Preveden.

Prpic, G. 1971. *The Croatian Immigrants in America.* New York: Philosophical Library.

———. 1978. *South Slavic Immigration in America.* Boston: Twayne.

Rachleff, P. 1985. "Ethnicity and Class among Croatian-Americans during the Great Depression: Packinghouse Workers in South St. Paul, Minnesota." Paper read at Northern Great Plains History Conference, October, at Minneapolis, Minn.

———. 1986. "Impact of Old World Politics on Croatian-Americans, 1915–1941." Paper read at Missouri Valley History Conference, March, at Omaha, Neb.

Raditch, S. 1928. "Autobiography of Stephen Raditch." Introduced by Charles Beard. *Current History* 29, no. 1 (October).

Rasporich, A. 1978. "Tomo Cacic: Rebel Without a Country." *Canadian Ethnic Studies* 10, no. 2.

Rothenberg, G. 1966. *The Military Border in Croatia, 1740–1881.* Chicago: University of Chicago Press.

Schereck, W., ed. 1957. *The Peoples of Wisconsin.* Madison: State Historical Society of Wisconsin.

Sheridan, F. 1907. "Italian, Slavic, and Hungarian Unskilled Laborers in the U.S." *Bulletin of the Bureau of Labor*, no. 72.

Soric, B. 1947. *The Life and Work of the Croatian People in Allegheny County, Pa., 1847–1947.* Pittsburgh, Pa.: Croatian Historical Research Bureau.

Spalatin, M. 1976. "Perspectives on the Croatian Concept of Liberty." *Journal of Croatian Studies* 17.

Stipanovich, J. 1978. *In Unity is Strength: Immigrant Workers and Immigrant Intellectuals in Progressive America: A History of the South Slav Social Democratic Movement, 1900–1918.* Ph.D. diss., University of Minnesota, Minneapolis.

———. 1980. "Collective Economic Activity Among Serb, Croat, and Slovene Immigrants." In *Self-Help in Urban America*, edited by Scott Cummings. Port Washington, N.Y.: Kennikat.

Tomasevich, J. 1955. *Peasants, Politics, and Economic Change in Yugoslavia.* Stanford: Stanford University Press.

Tomasic, D. 1962–63. "Ethnic Components of Croatian Nationhood." *Journal of Croatian Studies* 3–4.

Trouton, R. 1952. *Peasant Renaissance in Yugoslavia, 1900–1950.* London: Routledge & Kegan Paul.

U. S. Congress. Senate. Hearings before the Subcommittee on Immigration and Naturalization of the Committee of the Judiciary, 81 Cong., 1st sess. 1950. *Communist Activities among Aliens and National Groups.* Washington, D.C.: GPO.

Ward, F. 1904. *The Slav Invasion and the Mine Workers.* Philadephia: J. B. Lippincott.

Zajedničar. Major Croatian-American newspaper, published by the Croatian Fraternal Union. On microfilm at Immigration History Research Center, St. Paul, Minn.

Zapisnik, T. K. 1932. Proceedings of the CFU annual convention, Gary, Ind.

Zivich, E. 1977. *From Zadruga to Oil Refinery: Croatian Immigrants and Croatian-Americans in Whiting, Indiana, 1890–1950.* Ph.D. diss. SUNY-Binghamton.

6

The Interweave of Gender and Ethnicity: The Case of Greek-Americans

ALICE SCOURBY

While a considerable amount of attention has been paid to the complex relationship between class and ethnicity in recent research, comparable attention has not been devoted to the equally complicated interplay of gender and ethnicity. Whether Gordon's (1964) "ethclass" has proven to be a useful analytical tool is open to debate. It is, however, a clear indication that interpretive effort has been expended on explicating the interplay between these two shifting modes of identity. To date, no analogue—no development of a concept that might be dubbed "ethgender"—that would focus particular attention on the varied ways that gender shapes ethnic identity and vice versa has been forthcoming.

Recently, however, several studies have been published that attempt, in various ways, to focus on the manner that the prism of gender has shaped the experience of ethnicity. Diner's (1983) study of immigrant Irish women treats the ways in which ethnicity and gender identities can be seen as mutually reinforcing and how they come into conflict. She concluded that when push came to shove, ethnicity proved to be more salient than gender for "Erin's Daughters." Ewen (1986) has analyzed the challenges to received ethnic cultures posed by the American economy and by the advent of mass culture. While both studies have focused on the immigrant generation, di Leonardo (1984) has explored the role of gender in the ethnic experience of contemporary Italian-Americans, seeking to depict the various strategies used by women to respond to traditional sex-role expectations and to the goals of contemporary feminism.

This study explores the role of gender in shaping a sense of ethnic identity and in defining modes of ethnic expression among present-day Greek-Americans (Scourby 1973). Underpinning this analysis is my agreement with Shils's (1981) assessment of the significance of tradition. Criticizing the tendency to see tradition as essentially static, he has argued convincingly that tradition changes as it is transmitted from generation to generation; it is shaped and molded by those who receive it. To sever one's connectedness with tradition, as various currents of progressive thought would urge, is, according to Shils (1981, 326–28), "injurious because it deprives subsequent generations of the guiding charge which all human beings...need. ... An individual cannot chart the world himself." This is not to suggest that people do not have the potential for rejecting tradition; indeed, that is one option. The material that follows will provide a brief overview of the inherited culture, followed by an equally brief discussion of Greeks in American society, leading finally to an analysis of the varied responses to this tradition articulated by Greek-Americans during the past decade; I will seek, in particular, to highlight gender differences.

Greek Culture

Located on the periphery of the European economic system (Wallerstein 1974), the Greek economy in the late nineteenth and early twentieth centuries lacked the dynamism of core countries. As a consequence, the jarring cultural consequences of rapid economic development were not felt in Greece until relatively recently. In this regard, the Greek experience parallels that of other peripheral regions, perhaps most notably southern Italy.

Despite the presence of regional variations, Greek rural life shared the same core value system: the people were all at least nominal members of the Greek Orthodox church; they shared in an agrarian economy in which the role and status of each member was clearly defined (Burgess 1913; Fairchild 1911). Despite the role played by the church, the basic unit was the family, including strong patriarchal control and deeply binding extended kinship relationships. Similar to the concept of honor in Vecoli's (1964) description of the Contadini, the importance attached to defending family *philotimo* (honor) inhered in a code strong enough to support vendetta claims of individual family members. Individualism has been notably absent in Greek life. A Greek was born into a group whose members were interdependent. The focus was the family, not the child and certainly not the married couple. Individual interests and group interests were inseparable (Lee 1955, 74). In short, theirs was a world view characterized by a particular type of holism rather than by individualism.

The central importance of the concept of *philotimo* must be underscored. It literally means "love of honor." It implies that respect is given to one's honor by others and shapes images of self-esteem. Any insult, either direct or indirect, focused upon family members constitutes a serious offense and calls for retaliation. In the traditional village, community honor depended upon certain sex-linked virtues, strength in number of relatives, a well-ordered household, and wealth in land to support one's family. In the contemporary Greek village a modification has occurred, and honor is now reflected in the display of a style of life that emulates an urban sophistication (Campbell and Sherrard, 1969, 359–60; Pollis 1965). Despite this changing definition of honor, it is still the status of the family as a collective unit that forms the core of *philotimo*, not the individual who, in actuality, has little importance apart from the group. Protection against the violation of one's honor continues to motivate the actions of Greek men (Safilios-Rothschild 1972, 89–90; Safilios-Rothschild 1971–72, 1967).

This ideal of honor and family cohesion have also for centuries supported the institution of the *prika* (dowry), without which a marriage agreement could not be reached. Both father and brothers are responsible for providing an adequate dowry, and the brothers are obligated to postpone their own plans to marry until their sister(s) has a husband to protect her. According to Greek law, both daughters and sons have equal rights to their parents' property. The underlying assumption of the dowry system is that a young woman is not able to make a contribution to the marriage as breadwinner; the dowry, therefore, constitutes her contribution to the expenses of married life.

In this century Greece has developed a cash economy, and when money became central to a "successful" marriage, young girls often left their villages to seek employment in the cities as a way of meeting traditional demands. Educational achievement has now come to play a more prominent role in the assessment of a dowry, although it is still a secondary consideration (McNall 1974). It is ironic that women seek employment as a means of conforming to a traditional norm. Two different ideological worlds are thus welded together, a nontraditional pattern reinforcing a traditional one, while at the same time acting as a springboard for social change in the options available to women. The dowry, which for centuries was part of the marriage settlement, was finally abolished in 1983 by the socialist government, which also enacted other reforms that liberalized marriage and family laws. Nevertheless, it remains a potent force in marital alliances.

In addition to providing their daughters' dowries, parents were traditionally responsible, either directly or indirectly, for arranging suitable marriages for their children, sometimes through a *proxenetra* (matchmaker). The ideals of romantic love and companionate marriage were alien to Greek life. Free choice in mate selection, with its stress upon personal satisfaction and romantic love, was viewed as deleterious to the solidarity of the family; it would have meant a diminishing control over the individual, particularly the female, and a weakening of the obligatory bonds that held the family together.

In short, love is clearly dysfunctional for a family structure that subordinates the individual to the group. This family type, to use Banfield's (1967) characterization, is an "amoral family" in that it focuses primarily upon the immediate material interests of the nuclear family rather than upon communal, concerted action for the achievement of some common goal. In a study of a southern Italian village, it was found that a climate of economic scarcity and fear of destitution bred mistrust and mitigated against collective action (Vecoli 1964; Banfield 1967, 87). This applies to the Greek case as well. There is a self-fulfilling prophecy operating in this orientation: mistrust tends to strengthen family bonds, which, in turn, function to protect individual members against a potentially hostile environment. But what is it in the socialization process that causes the Greek villager to view the external world as hostile? What elements in the culture inculcate a sense of mistrust?

Indigenous to this culture is the belief that the world is a cosmic battleground where one must use all the resources at one's disposal to offset the ever-present potential for disaster. While Orthodoxy plays a very important part in the life of the villager, it does so at the institutional and not the ideational level (Kourvetaris 1976, 171). Christian theology is infused with a folk philosophy that makes the individual the victim of irrational and impersonal forces. It is a fatalistic world view. The villager believes that the world created by God is always in conflict with the Devil, who sends out demons and evil forces such as the evil eye to torment the individual, who is situated between the devil and God. Because the environment is perpetually testing man, threatening to defeat him, precautionary measures are taken to protect the individual. A baby is helpless against the evil forces of human envy, and "under these circumstances, external spiritual or even magical forces are believed to be necessary" (du Boulay 1974, 28). Though their importance in Greek life has declined in recent years, such strategies for controlling the unknown remain remarkably widespread throughout the society, but especially in rural Greece.

Honesty in the abstract is not a virtue and may even be regarded as foolish. Loyalty is never to something abstract like the government, which is equated with impersonal law. Responsibility is not social responsibility; it does not entail a polished sensibility involving a concern for the common good but is directed instead at the family, sometimes friends, and to a lesser extent, at the village. To take care of one's own, irrespective of merit, is one's duty (Lee 1955, 68). This attitude complements the concept of *meson* (contract), involving the use of an intermediary in order to exact from the government a specific favor or advantage, such as securing a job, gaining admission to a university, settling a property dispute, and so forth.

Two discernible patterns emerge with regard to Greek culture: on the one hand, deference is paid to authority as determined by a patriarchal kinship structure, and this pattern is extrapolated to define the rest of the world; on the other hand, the ideal of honor makes the individual vulnerable to the opinions, actions, and innuendoes of others. It is the "other" who has the power to expose the fragility of one's ego, an event that must be avoided at all costs. In this traditional society, a degree of social control is obtained through the inculcation of shame, brought by individuals either upon themselves or the primary group, although the two are for all intents and purposes indistinguishable. The "other" is important for both tradition- and other-directed types of social character. The latter, however, are forced to interpret the constantly changing norms of their society, while the tradition-directed individual's family and community govern appropriate attitudes and actions (Riesman 1950, 24–42; Bellah et al. 1985).

How does socialization of the Greek child reinforce this orientation? McNall (1974, 25) reported in his ethnographic study of two villages in the late sixties that when he asked villagers how many children they had, their answers invariably segregated female offspring, as in "Two children, and one daughter." The ethos of sexual egalitarianism is conspicuously absent in Greek culture. The conviction that men are superior to women finds its justification in the biblical story of Adam and Eve, which the Greeks believe relegates each sex to its appropriate role. Villagers believe that the Bible story documents the vulnerability of women to sensuality and thus their weakness, a weakness that is part of their nature and therefore unchangeable. In addition, the perceived power of a woman to contaminate through menstruation restricts certain of her activities during that time; for example, she is not permitted to light the candles in church, receive Holy Communion, or bake certain breads for the holy days. The male, however, is always clean, and because of this, more responsibility accrues to him. Physical strength becomes a third, albeit less symbolic, reason for the assertion of male superiority.

It is interesting to note that the woman, in her maternal role, cautions her son to beware of three basic evils of the world—fire, woman, and the sea. The internalization of both reverence and disdain for women cannot help but create ambivalence and mistrust in males.

The woman is regarded as essential to the formation of a household. A popular dictum states, "Without a woman there is no house." Absence from her house for an extended period of time constitutes a type of spiritual infidelity, because her absence damages the unity of the household (McNall 1974, 133).

It is the attribute of weakness, however, by which she is identified, and it is the norm of *endropi* (shame) that serves to enforce honorable behavior. This constraining norm is intended to protect her against her basic feminine sexuality. If she fails to live up to traditional expectations, it is attributed to a defect of nature, whereas a man's weakness is attributed to a defect of character. Despite evidence of erosion, the code of *endropi* still retains force; young girls in the village are still expected to be modest and chaste. Their eyes, however, "are no longer downcast." Modern-style dresses tend to be more revealing than the traditional homespun clothing that was intended to conceal their sexuality, but "a violator is still in mortal danger from the girl's family if he is not immediately arrested" (Campbell and Sherrard 1969, 341).

When, therefore, the villager equates children with sons, it is because the weakness of the girl places a heavy burden on the family, in terms not only of the dowry that has to be provided, but of the constant vigil that must be kept to see that she does not bring dishonor to the family. Her very nature has to be protected, which is one of the major reasons for her dependence upon men. A man does not require such surveillance, since he is free from inborn weakness. It is through a man, therefore, that a woman is validated and through motherhood that she is revered.

In summary, I have been considering a code of moral behavior governed by honor and its obverse, shame. This code is also a key to the moral order in other Mediterranean countries and seems to have its origin in certain ecological factors, religious beliefs, economic scarcity, and a weak or nonexistent central authority. In the case of Greece, these conditions yielded a strong autonomous nuclear family, with the head of the household assuming responsibility for its survival and enhancement. These cultural values were, in essence, adaptive mechanisms designed to strengthen the identity of the family and to enlist the loyalty of its members.

The Impact of Migration on Ethnic Values

Though various Greek-American organizations believe the figure significantly undercounts the number of Greeks of single or mixed ancestry, the U.S. Census Bureau (1983, 12) reported 959,856 in both these groups in 1980, representing .55 percent of the total population. A significant feature of the Greek exodus to America that distinguishes it from that of most other European-origin groups is that while the most important years for Greek migration were also the most significant for other eastern and southern European groups, with the peak years of migration occurring between 1890 and 1924, a substantial number of Greeks have migrated since World War II. A total of 46,000 arrived in the United States between 1946 and 1960, and since that time, especially after the passage of the Immigration Act of 1965, approximately 150,000 have entered the country (Saloutos 1980, 437). This raises the possibility that ethnic identity among the second and third generation might have been reinvigorated by the arrival of newcomers.

While the following section explores the salience of ethnicity among contemporary Greek-Americans, those who came of age during the period that Saloutos (1964, 362) has termed "the era of respectability," a bit of background is necessary to adequately contextualize changes that are occurring at the present time. The great influx of Greeks occurred in the first two decades of this century. After passing through Ellis Island, the Greek immigrant might have gone west to work in the mines, or to New England mill towns such as Lowell, Massachusetts. Most of them, however, settled in large cities and worked as peddlers, bootblacks in factories, or menials in restaurants (Moskos 1980, 13). Many saw their stay here as a temporary one, and large numbers returned home. They were paradigmatic sojourners (Bodnar 1985, 53; Handlin 1951). Previous experience with farming had not been a positive one in Greece, and after 1882, the United States was already a settled land. Moreover, the immigrant had no money to buy land, so that a majority settled of necessity in industrial towns and cities.

The immigrant generation formed communities by including all the Greeks of the local area and establishing a *koinotis* (community organization for mutual aid), which elected its own board of directors. The foremost aim was to raise money to build a local Greek Orthodox church. The Greek church grew out of the immigrant experience itself and was governed by immigrants in the early years of the century. Even though the church remained under the spiritual aegis of the Ecumenical Patriarchate of Constantinople, lay initiative proved important, in part due to jurisdictional disputes, in animating this central institution of the ethnic community.

The early community was composed overwhelmingly of men, raising immediate problems for any attempt to transplant the Greek family intact in the new milieu. It was not uncommon for men to return to

Greece in search of a wife. Women did not arrive in significant numbers until the 1920s. Usually they would come with a relative—a brother, sister, or cousin. But many women whose marriages were prearranged had to travel to the New World alone. One can only imagine the fear and apprehension these young women endured coming to a country alone without knowledge of the language while fearing that they might be suspected of violating the moral code of their people. And, yet, they were confronted with a new freedom, being left alone without parental direction and support to chart their own lives. They helped stabilize the Greek community in America, enveloping family life, religion, language, and customs, and re-creating the Old World in the process.

Women were instrumental in building the formal structure of the ethnic community: the church, fraternal organizations, ethnic newspapers, Sunday schools, Greek afternoon schools, and ethnic social functions, usually centered around the church. They were the key in creating the ethnic enclave that both maintained and transformed tradition.

The progress of these communities and the ascent of Greek men into the middle class by the 1920s were eclipsed by the depression of the 1930s.

The role of women in shaping the ethnic community was reinforced by their low level of involvement in the labor force. As Bodnar (1985, 79) notes, "Greek families actually considered it a disgrace for a wife, and sometimes for a sister, to work outside the home." While men coped with "industrial time," women shaped "family time" (Hareven 1982). During the first three decades of this century many Greeks were repatriated, but for those who remained, a new type of community began to emerge over the next two decades, one that blended with the larger American community and brought into existence the Greek-American. The role played by Greece as an ally of the United States in the Second World War enhanced the self-image of the Greeks; ethnic identity and patriotism merged. By the 1950s it was clear that the Greeks had established themselves in the middle class. The mobility between the first and second generation shows that the educational achievement of first-generation Greek males was limited to a primary education, while one-half of their sons completed college. Greek fathers of the first generation were determined that their sons would exceed them, not succeed them. For the Greek, manual work was and is regarded as demeaning; a manual worker could not expect to be accorded respect or prestige within the subcommunity. It is, therefore, not surprising to find that the native born of Greek descent are to be found in white-collar occupations. A look at data accessed from the 1980 census tapes shows that in a sample of 578 individuals of Greek descent, 26.9 percent of the males were found in the managerial and professional category, and 25.9 percent, in technical, sales, and administrative categories. By the third generation, women's participation in the labor force grew. At present, females of Greek descent (51.9 percent of Greek-Americans) are mainly in the sales and technical categories, conforming to the national trend that finds women largely represented in those occupational categories.

The upward mobility of Greek-Americans has not been impaired by new arrivals, since they have tended to be better educated and more cosmopolitan than earlier immigrants. While many have followed the old path of vendors and small businesses, many others have moved into new areas of work such as painting, construction, and maintenance. Unlike the earlier immigrants who admonished their wives to stay home, now both husband and wife may be blue-collar workers. They, too, have found their way to ethnic centers in urban America. Many of these immigrants were from the middle class. Kourvetaris (1976, 169; Kourvetaris 1973) reports that between 1962 and 1971, 4,517 Greeks with professional and technical skills migrated, constituting a significant "brain drain." Between 1957 and 1961 Greece lost over one-fifth of all its engineers with first degrees to the United States (Coutsoumaris 1968, 169). According to a National Science Foundation study, from 1962 to 1969, 1,066 scientists emigrated to this country. Thus, the fifties and sixties introduced a category of immigrants significantly different from the early immigrants and from the majority of new immigrants as well (Sandis 1982).

Shifting Gender Roles and Their Impact on the Family

In a society that stresses achievement over ascription and universalistic values over particularistic ones, and for a group intent on succeeding economically in the host society (in contrast, for example, with groups that consciously choose to remain aloof, such as the Amish), a major question arises: How flexible is the traditional culture that has been transplanted (Yans-McLaughlin 1974)? Can it be shaped to meet the demands of the migration environment or does it have to be dispensed with?

Clearly, the inherited culture has not simply been reproduced in the United States. Due to the shortage of women prior to the 1920s, exogamous marriages were not infrequent. Saloutos (1964, 317) reports that second-generation males rebelled against arranged marriages, often describing the practice as "barbarous and uncivilized." As a consequence of their rejection of this tradition, it is not surprising that males were more inclined to marry outside the group than females. Greeks, because of their religious allegiances (Scourby 1980), did not fit into the "triple melting pot" scheme (Kennedy 1944; Herberg 1955), creating a somewhat unique situation for them. Nonetheless, exogamous marriages reflected a common generational challenge. Warner and Srole (1945, 148) reported that in Yankee City, interviews with Greek immigrant fathers revealed that they felt they had "lost ground in their effort to maintain the traditional inclusive controls." These reported changes generally referred solely to males.

Women, however, were not immune to change. Many women played roles that were not part of the traditional normative standards for a variety of reasons. To be sure, there were the manipulators, the schemers, the prodders, but there were also those who might have preferred not to assume economic responsibility for the family but who were cast in new roles by financial hardship or widowhood. Others had husbands who, because of personality problems or other reasons, were unable to assume the role of economic provider. The relinquishment of the passive role undoubtedly had a profound impact; these women served as models for their second-generation daughters, particularly those first-generation women who felt a sense of pride and accomplishment in their work.

There were also those women who were energetic and resourceful but who accepted a subordinate role in the family where the husband demanded subservience. Often the ambitions of these mothers were actualized through their daughters, so that they became role models in a different sense.

Young adults of Greek or Greek-American descent have been exposed for all or most of their lives to a value system at odds with traditional codes of conduct, this being especially the case regarding the issue of egalitarian sex roles. A study addressed two questions: (1) To what extent has there been a rejection of traditional role expectations, and (2) To what extent are gender differences significant? To assess these questions, a sample of males and females was drawn from three generations of college students. The seventy-six students attended four colleges in the New York metropolitan area ($N = 31$ males, 45 females). Attitudes toward the church, family, and ethnicity were elicited. While caution is required in drawing conclusions because of the small size, the results are nonetheless highly suggestive, and they tend to reinforce the conclusions of previous research (Kourvetaris 1976; Capanidou 1961).

The findings disclosed that students of Greek descent showed some differences in conformity to traditional norms. Their views varied sometimes according to generation, sometimes according to sex, and at other times, both were irrelevant. While the females of all generations indicated a favorable attitude toward the church, for examples, they overwhelmingly wanted the word *obey* removed from the marriage service. Thus, on the one hand, there was traditional adherence to the ethnic church but, on the other, a nontraditional rejection of female deference. The opposite result obtained with the males, who were less favorable toward the church but strongly opposed to removing *obey* from the marriage service. Along the generational continuum, first-generation men tended to be more conservative than either their second- or third-generation successors. Contrary to expectations, the relationship between attachment to the church and conservatism was not predictable.

The female's stronger attachment to a traditional value orientation was exemplified in responses designed to elicit the degree of ethnic identification. Women tended to identify as "Greek Orthodox" or "Greek American," reaffirming their positive response to the church. This, parenthetically, emphasizes the interplay between relinquished ethnicity and religion. Although Eastern-rite churches in theory do not fuse ethnicity and Orthodoxy, in practice this has tended to be the case (Burgess 1913), especially due to Greek-Slav tensions. As the largest Orthodox constituency (Ahlstrom 1972, 992), Greeks have played a dominant role in Orthodoxy in America. The female respondents were also inclined to be less critical of the church, although some differences were discerned among generations. The second and third generations were less critical of the church than was the first generation of both sexes. This may have been due to different cultural perceptions regarding the appropriate role of the church. The native-born students were more apt to see it as the locus of identity in a pluralist society, whereas the first generation continued to identify nationalism with religion in a taken-for-granted manner.

Endogamy, generally seen as one of the most important indices of assimilation (Gordon 1964; Bernard 1980), elicited quite different responses from males and females. Most of the males, irrespective of generation, were in favor of exogamy. The vast number of females, however, expressed a preference for marriage within the ethnic group. It is not surprising that intermarriages continue to be of great concern to the Greek Orthodox church, which to a great extent still tends to perceive itself as an ethnic church, although increasingly there are critics of this position who insist that Orthodoxy per se must take precedence over the ethnic component. Out of 5,143 weddings performed by the church from 1 January to 31 December 1984, 1,821 were endogamous and 3,322 involved mixed couples, almost double the number of in-group marriages (Greek Orthodox Archdiocese 1986, 101). There are no data on marriages that take place outside the church. To combat mixed marriage the church has encouraged conversion on the part of the non-Orthodox partner and, although solid evidence on the success of this approach is not readily available, it would appear that conversions to Orthodoxy occur with greater frequency than conversions from Orthodoxy.

The weaker attachment of men to the church and to ethnic identity and their attitude toward exogamy suggest a more rapid assimilation to the success goals of American society. Men are inclined to deviate from those ethnic norms which tend to curtail fulfillment of their instrumental role as the provider, the ambitious, self-reliant, assertive male.

In open-ended interviews following the completion of the questionnaire, several points emerged with considerable frequency. One concerned equality between the sexes. The females of all generations were generally sympathetic to many goals of the women's movement, particularly in regard to job opportunity. But they did not subscribe to full equality between the sexes in all spheres of life. Although they were all motivated to find employment after graduation, they also expected to marry, remain home during the child-rearing years, and eventually re-enter the work force. The idea of a dual-career family during early childhood years did not appear feasible to them.

In short, while influenced by the politics of the women's movement, they sought to define their own understanding of "personal politics" (Evans 1979). The men were divided in their attitudes toward the women's movement. The first-generation men were overwhelmingly opposed to the goals of the movement; the second- and third-generation men tended to be more sympathetic, showing a greater openness to a more egalitarian family structure. All three generations of males believed that premarital sex should not stigmatize the female. Paradoxically, as noted earlier, they were averse to removing the word *obey* from the marriage service. One might conceivably view the aformentioned liberalism on premarital sex as self-serving, or view the contradictory stance as part of a "lagging emulation." Whatever the reasons, this marks a significant departure from the past. Their world no longer resonates with the double standard so poignantly depicted in the work of Harry Mark Petrakis (1978). In his short story "The Ballad of Daphne and Apollo," Daphne is not permitted to enjoy happiness with the man she loves because of her prior sexual experiences. Apollo cannot reconcile her past with his love for her. In this case, tradition triumphs over romantic love. Finding no solution, Daphne finally commits suicide.

The males perceived their primary role to be that of breadwinners. It seems probable that the sex-role stereotyping in the Greek family has encouraged the male's upward mobility. Bernard Rosen's (1959, 40) study confirmed that Greeks and Jews have attained middle-class status more rapidly than most of their fellow immigrants. "In this country," Rosen wrote, "the Greek is expected to be a credit to his group."

During the interviews referred to earlier, both sexes articulated strong attachments to their mothers, which surfaced in expressions of not wanting to displease them. All generations articulated a gnawing sense of guilt over this issue. The sentiments expressed by the female respondents, irrespective of generation, were: "I know my mother does what's best for me, I don't want to hurt her"; "I would like to live away from home, but my mother would really be crushed." Another added, "I don't think my mother means to do it, but she always makes me feel guilty," and "I find myself thinking about how something I do will make her feel before I do it."

Two first-generation males had already assumed economic responsibility for their widowed mothers, one adding, "I still have to think of my sister in Greece and help with the dowry." The father was not consciously perceived as forming an integral part of this emotional matrix described by both males and females.

The attachment of the daughter to the mother is a very interesting one. In the early seventies, a study of sixty first-generation recent immigrant women who were seriously maladjusted was undertaken. The research revealed that their pathology was directly related to the fact that their strongest loyalty was not to their husbands but to their mothers who had remained in Greece. Their need was for love and approval from their mothers rather than from their husbands. This "Persephone syndrome" was one that the female respondents understood very well (Dunkus and Nikelly 1978).

Although the females in the sample had been urged toward a certain amount of self-determination, that is, to do well academically, they may also have been encouraged to develop a type of dominant-dependent personality that thwarts autonomy. The daughters may have been the recipients of two different messages—one demanding achievement, the other demanding submission. While the individual may be taught to value self-reliance, the dependence bond remains. The Greek female, compared with the Greek male, seems particularly vulnerable to this "dependency hang-up" (Whiting 1977).

It may be that the "fear of success" that operates to thwart the ascendancy drives in the Greek case stems from a fear of negative consequences that include emotional rejection as well as feelings of being unfeminine (Horner 1972). The daughter's success in meeting two equally imperative needs, self-reliance and affection, may engender both pride and apprehension in the mother. The fear of being abandoned, which forms the crux of the mother's apprehension, may result in a subtle form of rejection and ultimately in her withholding total approval. This solution to the mother's dilemma may very well function to preserve the dependency bond and limit the daughter's achievement.

The mother-daughter relationship must be understood within the patriarchal framework of Greek life as well as in the larger American patriarchal value system. Whether the mother is idolized or blamed, it is always the mother who appears responsible for either overcoming or perpetuating the problem of female victimization. While she herself may be a victim—victimized by her own mother and so on and so on—the victimization *appears* to be produced and perpetuated by women. To be sure, the interaction between mothers and daughters may, and probably does, perpetuate a particular female personality structure from generation to generation. What is critical, however, is that identification with the mother takes place within a patriarchal value system. The devaluation of women within that particular authority system perpetuates the dependency chain of mother-daughter relationships.

It is not only the daughter who identifies with the mother but also the mother who identifies with the daughter, far more than she does with the son. As a result, she does not allow her daughter to separate herself as much from her and achieve independence. In the experience of mothering, a double identification takes place. "A woman identifies with her own mother, and through identification with her child, she re-experiences herself as a cared for child" (Chodorow 1974, 43). In identifying with both her mother and her daughter, a woman will reproduce her own mother's caring for her as a child. Despite efforts to socialize daughters differently, this double identification allows for interaction patterns to be perpetuated from generation to generation.

Clearly, this relationship is linked to gender learning. By remaining close to the daughter and not encouraging the independence she gives a son, the mother keeps her daughter's ego confounded with her own. As a result, the daughter does not develop a clear sense of who she is. This ego-boundary weakness compels the daughter to define herself in terms of others, a pattern in keeping with the relational system that has characterized Greek family life. This very dependence results in a sense of responsibility for the welfare of others. If something goes wrong, the mother feels responsible, even though the event may not have been caused by her. She is caught in an "inescapable embedded-

ness in relationships to others" (Chodorow 1974, 58). The subculture
of Greek life and American culture reinforce these gender-related
patterns, so that the dependent daughter becomes the dependent wife
and then becomes the dependent mother. What has to be made clear
is that the psychological component is itself embedded in a male-
defined milieu that perpetuates the context in which mother and
daughter relate. The double standard generates both responsibility
and powerlessness on the part of the female. With limited options, the
need of the mother to remain close to her daughter is exacerbated and
thereby creates and reinforces the contradiction between submission
and refusal, between patriarchal domination and female autonomy
(Rich 1976, 195).

In order to shed more light on the relations between gender-role
expectations and achievement drives among Greek female immigrants
attending college, we administered the Bem Sex Role Inventory to
eleven first-generation students who were part of our larger sample of
seventy-six. This was followed by in-depth interviews. The majority of
the fathers were blue collar; three were designated as white collar.
The mothers' occupations were divided equally between blue-collar
work and homemaking (Scourby 1984, 135–39).

The Bem Sex Role Inventory (Bem 1974) consists of sixty mas-
culine traits (ambitious, self-reliant, assertive); twenty traditionally
feminine traits (affectionate, gentle, understanding, sensitive to the
needs of others), and twenty neutral traits (truthful, friendly, likable).
An individual receives a masculinity score, a femininity score, and an
androgynous score. Underpinning this analysis is an assumption that
traditional concepts of masculinity and femininity tend to limit a person's behavior in important ways, while an androgynous sex-role
orientation frees individuals from rigid sex-role identification and
gender stereotyping.

The masculinity and femininity scores of ten students were approximately equal, indicating that they had internalized an androgynous
sex role. The eleventh student had a high femininity score. Whether
the students who perceived themselves as androgynous actually
behaved androgynously was explored. In probing this question, the
students were asked to respond to a variety of issues. One question
explored their attitude toward the women's liberation movement.
Although none was an active member, all were sympathetic to most of
its goals. In response to the statement "Women can be too bright for
their own good," only one student was undecided. All agreed that the
media degrade women by portraying them as sex objects. In response
to the statement "Raising a child provides many rewards, but as a
full-time job, it cannot keep most women satisfied," all students

agreed. When asked to respond to the statement "Men and women are born with the same human nature; it's the way they are brought up that makes them different," all agreed. And to the statement "When both husband and wife work, household chores should be shared equally," they again concurred. All agreed that "women should be as free as men to take the initiative in sex relations."

But when asked to consider whether "it is only right that women be allowed to become priests in the Greek Orthodox church," only one student agreed; eight were undecided and two disagreed. Up to this point, the responses elicited were consistent with the androgyny scores on the Bem Sex Role Inventory; however, this response and further probing disclosed some inconsistencies in the students' viewpoints. For example, eleven favored endogamous marriages for themselves, even though they agreed that Greek men tend to feel superior to women and would refuse to share equally in household chores if both spouses were employed. As one young women put it, "No matter how you cut the cake, you will always be subservient to a Greek male. Maybe not the way our mothers were, but we would be submitting unconsciously." They described the Greek male as "domineering," "jealous," "antagonistic," "prejudiced," "one who tends to relegate women to subordinate jobs." On the other hand, he was also regarded as "gregarious," "generous," "hardworking," "family oriented," and "affectionate." They explained that it was important for Greek men to be in control; their masculinity depended upon a superordinate-subordinate relationship, a norm in conflict with the responses they gave on the Bem Scale and with the newer mode of intellectual companionship between the sexes.

The students agreed that even though their parents supported their educational achievements, they were expected to play a deferential role at home. Examples given were serving their fathers and brothers before anyone else and being generally attentive to their needs. One of the girls remarked, "We just hope that the Greek men we marry will be different or that they will change after marriage."

In discussing alternate lifestyles such as singleness and premarital cohabitation, the students agreed that living with someone outside of marriage was not acceptable. They might, they reasoned, do so if they lived away from family and the Greek community, but, clearly, the constraints of group norms prevented them from considering it as an alternative lifestyle or as a precursor to marriage. There was general agreement that their own socialization stressed "femininity," which they defined as not taking risks. At this point, the relationship of mother to daughter again surfaced as a very close one. Taking any action that their mothers opposed caused such extreme guilt that the consensus was, "It's just not worth it." Thus, the control imposed by the family limited their endorsement of the "new social ethnic" (Yankelovich 1981), a concept that emphasizes self-exploration and personal growth.

Since risk taking is an integral part of the motive to achieve and since the students expected to utilize the skills they were developing in college, they were asked if they would seek educational or occupational advancement in another state. Their response was that they regarded the present ethnic community as central to their identity and would not wish to leave it. One student said, "I feel safe and secure when I'm with the family; I feel nothing can happen to me." One young woman spoke for all of them when she said, "My friends and I tend to be conservative regarding marriage and family life and have put our priorities in marriage."

While it is true that the traditional view of boys as an economic asset and girls as a dowry problem has diminished, the legacy of male supremacy is still evident, though there is also a willingness to challenge it. In an effort to ascertain if the traditional preference for a male child persisted, the students were asked what their own preference would be. One respondent volunteered, "I would prefer to have a boy. I am more certain of what traits a male should have. If it's a boy, he can make many of his own decisions. I'm afraid that I'll bring a girl up to be like a boy." Another added, "I would like a girl in order to socialize her to an alternative she can have, alternatives I don't think I have." Still another said, "I know what a male is, but not a female. It would bother me if I had a passive little girl."

Reflected in these responses is a considerable degree of ambivalence. Ethnicity, particularly as transmitted through the family, remains an important variable in the lives of these young adults—especially, for reasons we have explored, for young women. Nonetheless, ethnicity combined with the ethnic family does not have the same ability to coerce the young as it did even a generation ago. While these individuals clearly feel the power of traditional Greek cultural values and also feel the tension that exists between them and the values of an achievement-oriented society, there is also a sense expressed here that people have options: affiliation with one's ethnic background increasingly requires a voluntary commitment on the part of individuals. To the extent that ethnicity no longer remains the most salient force shaping behavior, manifestations of ethnic identity increasingly take on the characteristics Gans (1979) has described as "symbolic ethnicity."

This article has sought to indicate that this trend is not as pronounced among Greek-Americans as it is among many other

European-origin groups. While one reason for this is the role played by recent immigrants in reviving the ethnic community, it has been argued herein that social-psychological features of the Greek family have played a critical role in preserving an ethnicity with behavioral consequences. Furthermore, because of sex-specific types of socialization, it is women who have been the primary bearers of ethnic allegiance. They are chiefly responsible for subverting tendencies toward complete assimilation. Whether the generation currently coming of age will choose to bear that burden remains an open question.

References

Ahlstrom, S. 1972. *A Religious History of the American People.* New Haven: Yale University Press.

Banfield, E. 1967. *The Moral Basis of a Backward Society.* New York: Free Press.

Behr-Sigel, E. 1976. "The Meaning of the Participation of Women in the Life of the Church." Paper presented at the World Council of Churches meeting, Agapia, Rumania.

Bellah, R., et al. 1985. *Habits of the Heart.* Berkeley and Los Angeles: University of California Press.

Bem, S. 1974. "The Measurement of Psychological Androgyny." *Journal of Consulting and Clinical Psychology* 42, no. 2.

Bernard, R. 1980. *The Melting Pot and the Altar.* Minneapolis: University of Minnesota Press.

Bodnar, J. 1985. *The Transplanted.* Bloomington: University of Indiana Press.

Burgess, T. 1913. *Greeks in America.* Boston: Sherman, French.

Campbell, J., and P. Sherrard. 1969. *Modern Greece.* New York: Praeger.

Capanidou, L. 1961. "Cultural Change among Three Generations of Greeks." *American Catholic Review* 22 (Fall).

Chodorow, N. 1974. "Family Structure and Feminine Personality." In *Women, Culture and Society,* edited by M. Z. Rosaldo and L. Lamphere. Berkeley and Los Angeles: University of California Press.

Coutsoumaris, G. 1968. "Greece." In *The Brain Drain,* edited by W. Adams. New York: Macmillan.

di Leonardo, M. 1984. *The Varieties of Ethnic Experience.* Ithaca: Cornell University Press.

Diner, H. 1983. *Erin's Daughters in America.* Baltimore: Johns Hopkins University Press.

du Boulay, J. 1974. *Portrait of a Greek Mountain Village.* New York: Oxford University Press.

Dunkas, N., and A. Nikelly. 1978. "The Persephone Syndrome." *Social Psychiatry* 7.

Evans, S. 1979. *Personal Politics.* New York: Alfred A. Knopf.

Ewen, E. 1986. *Immigrant Women in the Land of Dollars.* New York: Monthly Review Press.

Fairchild, H. P. 1911. *Greek Immigration to the United States*. New Haven: Yale University Press.

Gans, H. 1979. "Symbolic Ethnicity: The Future of Ethnic Groups and Cultures in America." *Ethnic and Racial Studies* 2, no. 1.

Gordon, M. 1964. *Assimilation in American Life*. New York: Oxford University Press.

Greek Orthodox Archdiocese of North and South America. 1986. *Yearbook*, Vital Statistics. N.p.

Handlin, O. 1951. *The Uprooted*. Boston: Little, Brown.

Hareven, T. 1982. *Family Time and Industrial Time*. Cambridge: Cambridge University Press.

Herberg, W. 1955. *Protestant-Catholic-Jew*. Garden City, N.Y.: Doubleday.

Horner, M. S. 1972. "Toward an Understanding of Achievement-Related Conflicts." *Journal of Social Issues* 28.

Kennedy, R. J. 1944. "Single or Triple Melting Pot?: Intermarriage Trends in New Haven." *American Journal of Sociology* 49, no. 4.

Kourvetaris, G. 1973. "Brain Drain and the International Migration of Scientists: The Case of Greece." *Greek Review of Social Research* 15–16.

———. 1976. "The Greek American Family." In *Ethnic Families in America*, edited by C. Mindel and R. Habenstein. New York: Elsevier.

Lee, D. D. 1955. "Greece." In *Cultural Patterns and Technical Change*, edited by M. Mead. New York: Harper and Row.

McNall, S. 1974. *The Greek Peasant*. Washington, D.C.: American Sociological Association, Ross Series.

Meyendorff, J. 1973. *The Orthodox Church*. New York: Pantheon.

Moskos, C. 1980. *Greek Americans: Struggle and Success*. Englewood Cliffs, N.J.: Prentice-Hall.

Petrakis, H. M. 1978. *A Petrakis Reader*. Garden City, N.Y.: Doubleday.

Pollis, A. 1965. "Political Implications of the Modern Greek Concept of Self." *British Journal of Sociology* 16.

Rich, A. 1976. *Of Woman Born: Motherhood as Experience and Institution*. New York: W. W. Norton.

Riesman, D. 1950. *The Lonely Crowd*. New York: Doubleday.

Rosen, B. 1959. "Race, Ethnicity, and the Achievement Syndrome." *American Sociological Review* 24, no. 1.

Safilios-Rothschild, C. 1967. "Class Positions and Success Stereotypes in Greek and American Cultures." *Social Forces* 45 (March).

———. 1971–72. "The Options of Greek Men and Women." *Sociological Focus* 5 (Winter).

———. 1972. "Honor Crimes in Contemporary Greece." In *Toward a Sociology of Women*, edited by C. Safilios-Rothschild. New York: John Wiley.

Saloutos, T. 1964. *The Greeks in the United States*. Cambridge: Harvard University Press.

———. 1980. "Greeks." In *Harvard Encyclopedia of American Ethnic Groups*, edited by S. Thernstrom. Cambridge: Harvard University Press.

Sandis, E. 1982. "The Greek Population of New York City." In *The Greek American Community in Transition*, edited by H. Psomiades and A. Scourby. New York: Pella.

The Interweave of Gender and Ethnicity **133**

Scourby, A. 1973. "Three Generations of Greek Americans: A Study in Ethnicity." *International Migration Review* 7, no. 4.

————. 1980. *Third Generation Greek Americans: A Study of Religious Attitudes*. New York: Arno.

————. 1984. *The Greek Americans*. Boston: Twayne.

Shils, E. 1981. *Tradition*. Chicago: University of Chicago Press.

U.S. Bureau of the Census. 1983. *Ancestry of the Population by State: 1980*. Washington, D.C.: GPO.

Vecoli, R. 1964. "Contadini in Chicago: A Critique of *The Uprooted*." *Journal of American History* 51.

Wallerstein, I. 1974. *The Modern World System*. New York: Academic Press.

Warner, L., and L. Srole. 1945. *The Social Systems of American Ethnic Groups*. New Haven: Yale University Press.

Whiting, B. 1977. "The Dependency Hang-up and Alternative Life Styles." Paper read at the American Sociological Association Annual Meeting, Chicago.

Yankelovich, D. 1981. *New Rules: Searching for Self-Fulfillment in a World Turned Upside Down*. New York: Random House.

Yans-McLaughlin, V. 1974. "A Flexible Tradition: South Italian Immigrants Confront a New Work Experience." *Journal of Social History* 8.

7

Constructing an Ethnic Identity: The Case of the Swedish-Americans

DAG BLANCK

Previous research in American immigration history has only infrequently dealt explicitly with those factors which determined the contents of the ethnic identities of the various immigrant groups. It is, however, possible to discern two major approaches: the emphasis has either been on the influence of the new (and often urban) American environment or on the significance of the European background. The classic statement of the overwhelming role of the new American setting is Oscar Handlin's *The Uprooted* (1951), in which the immigrants were assumed to have completely severed their cultural and social ties with the old country. Handlin's almost archetypal portrayal left very little room for the immigrant's Old World heritage, insisting instead on the influence of the new, urban environment in shaping immigrant beliefs and behavior in the United States.

The simultaneous rise of the "new social history" and "the ethnic revival" in the 1960s saw a break with this view, and a long series of studies reached the conclusion that instead of being uprooted, the immigrant groups experienced a remarkable degree of cultural continuity in the United States. The first, and now very influential, formulation of this view was Rudolph Vecoli's (1964) article "Contadini in Chicago: A Critique of *The Uprooted*," which showed how south Italian peasants in Chicago resisted assimilation and Americanization and instead maintained their traditional behavior and value systems.

Both of these views, however, seem to give little room for an appreciation of what many immigrants themselves seem to have been acutely aware, namely, that the ethnic identity that emerged in the United States, instead of being shaped solely by either the new American environment or the European background, consisted of a combination of the two. The Swedish-American writer and journalist Johan Person (1912, 9–10) expressed this view very well when he depicted Swedish-

134

Americans as "neither Swedish, nor American, but a mixture of both." A recent scholar who has noted this fact is Peter Kivisto (1984, 37); he contends in a study of Finnish-American radicalism that

> the sea change . . . neither resulted in the thorough deracination of social organizations . . . , nor the mere transplantation of the Old World in the New. Instead the relationship is best seen as a dialectical one, in which immigrants, to the extent that they were able, constructed a meaningful social reality out of the old world and the new.

A study of this "new meaningful social reality" created by the various immigrant groups in the United States would, then, appreciate both the Old World heritage as well as the conditions under which the immigrants lived in the New World. It would analyze the reciprocal interplay between the received culture and forces at play in the relationship between the Old World heritage and the American environment. Nonetheless, the factors that influence the precise contents of the ethnic culture and identity still remain obscure and need to be discussed further (cf. Albares 1981).

An interesting attempt to more precisely identify the salient factors at work in the creation of the ethnic identities among American immigrant groups was made by the sociolinguists Joshua Fishman and Vladimir Nahirny (1965, 1966), who used the generational perspective introduced by Marcus Lee Hansen (1938) but added some important modifications. They recognized the fact that different generations may differ in their degree of ethnic identification. This, however, assumes "that the concept of ethnic identification lends itself to an analysis along a unidimensional attitudinal continuum" that "ignores the central fact that (the generations) . . . may differ among themselves not only in *degree* but also in the *nature* of their identification with ethnicity" (Fishman and Nahirny 1965, 312). To remedy this situation, Fishman and Nahirny developed a model, which takes into account both the "degree and mode" of ethnic identification within the various ethnic groups in the United States.

For members of the first generation, ethnicity provided "an *ersatz*-framework within which they could and did recreate their common past experience." Only the first generation, which had personally experienced the Old World heritage, "embedded as it was in the local scenery with its fjords, orchards or white peasant huts" (Fishman and Nahirny 1966, 346), could genuinely appreciate this tangible and often highly local and regional ethnicity. Since these personal and concrete experiences remained inaccessible to members of the second generation, to them the ethnic heritage became "a set of ideals," which they used in the forging of their ethnic identity in the United States. Their ancestral heritage became a "usable past" from which appropriate elements were manipulated. The authors call the second generation's ethnic identity "transmuted," or an "ideology," transcending the "tangible elements of the traditional ethnicity" of the first generation and seeking to "embrace the intangible values" of the ancestral past (Fishman and Nahirny 1965, 321). It is, thus, a "highly selected and transmuted past," relying on "the heritage of more 'distant ancestors'—from Plato to Buber, from Columbus to Kosciusko" instead of "the actual heritage of their 'close' ancestors" (Fishman and Nahirny 1965, 350). These idealized versions of ethnic pasts need not be historically accurate. Historical authenticity is of less significance than the way in which the elements of the past have been used in the construction of ethnic identity.

While Fishman and Nahirny focus on generational differences, they note that there has been some discussion about whether the "creators of the ethnic past" were from the first, second, or third generation, but they contend that it is the "elective affinity" resulting in the "transmuted past" that is most significant, not "the generational composition of the authors" (1966, 350). If the generational classification thus seems to be of less importance, the actual way in which the ethnic "ideology" was constructed and the role of "the creators of the ethnic past" seems of greater significance. In this regard, the contribution of ethnic leadership must be recognized. John Higham (1980, 642) has pointed out that ethnic leaders assumed a special role in the "amorphous" American social structure, characterized by "pervasive mobility and . . . shifting, multiple allegiances," leaving them with the task of "focus[ing] the consciousness of an ethnic group and in doing so mak[ing] its identity visible."

In a study of the establishment of four ethnic communities in Chicago, Victor Greene (1977, 144–75) has also highlighted the role of the leaders in these communities as "mediating brokers" between the immigrant community and mainsteam American society, assigning them the dual role of preservers of tradition through assisting in efforts to maintain the old country heritage and promoters of their people's participation in American life. In this way, they played a highly influential role by functioning as "brokers" between the immigrants' two worlds and by focusing and defining their new, American ethnic identity.

In the case of Swedes, the construction of an ethnic identity in America was shaped by the fact that Swedes, as white Protestants, did not confront the intense nativist hostility that many other groups did. As Charles Anderson (1970, 55) has written, "the Swedes were never the object of intense prejudice or systematic discrimination." As a consequence, they were not forced to assume a defensive posture but found themselves in a position to be much more assertive in proclaiming an integral place for themselves in American society. Taking the previous discussion about ethnic ideologies as a point of departure, the following pages will provide empirical examples of the way in which members of a segment of the Swedish-American community, the religious sector associated with the Augustana Synod, sought to carve out a niche for themselves in American society while simultaneously forging a distinctive Swedish-American ethnic identity.

Between 1850 and 1930, some 1.3 million Swedes migrated to the United States, and at the beginning of the twentieth century roughly a fifth of all Swedes lived in the United States. Sweden experienced the third highest rate of emigration per capita in Europe, after Ireland and Norway (cf. Gjerde 1985 on Norwegians). The Swedish immigrants settled primarily in the Midwest, which in 1880 contained 77 percent of all Swedish-born residents in the United States. The figure gradually declined, but it was still 64 percent in 1900 and 56 percent in 1920 (Lindmark 1971, 27–29). In the early years of immigration, the agricultural sector attracted a large number of Swedes, especially after the adoption of the Homestead Act in 1862. The image of Swedes as primarily farmers (made popular by Vilhelm Moberg's trilogy *The Emigrants* from the late 1950s) is, however, incorrect. As early as 1890 a third of the Swedish-born population lived in cities, and when it reached its peak in 1910, 61 percent were urbanites (Beijbom 1971, 11). The occupational structure of the Swedish immigrants also reflects this gradual urbanization process. At the turn of the century, a third of the Swedish-born still worked in the agricultural sector, while another third worked in industry. As was the case with most immigrant groups, the shift toward urban-industrial occupations continued as the twentieth century progressed, although precise figures are not readily available (Hasselmo 1974, 23; Lindmark 1971, 35; Hutchinson 1956, 242f).

Soon after the arrival of the Swedish immigrants, a Swedish-American community was created. As Sture Lindmark (1971, 37) has pointed out, instead of being a geographical entity, "Swedish-America" was an essentially abstract notion, "a collective description of the culture and religious heritage" brought to the United States by Swedish immigrants and largely preserved through a variety of ethnic institutions. The major Swedish-American communal institutions encompassed the different immigrant church bodies and various secular organizations, including mutual aid societies, social clubs, singing societies, labor unions, and the like. Among the religious bodies, the

Lutheran Augustana Synod (founded in 1860) was by far the largest, with a membership of some 290,000 in 1920. This also made it the single largest Swedish ethnic organization in the United States and assured it a place of great influence in Swedish-America. Other major Swedish-American churches included the Swedish Mission Covenant Church, the Swedish Baptist Church, and the Swedish Methodist Church. It has been estimated that the total membership of all the Swedish-American denominations around 1920 was between 350,000 and 400,000, or around 25 percent of the approximately 1.6 million first- and second-generation Swedes (Lindmark 1971, 238).

Secular organizations and societies were also numerous. It is hard to determine the exact number and membership figures, but Ulf Beijbom (1986) has estimated that at least two thousand nonreligious clubs, organizations, and lodges have existed among the Swedes and their descendants in the United States. Among the larger mutual aid societies in 1930, the Vasa Order of America had 70,000 members and the Scandinavian Fraternity of America included 50,000, while the Independent Order of Svithiod and the Order of the Vikings counted 15,000 members each.

It is clear, however, that the Swedish-American community was divided into at least two main catagories. On the one hand, there was a religiously influenced sector, largely dominated by the Augustana Synod and its ministers and rooted in the rural areas. The opposite side of the spectrum was an urban-based and secularized cohort, often with middle-class leadership, making for a strong dichotomy between the religious and secular spheres in Swedish-America (Beijbom 1986; Beijbom 1971, 343–46).

In the religious sphere of Swedish-America, the Augustana Synod played a highly significant role in shaping the Swedish-American identity. At the Synod's colleges and academies, its leadership was educated and presented with what can be called the "Augustana version" of the Swedish-American ethnic identity. As ministers to Augustana congregations, teachers in other Augustana colleges or academies, or journalists at one of the Augustana Swedish-language newspapers, these persons were instrumental in spreading the Augustana Swedish-American identity to a larger Swedish-American audience.

Augustana College was the central institution for disseminating this viewpoint. Most of the students at the school had come to America without any real sense of a national Swedish identity. Instead, their loyalties tended to be local and regional, tied to a particular province or district in Sweden, and it was not until they came to Augustana that they were exposed to the national Swedish cultural heritage. The same was of course true for the second-generation Swedish-American students, born in the United States to Swedish parents, who by the end of the nineteenth century constituted the majority of the students at the school (Bergendoff 1969, 83–109; Augustana College Catalogs, 1875–1900).

One important source of this identity was a specific and positive view of the Swedish language and Swedish-American history, explicitly spelling out the role of the Swedes and Swedish-Americans. Since in the first decades of the school's existence the majority of the students were Swedish-born, and as an examination of the position of the subject of Swedish in the college's curriculum shows, from the very beginning Swedish obviously occupied a prominent position at Augustana. Until the mideighties, much of the actual instruction was also carried out in the Swedish language (Augustana College Catalog, 1881–82). It is also clear, however, that the early leadership at the school wanted to encourage a rapid change to English. Erik Norelius (1942, 127), a prominent member of the Augustana Synod, wrote in 1860 that "we [the Augustana Swedes] are not and will never be shut up within our own nationality" and that "[we] will become more and more Americanized every day." The strong man of the synod and the president of the college, T. N. Hasselquist (1863), agreed with Norelius. He wrote in the leading Swedish-American newspaper *Hemlandet* that the Scandinavian immigrants in the United States "in the long run, cannot remain Scandinavians."

This attitude is reflected in the Augustana college curriculum, which from the beginning called for one English-speaking teacher (the other two were to be speakers of Swedish and Norwegian; however, the Norwegians withdrew from the school in 1870). During the eighties, a series of curricular changes led to the establishment of two tracks of study, one including the study of Swedish and one without. By 1888, it had become possible to graduate from Augustana without having studied Swedish.

A look at the situation in the nineties and at the turn of the century, however, reveals that this emphasis on English with its overt promotion of rapid assimilation was becoming less significant. During the first ten years after the introduction of the non-Swedish track, only roughly 5 percent of the college students gave up the study of Swedish. The great majority kept Swedish language and literature in their curriculum. The official position concerning Swedish also seems to have undergone a marked change by this time. In his commencement address of 1896, President Olof Olsson (1896, 10–14) posed what seems to have been a criticism of Americanization in offering a defense for the study of Swedish. He said that the school was not "ashamed of being called a Swede college" and asked rhetorically, "Does it reduce the honor of Longfellow that he counted Swedish as one of the civilized languages of the world?"

Olsson's successor, Gustav Andreen (1901, 18), voiced similar opinions when he wrote that "our fathers thought that the Swedish language would be dead in 20 years, or surely 30 or 50 years. Swedish is now spoken and read by more people in America than ever. . . . A language does not die easily."

It seems, then, that the position of Swedish in the Augustana curriculum changed, moving from a less emphasized status in the early years, when it was assumed that it would die out, to a much stronger and also defended position around the turn of the century. As Olsson's statement suggests, the school leadership at this later point took more pride in the school's Swedish character, and I think that this renewed emphasis can be interpreted as a growing awareness that the Swedes at Augustana had become Swedish-Americans, and thus that a Swedish-American consciousness was being created at the school. This issue was addressed explicitly by a student organization at the school, *Svenska Vitterhetsällskapet* (The Swedish society of belles lettres), when it maintained that America was not "one single integer" but "the sum of all immigrant cultures" and that it was the members' "duty as true Americans to bring forth to the altar of our new homeland, as our most precious gift, the best of Swedish culture" (Blanck 1986, 98).

At the same time as the position of Swedish was strengthened in the college curriculum, Swedish course content also changed. An examination of the textbooks used in Swedish as well as those authors who received particular attention in the Swedish curriculum will illustrate this point. This examination is based on the textbook listings and the course descriptions that appear in the college catalogs between 1870 and 1901.

Prior to 1890, three principal textbooks in Swedish were used at Augustana. They were Sunden and Modin's *Svensk läsebok för elementarläroverken*, Herman Bjursten's *Översikt över svenska språkets och litteraturens historia*, and Claesson's *Svenska språkets och litteraturens historia*. The authors included in these books were mainly from the nineteenth century and belonged almost exclusively to the romantic and neo-romantic periods. Two authors seem to have occupied a particularly important position in the Augustana curriculum, in that their names and certain of their works are specifically mentioned in the course descriptions. They were Esaias Tegnér, the leading romantic Swedish author in the early part of the nineteenth century, and the romantic Finnish-Swedish poet and patriot Johan Ludvig Runeberg.

The most popular work was *Fritiofs Saga* by Tegnér, set in the Viking past, and Runeberg's *Fanrik Ståls Sagner* (The tales of Ensign Stål), which depicts in heroic terms the disastrous War of 1808–1809, when Sweden had to cede the province of Finland, for centuries a part of the realm, to Russia.

Around 1890, the textbooks in Swedish were changed and new courses were introduced. The three earlier textbooks were replaced by Ekerman's *Läsebok till svenska litteraturhistorien*. The selections in Ekerman are similar to those in the earlier books in that the nineteenth-century romantics are still given a prominent position. The period covered is extended backward, however, to include the eighteenth and seventeenth centuries, as well as a substantial selection from the Icelandic sagas.

The change is even more visible in the particular authors and books that were introduced into the curriculum. In 1886, P. A. Gödecke's Swedish translation of the *Edda* made its appearance in the Augustana Swedish curriculum. Together with this book, a number of texts dealing with the Viking age, Old Norse mythology, and the Icelandic sagas were used in the Swedish classes after 1890. In that year, Sunden's *Översikt av nordisk mytologi* (*A survey of Nordic mythology*), Viktor Rydberg's *Fädernas Gudasagor* (Ancient sagas about the gods) and the sagas of Volupsa, Heimskringla, and Havamal found their way into the Swedish classes. The extension backward in time, did not, however, mean that the nineteenth-century romantics were dropped, as Tegnér and Runeberg remained prominent in the curriculum. *Fritiofs Saga* was as popular as ever at Augustana.

At a time, then, when the Swedish heritage seems to have been re-emphasized and the college leadership no longer spoke of it as something that inevitably would disappear, the content of what made up this heritage was extended backward in time, toward a period in Swedish history when the country, through its Viking expansion, played a significant role in European history. The lasting literary contribution of the Icelandic sagas was also included in this heritage, as well as Old Norse mythology, a religion unique to Sweden and Scandinavia. If the strengthened position of Swedish at Augustana signified the beginnings of a Swedish-American identity, the aspects of Swedish history and literature that were taught can be said to have formed the basis for this Swedish-American consciousness.

A sense of identity can be observed in the concerns of the leading literary and debating club at the school, the Phrenokosmian Society (facts in the following section are from the Phrenokosmian Society Archives). This club met once a week and presented programs that were often historical and cultural in nature. From the mid 1880s and

onward, programs dealing with Swedish history became fairly common. Examples of topics include "Sweden During the Folkung Era"
(thirteenth-century Swedish history) and discussions of the prominent
kings Gustavus Vasa (1521–1560), Gustavus Adolphus (1611–1632),
and Charles XII (1699–1718). Gustavus Adolphus was a particularly
popular person in the discussions of the society, since he could be seen
both as a heroic king, promoting the glory of Sweden on the battlefields of Germany, and as a religious leader on the Protestant side
during the Thirty Years' War. On 6 November 1896 (the anniversary
of the king's death in the battle at Lützen in 1632), for example, a
special meeting was held in Gustavus's honor at which "patriotic
songs" and several orations about the king's life were featured.

As was noted earlier, the role of key leaders was crucial in shaping
a Swedish consciousness. In this regard, one particular case can be
instructive. One of the most influential members of the Augustana
Synod was Johan Alfred Enander. He was born in Sweden in 1842
and emigrated, at the age of twenty-seven, in 1869. After studying at
Augustana College and Theological Seminary, he became the editor
of the synod's largest and one of the most influential Swedish-
language newspapers in the United States, *Hemlandet* (The homeland)
in Chicago. As editor of *Hemlandet*, he wrote prolifically on Sweden's
and Swedish-America's history and culture. In the early 1890s, he
became professor of Swedish at Augustana College and shaped the
Swedish curriculum at the school. When he died in 1910, one obituary
recognized his importance by saying that "one of the chieftains of
Swedish culture has fallen," a man who had devoted his entire life to
"the preservation of Swedishness in America" and to whom "being a
Swedish-American was second only to being a human being" (Schön
1910, 372; see also Beijbom 1977, 21–24; Barton 1984, 288–92; Runblom 1985, 141–43). An analysis of Enander's views on Sweden and
Swedish-America will provide further indications of the components
that were included in the Augustana version of the Swedish-American
identity.

Enander expressed his views both in print and in public speeches. A
manuscript of a major address on "The Role of Sweden in World
History" (which, despite its title, deals only with Sweden's influence
on United States history) has recently been found. From internal evidence one can conclude that the speech was presented to a meeting of
Swedish-Americans, possibly at Augustana College, sometime shortly
before 1891. It summarizes Enander's views well and, supplemented
by some of Enander's published writings from the period, will form
the basis for what follows.

What was the significance of Sweden in American history according to Enander? He speaks of two roles, the direct and the indirect. The indirect has to do with the influence of Sweden on England, from which country the founders of the United States and the ideas that shaped the nation are said to have come. The direct role is concerned with the explicit influence of Sweden on the United States, primarily through the New Sweden colony (1638–1658) on the Delaware River and the nineteenth-century mass immigration.

When Enander discusses the roles played by Sweden in the formation of the United States, there are a number of recurring themes. The first concerns an emphasis on freedom. In the very opening sentence of the above-mentioned address, Enander states that "during the ice-gray antiquity" there lived a people in "a country close to the Polar Star" who were untouched by foreign foes as well as by the "shameful chains of domestic slavery." This is, according to Enander, the country from which much of the political and constitutional freedom in the world in general and in the United States in particular stems, since, as he puts it, "The American tree of freedom found one of its deepest roots in this by us all so beloved country, long before the Star Spangled Banner flew over a free people in old Vinland [the old Viking name for America]."

This freedom was spread throughout the world via the Vikings, who, "following the decrees and judgement of a higher Divinity pushed and paved the way for a new society." First it reached Normandy, was transplanted to England after 1066, and eventually arrived in America, where this "spirit of freedom" grew stronger "than in any other country" and "laid the foundations of the empire of which we are citizens today."

Enander describes the character of the freedom that spread over the world from Sweden in his discussion of the conquest of France in 911, when the Viking chief Rolf asked his men who their king and lord was. The answer given was, according to Enander's fabricated account, "the very opening words of the Declaration of Independence of the United States—865 years before their inclusion in the letter of rupture between our adopted country and England," namely, "We have no master or king, we are all equals."

But freedom and equality were not only brought indirectly to the United States through the Vikings and Normans. The colony of New Sweden, established in 1638 on the Delaware River, played an equally important role. According to Enander, an American author called these colonists "a model for all other nationalities," and Enander maintains that they exercised a "considerable and beneficial influence on their neighbors." At a time when the English colonists "had begun to blacken the conscience for reason of greed" with that "awful institution of slavery," Enander writes, the freedom of the individual in America was only defended by "the freedom-loving yeomen from Sweden" and by a few Germans. The Swedish colony also provided freedom and protection for people of various religious persuasions while the prisons in the English colonies were full of "sighs and lamentations from the victims of religious intolerance and superstition." Finally, the Swedes peacefully interacted with the Indians, bringing "peace and civilization" to them, while the "English colonists—the forefathers of our present-day yankees—hunted them like wild animals in the woods."

The final contribution to American freedom by Swedes came from Enander's contemporaries. Thousands of Swedes participated in the Civil War, during which they "drew the swords for the father-land, freedom and human rights and fought with Viking bravery year after year on the bloody battlefields of the South." In addition, the Swedish-American John Ericsson turned defeat into victory and saved "the entire fleet of the country and the most prominent Northern coastal cities" by the construction of the *Monitor*, victorious at the Battle of Hampton Roads, "an influence," Enander concludes, "whose memory never will be erased from the pages of history."

Another main contribution by Swedes to the development of the American republic was, according to Enander, the combination of independence and legality. It was again the Vikings who, through their conquests and settlements on the European continent, spread "self-governance and a society built on just laws." The Viking influence was most noticeable in the political and constitutional development of England. Following the Viking attacks in 753, large parts of England eventually came under Nordic rule under King Canute. His government was "wise and just" and brought "the judicial system and army in excellent order." "Never before," Enander states, "had such a spirit of freedom and self-governance reigned in the country and the Anglo-Saxons and the Viking descendants gradually melted into one people." Yet another Nordic influence was introduced in England after 1066 and the victory of the Norman king William at the Battle of Hastings. In this way a new nationality emerged in England—the English—consisting of the Anglo-Saxons, Viking descendants, and the Normans, all profoundly shaped by the Nordic heritage.

The influence of this heritage of political independence and legality can be clearly seen when King John (1199–1216), known as John Lackland, lost large parts of the realm and became indebted to the Pope. At this point, Enander writes, "the Norman descendants in the country could no longer stand the shame and dishonor brought upon the country, and their old love for freedom and independence, which could stand abuse from neither King nor Pope, came into the fore." They "seized power" and forced "the godless and cowardly King" to issue the Magna Charta in 1215. The constitutional and political liberties in England can, according to Enander, be traced to this point, and he concludes that "the seed of freedom planted by Viking descendants and Normans thus bore rich fruit" and that "the people of England was fostered to freedom and self-governance through laws which originally had been formulated by descendants from the original home of freedom—from the Far North."

When the "restless spirit of freedom" no longer could thrive properly in an English society "characterized by oppression and violence against dissidents," a westward emigration began and "thousands upon thousands" sought refuge in America to "live like a free people under their own laws." In this way, "the spirit of freedom and self-governance which once resided in the Viking halls, decorated with shields, and in the Normans' impressive castles, now lived quietly in the low block-houses and the dugouts of the untamed American forests," assuring that the American political and legal system bore the imprints of the Nordic heritage.

Swedish independence and self-government were not only brought to American soil indirectly, through the Viking and Norman heritage. The Swedish nineteenth-century immigrants had, according to Enander, contributed just as significantly to the growth of American society. He speaks of the Swedish settlers in "the Far West," where previously unused land has now been "tamed by the Swedish-American plow" and where significant settlements have been founded. These settlements constitute the advance of civilization and ordered society, which will continue to grow to become the cities and states of the future. In this way, Enander and his fellow Swedes, although they form a relatively small part of the American people, "will follow in the foot-steps of the first colonists" and continue to add the highly beneficial elements of freedom, self-governance, and an orderly society to the American republic.

The third aspect of the Swedish role in American history that plays a prominent role in Enander's thinking concerns the early Swedish presence on the American continent. Fishman and Nahirny (1966, 350) have noted this way of establishing "a bilateral line of descent . . . to the American colonial past" as well as to the old country among many immigrant groups, who have discovered their respective ancestors "among the contemporaries of John Smith, George Washington and Abraham Lincoln." Enander's extensive treatment of the New Sweden colony, whose residents settled on American soil a mere eighteen years after the landing of the *Mayflower*, is one example of this. In Chicago in September 1890 Enander gave a speech he titled "A Dream" (published in his *Selected Works*), in which he highlights other Swedish contributions to American colonial history. He conjures up the picture of Philadelphia in July 1776 when the vote on the Declaration of Independence was taken. The deciding vote was, according to Enander (1892, 24), cast by a delegate from Pennsylvania, "the respectable Swedish-American John Morton," thus placing that state on the affirmative side and "determining the future of the fatherland." Moreover, the Swedes played an important role during the War of Independence, and "Swedish-American troops" were in the forefront at the Battle of Trenton. According to Enander (1892, 25), their outstanding performance caused George Washington to reflect: "If only all my troops were such heroes as these descendants of Swedes, to whom no undertaking is too difficult, no obstacle insurmountable or no duty too heavy."

To Enander (1892, 15), the most important aspect of the early Swedish presence on the American continent was the fact that "the first European to set foot on American soil was not an Italian, but a Scandinavian." Enander is here referring to the alleged Viking journeys to America under Leif Eriksson and the subsequent colonies on Newfoundland, which always have played (and still play) an important role in Swedish-American ethnicity. Enander spent a great deal of time and effort to prove that the Vikings not only had landed in Newfoundland but also had established a colony there. In 1893, his efforts were capped by publication of his book in Swedish on the subject. Its subtitle, translated as "An historic tract in view of the Columbian festivities in Chicago 1892–1893," refers to Chicago's Columbian Exposition, commemorating the 400th anniversary of Columbus's landing in the Western Hemisphere. The book gives a detailed description of the arrival of the Vikings and their subsequent settlements, and it takes issue with "Anglo-American" scholars who dispute the Viking presence in America. In the conclusion, Enander (1893, 65–66) laments the fact that his views have not been accepted, and he attributes this to the strong influence of the Italians in the United States and to the Pope, who had declared "that the saint-like Columbus, inspired by the Holy Ghost and protected by the Virgin Mary," was the first European to reach America, which has resulted in a situation in which it is "considered High Treason" to voice dissenting opinions. The "historic truth," however, lives on, and long after the speeches to Columbus have been forgotten, the fact will remain "that the Norsemen discovered America and founded lasting colonies there 500 years before Columbus saw the light of day" (Enander 1893, 66; see Albares 1981 for a comparison of German-American ethnic sentiments in conjunction with the Franco-Prussian War [1870–71]).

Another instance of use of the Swedish past by Swedish-Americans was at the fiftieth anniversary of the college and the church in 1910. The Jubilee festivities lasted for ten days and attracted a great number of prominent visitors from both Swedish-America and Sweden, giving the celebration a very official character. The Swedish representatives included a delegation from the Church of Sweden, headed by Bishop K. G. von Schéele and the Rector of Uppsala University, Henrik Schück.

At one of the events, Ernst W. Olson, a leading lay member of the Augustana Synod, recited a poem specially written for the occasion, in which he posed the question "What is our heritage?" (for the poem in its entirety, see Olson 1911). The answer is that the history of Sweden represents "Faith, Freedom and Light," and that the Swedish immigrants have brought this heritage to America and placed it "upon Columbia's threshold." In some thirty-odd stanzas the author shows how these characteristics have permeated Swedish history, beginning with the ancient knowledge of the sagas: "Put down on Saga's yellowed page. . . / For us from Urd's unfathomable well / The waves of ancient wisdom flow, and ever shall / Fresh, wholesome, lucid, deep and cold withal." This Swedish tradition of dedication to knowledge and learning is evidenced, among other things, by the well-educated Swedish population in America, participating in public life and thus contributing to the welfare of the American republic.

Next, Olson introduces the theme of freedom. The Swedish freedom was, according to Olson, rooted in the never subjugated and independent Swedish peasantry, and since the majority of the Swedish immigrants, and particularly those who joined the Augustana churches, had been peasants before coming to America, this perspective became especially appropriate for Olson. He writes: "When Europe all gave servile fealty / To feudal lords, the Swedish commonalty / Ruled at the people's open Thing / And freely spoke his mind to jarl and king." This society was ruled by the "Consensus of the Swedish yeoman's will," which for "a thousand years" had taught the Swedish peasantry to "govern and obey," a legacy that now had been transplanted to America as "[a] million of these governors are thine to-day."

The last Swedish characteristic is "Faith," which in Olson's poem means the Lutheran faith. The Reformation was carried out in Sweden by Gustavus Vasa, who challenged "the Roman leopard" and "pried him from his loot-encumbered den / where he grew fat from feeding to excess / on the monk-ridden, tithe-taxed populace," and was defended by his grandson Gustavus Adolphus who, by intervening in the Thirty Years' War, "killed the northern brood of the marauder's league" and "refilled the lamp that Luther lit."

Olson, like Enander, then sought to indicate how these traits played a beneficial role in the American republic. In his poem he also includes John Morton, who in Philadelphia in 1776 "sat in council with the wise" and cast the decisive vote in the Pennsylvania delegation in favor of the Declaration of Independence, which leads Olson to conclude: "When half the chamber cowered to declare / For liberty it took a Swede to dare." Moreover, Swedes played an active part in the War of Independence, since "[b]eneath this standard, borne by Washington / with Fersen and with Stedingk we marched on," as well as in the Civil War; "[w]hen Lincoln's call rang out across the farms / Many a Swedish Cincinnatus flew to arms." The best example of early Swedes in America was, once again, the colony of New Sweden on the Delaware River, which belonged to Sweden from 1638 to 1654. Indeed, these sixteen years of Swedish-American colonial history assumed a special significance after 1888, when the 250th anniversary of the establishment of the colony was celebrated by fifteen thousand persons at ceremonies in Minneapolis (Mattson 1888).

To be a Swedish-American, however, did not only mean celebrating the Swedish past. Augustana students studied the history and the literature of their adopted country as well. English, American history, and civics had been subjects in the Augustana curriculum from the very beginning, and all Augustana students had to take courses in "the American subjects." American topics were also common in the debates of the Phrenokosmian Society. In 1880, the question posed for general discussion was "Who was the most praiseworthy: Washington, La Fayette, Lincoln or Grant?" In 1887 one evening was devoted to speeches and orations about the life of President Lincoln, and later that year the theme for one meeting was "The Revolutionary War," with a program consisting of "patriotic songs," a declamation of the Declaration of Independence, and speeches about the battles of Saratoga and Yorktown.

The Swedish and American pasts were sometimes directly combined at Augustana. At an 1897 meeting of the Phrenokosmian Society devoted to "famous battles," the discussion focused on two decisive engagements, the Battle at Hampton Roads during the American Civil War, considered by the participants to have "saved the Union fleet," and the Battle of Breitenfeld during the Thirty Years' War, in which the Swedish troops were victorious. Another example of this juxtaposition of Swedish and American elements comes from an all-school celebration of Washington's Birthday in 1888. The festivities took place in the college chapel where, according to a description of the event, "above the speakers, the banners of the American and Swedish Nations were displayed intertwined . . . [and] a picture of Washington symbolized the Union." Even the program itself reflects this duality; it opened with "The Star Spangled Banner," continued after a prayer with "Vårt Land" (Our country, a Finland-Swedish patriotic song), and, following an oration about George Washington, closed with "My Country 'Tis of Thee."

How is one to interpret the claims that have been made and the concerns that have been expressed? Clearly, what Enander and Olson and their colleagues and students in the Augustana Synod were involved in was what Eric Hobsbawm (1983, 1) has referred to as the production of an "invented tradition," which he defines as "a set of practices, normally governed by overtly or tacitly accepted rules and by rituals of a symbolic nature, which seek to inculcate certain values and norms of behavior." They are, according to Hobsbawm (1983, 4, 12) constructed and found in all societies and times, but are particularly frequent in periods of rapid societal change, which "weakens or destroys the social patterns for which 'old' traditions had been designed." A prominent characteristic of these invented traditions is that "as far as possible" history is used as a "legitimator of action and cement of group cohesion."

Examining the Swedish-American way of life as it existed at around the turn of the century, when Swedish immigrants had been coming to the United States for a half century, reveals the emergence of a specific Swedish-American ethnic identity. By this time, "Swedish-America" was well established, with numerous institutions, both secular and religious, as well as a great number of newspapers, all helping in some way to produce and implant this identity among the Swedish immigrants and their children. In this essay, I have examined some of the components in the Swedish-American identity such as it was presented by the Augustana Synod (cf. Blanck 1986).

It is important to realize that although the Augustana Synod was a dominating force within Swedish-America, and its influence was widespread, the Swedish-American identity that emanated from its central institutional organs and spokespersons was not embraced by all of Swedish-America. As has already been mentioned, there was a dichotomy between the secular and religious spheres within Swedish-America, and although the cultural differences grew less significant with time, the Augustana Swedish-American identity was clearly distinct from its secular counterparts. In addition, there was a small but vocal group of radical Swedish-Americans, associated with labor unions and various socialist parties. Although this part of Swedish-

America is virtually unexplored, it is clear that the radical Swedes distanced themselves from and developed a markedly different ethnic identity than the rest of Swedish-America, be it religious or secular (Bengston 1955).

As has been noted, segments of the historical past were chosen in a highly selective manner, "transmuted" into something new, and incorporated in the emerging Swedish-American culture and identity. The elements included are highly idealized and "intangible"—the Swedish "spirit of freedom and equality" and the notion of self-governance and an ordered society governed by just laws laid down by the people itself; they made their way to America both indirectly via Swedish influence on England and directly through Swedish immigration to the United States. In addition, Enander and Olson spent a great deal of effort trying to establish a Swedish birthright in the United States. Here, the establishment of the New Sweden colony and the alleged Viking "discovery" of America and subsequent settlements on the American continent played a role that is hard to over-estimate. What emerged, then, fits well with Joshua Fishman and Vladimir Nahirny's (1966) notion of an ethnic "ideology." It was created in the tension between the heritage of the Old World and the demands of the New, and can thus be called a Swedish-American ideology.

Swedes were, of course, at a distinct advantage in comparison with many other groups, particularly those arriving from eastern and southern Europe between 1880 and 1924. In part, this had to do with timing: Swedes arrived somewhat earlier and, therefore, were able to carve out a niche for themselves in the expanding American economic order. Cultural and religious similarities with the hegemonic British-origin population also proved to be of crucial importance. In the first place, Swedes found themselves in the enviable position of not having to spend as much energy as many groups in providing explanations, justifications, or excuses for their Old World traits. They did not have to defend themselves against periodic outpourings of nativist hostility, for they were not viewed, in Higham's (1963) phrase, as "strangers in the land." Second, by settling in the frontier developments of the Midwest, they were able to depict themselves as an integral element in the creation of new American communities. The aggressive claims they made about their own importance in American history can be understood as a concerted effort to enhance their status (cf. Mintz 1978). By creating an idealized image of the ethnic community, they sought to succeed in America on its terms. By seeking to instill a sense of pride in being Swedish-American, however, they sought to achieve success without succumbing to an assimilation that would sever forever the ties to the homeland and its culture.

References

Albares, R. 1981. *The Structural Ambivalence of German Ethnicity in Chicago*. Ph.D. diss. University of Chicago.

Anderson, C. 1970. *White Protestant Americans*. Englewood Cliffs, N.J.: Prentice-Hall.

Andreen, G. 1901. *Det svenska språket i Amerika*. Stockholm: Bonniers.

Augustana College Catalogs. 1870–1900. Rock Island, Illinois.

Barton, H. 1984. "The Life and Times of Swedish-America" *Swedish-American Historical Quarterly* 35.

Beijbom, U. 1971. *Swedes in Chicago: A Demographic and Social Study of the 1846–1888 Immigration*. Studia Historica Upsaliensa 38. Stockholm: Läromdelsförlagen.

———. 1977. "Clio i Svensk-Amerika" (Clio in Swedish-America). In *Historieforskning på nya vägar: Studier tillägnade Sten Carlsson 17.12 1977*, edited by Lars-Göran Tedebrand. Lund: Studentlitteratur.

———. 1986. "Swedish-American Organizations." In *Scandinavia Overseas: Patterns of Cultural Transformation in North America and Australia*, edited by Harald Runblom and Dag Blanck. Uppsala Multiethnic Papers 7. Uppsala: Centre for Multi-Ethnic Research.

Bengston, H. 1955. *Skandinaver på vänsterflygeln i USA* (Scandinavians on the left wing in the U.S.A.). Stockholm: Kooperativa Förbundets Förlag.

Bergendoff, C. 1969. *Augustana: A Profession of Faith* (Rock Island, Ill.: Augustana College Library).

Blanck, D. 1986. "At Home Abroad: The Creation of a Swedish-American Consciousness at Augustana College, 1860–1900." In *Scandinavia Overseas: Patterns of Cultural Transformation in North America and Australia*, edited by Harald Runblom and Dag Blanck. Uppsala Multiethnic Papers 7. Uppsala: Centre for Multi-Ethnic Research.

Enander, J. N.d. "Sveriges roll i världshistorien" (The role of Sweden in world history). MS in *Riksföreningen för svenskhetens bevarande i utlandets arkiv* (Archives of The Society for the Preservation of Swedishness Abroad), *Landsarkivet i Goteborg* (Provincial archives), Gothenburg, Sweden.

———. 1892. *Valda Skrifter*. Vol. 1, *Selected Works* Rock Island, Ill.: Augustana Book Concern.

———. 1893. *Nordmännen i Amerika eller Amerikas upptäckt: Historisk afhandling med anledning af Columbiafesterna i Chicago 1892–1893* (The Norsemen in America or the discovery of America: An historic tract in view of the Columbian festivities in Chicago 1892–1893), Rock Island, Ill.: Augustana Book Concern.

Fishman, J., and V. Nahirny. 1965. "American Immigrant Groups: Ethnic Identification and the Problem of Generations." *Sociological Review* 13.

———. 1966. "Ukranian Language Maintenance Efforts in the United States." In *Language Loyalty in the United States*, edited by Joshua Fishman. The Hague: Mouton.

Gjerde, J. 1985. *From Peasants to Farmers: The Migration from Balestrand, Norway to the Upper Middle West*. Cambridge: Cambridge University Press.

Greene, V. 1977. "'Becoming American': The Role of Ethnic Leaders—Swedes, Poles, Italians, Jews." In *The Ethnic Frontier: Essays in the History of Group Survival in Chicago and the Midwest*, edited by Melvin G. Holli and Peter d'A. Jones. Grand Rapids, Mich.: William B. Eerdmans.

Handlin, O. 1951. *The Uprooted*. Boston: Little, Brown.

Hansen, M. 1938. *The Problem of the Third Generation Immigrant.* Rock Island, Ill.: Augustana Historical Society.

Hasselmo, N. 1971. *Amerikasvenska: En bok om språkutvecklingen i Svensk-Amerika* (American Swedish: A book on the linguistic development in Swedish-America). Stockholm: Esselte.

Hasselquist, T. 1863. *Hemlandet.* Swenson Swedish Immigration Research Center, Rock Island, Ill.

Henretta, J. 1977. "The Study of Social Mobility: Ideological Assumptions and Conceptual Bias." *Labor History* 18.

Higham, J. 1963. *Strangers in the Land.* New York: Atheneum.

————.1980. "Leadership." In *Harvard Encyclopedia of American Ethnic Groups*, edited by Stephan Thernstrom. Cambridge: Harvard University Press.

Hobsbawm, E. 1983. "Introduction: Inventing Traditions." In *The Invention of Tradition*, edited by Eric Hobsbawm and Terence Rangers. Cambridge: Cambridge University Press.

Hutchinson, E. 1956. *Immigrants and Their Children, 1850–1950.* New York: John Wiley.

Kivisto, P. 1984. *Immigrant Socialists in the United States: The Case of the Finns and the Left.* Cranbury, N.J.: Fairleigh Dickinson University Press.

Lindmark, S. 1971. *Swedish America, 1914–1932: Studies in Ethnicity with Emphasis on Illinois and Minnesota.* Studia Historica Upsaliensa 37. Stockholm: Laromdelsforlagen.

Mattson, H. 1888. *250th Anniversary of the First Swedish Settlement in America.* Minneapolis: Privately printed.

Mintz, S. 1978. "Ethnicity and Leadership." In *Ethnic Leadership in America*, edited by John Higham. Baltimore: Johns Hopkins University Press.

Norelius, E. 1942. "The Missionary." In *The American Origin of the Augustana Synod*, edited by Fritiof Ander and Oscar Nordstorm. Rock Island, Ill.: Augustana Book Concern.

Olson, E. W. 1911. "A Poem." In *Minnen från Jubelfesten* (Memories from the Jubilee). Rock Island, Ill.: Augustana Book Concern.

Olsson, O. 1896. *A Pilgrim Story from Augustana College.* Rock Island, Ill.: Augustana Book Concern.

Person, J. 1912. *Svensk-amerikanska studier* (Swedish-American Studies). Rock Island, Ill.: Augustana Book Concern.

Phrenokosmian Society Archives. MS in Special Collections, Augustana College Library, Rock Island, Illinois.

Runblom, H. 1985. "Emigranten och fosterlandet: Svensk-amerikanernas bild av Sverige" (The emigrant and the fatherland: The Swedish-Americans' image of Sweden"). In *Att vara svensk.* Vitterhets Historie och Antikvitets Akademien. Stockholm: Kungl.

Schön, A. 1910, "Joh. A. Enander: Kort minnesruna for Ungdomsvännen" (Joh. A. Enander: A short obituary for Ungdomsvännen"). *Ungdomsvännen.* Swenson Swedish Immigration Research Center, Rock Island, Ill.

Vecoli, R. 1964. "Contadini in Chicago: A Critique of *The Uprooted.*" *Journal of American History* 51, no. 3 (December).

8

The Honest War: Communal Religious Life in a Dutch-American Protestant Community

LAWRENCE J. TAYLOR

"The Church is a very big part of people's lives here. They came here because of the bay...but they stayed together because of the church." So spoke an elder of the Christian Reformed Church of West Sayville, a small Dutch-American shellfishing community on Long Island, in 1979. His words resonate with one great tradition of sociological thought about the role of religion in providing the moral glue necessary to the survival of social systems. There is, however, an old Dutch proverb that throws an altogether different light on the effects of religion on communal cohesion: "One Dutchman—a theologian. Two Dutchmen—a church. Three Dutchmen—a schism."

In 1849 the DeWaal and Hage families left their village of Bruinisse in the Dutch province of Zeeland for America. According to the local oral tradition, their intention was to go to Michigan where large numbers of their compatriots were settling in order to farm. When they arrived in New York, however, they heard about the abundant oysters in nearby Long Island's Great South Bay, and having been raised as oystermen back in the Netherlands, the brothers-in-law decided to try to find a living on that nearer frontier, fifty miles east of New York City. They evidently found what they were looking for, and they were followed by a steady trickle of their relations and Old World neighbors. By the 1870s, these Dutch immigrants had come together in the hamlet of West Sayville, which was fast becoming the center of the shellfish industry that would make "Blue Point" oysters a prized delicacy on both sides of the Atlantic. While the waterfront was one focus of communal activity and interest, the church—and, eventually, churches—was certainly another. If the bay was the scene of dispute and tension over access to the precious shellfish, the religious domain evidently offered little respite. From the outset, organized religious life was as agonistic as it was pious.

On Wednesday, 13 September 1876, eight "separatists" met in the house of Arie Beebe, where, with the help of two schismatic dominies (ministers)—the Reverend Rietdyk and the Reverend Vanden Bosch—up from New Jersey for the occasion, they confessed their newly found faith and formed a congregation of the True Holland (later Christian) Reformed church. This schism, so calmly noted in the local Dutch Reformed Church consistory records, followed years of apparently bitter disputes between factions and individuals. Such battles, in a hamlet of 150 to 200 culturally isolated immigrants, could have left deep scars if not festering wounds. The first Hollanders had arrived twenty-five years before, but the church and settlement that was to be called West Sayville (the community, in other words) was not yet a decade old when thus acrimoniously rent asunder. The Dutchmen were apparently divided into two hostile camps and were determined to pursue their internecine theological struggles amid their puzzled or unconcerned American neighbors.[1]

The schism of the Dutch Reformed congregation in West Sayville was a local event, but certainly not an isolated one, as the presence of the outside agitators (as they appeared from the nonseceder perspective) attests. In fact, the split was national,[2] having begun in Michigan with the founding of the True Holland Reformed Church in 1857, but soon spreading to the various Dutch immigrant communities across the country. Why should such schisms have transpired, so often splitting small, struggling communities in two? What can an exploration of these disputes in a place like West Sayville add to an understanding of the role of religion in an American immigrant community?

From the point of view of the separatists themselves, there is no puzzle about the reasons for the schism. They were, for the most part, straightforward disagreements about the right doctrine and practice. The dissatisfied among the immigrants complained of "the neglect of preaching each Sunday from the Heidelberg Catechism, a tendency to ignore the doctrine of predestination, tolerance of membership in the Masonic Lodge, participation in other church services, a preference for hymns over psalms, neglect of catechetical instruction, choir singing (which discouraged congregational singing), and the baptizing of infants in consistory chambers and in private homes, rather than in the presence of the congregation" (Lucas 1955, 511). Several of these issues were raised in West Sayville's church disputes, yet in neither the national nor the local cases can one presume that confrontation and conflict expressed in theological terms necessarily have their roots only in religious matters. The immigrants were happy to receive the help of American Reformed ministers and congregations. Once they had settled into their new life some of these Hollanders, particularly those who had been "seceders" in the old country, began to grow less satisfied with an American church they felt suffered from many of the same faults that had driven them from the established church in Holland. Yet there was more to it than that, as an examination of life in the immigrant churches reveals. An identification of ethnicity with religion permitted Dutch-Americans to translate general cultural tensions into religious issues. Those who were less at home in the encompassing American society might focus their anxiety on the relationship between their congregation and the governing American church hierarchy. This, as will become evident, was very much the case in West Sayville.

There is a difficulty with explaining this schism as solely due to the stresses of life in America, for churches in the Netherlands were undergoing their own great upheavals throughout the nineteenth century. Although their problems were not directly connected to those of the American Reformed church, they took much the same form; in Holland, too, various brands of separatists claimed a more orthodox Calvinism and sought a covenant at once more democratic and totalitarian. Whatever causes are elicited to explain events in the American context should apply as well to the Dutch case.

Beyond that, the American schism did not take whole immigrant communities out of their church so often as it rent them in two, thus pitting Dutchmen against Dutchmen. Why were some of these men and women attracted to the schismatic sect, while others remained in the Dutch Reformed church? Historian Robert Swierenga (1980) has proposed an answer to this problem, based on a statistical treatment of the Dutch regional origins of the immigrants. He argues, with the aid of Robert Merton's (1949) categorical dichotomy of "locals" and "cosmopolitans," that those Dutch who joined the new and more reactionary True Holland church were more likely to have come from the less-urban-influenced areas of Holland, where the populace was "local" in cultural outlook. Those who remained in the Dutch Reformed church, conversely, he shows to have been more often from regions where city influences encouraged a more "cosmopolitan" world view. This approach locates the causes of the schism outside the American context and thus may shed some light on the Dutch schisms as well.

The static dichotomy of "locals" and "cosmopolitans," however, is only a system of labels and is not much help in explaining the dynamic process of constant internal fission characterizing Dutch Reformed religion in both Holland and America. Verrips's (1973) account of intracommunity factions in a modern Dutch town, and the

example of West Sayville, suggest that whatever labels are attached
to the individuals choosing one church over the other, there is also
a community dynamic involved in church fission and factions. The
nature of that process is manifest not through a consideration of the
individual characteristics of the immigrants but through an analysis
of their interaction—and that is revealed, in part at least, in the
records of the church consistory, where a number of colorful social
dramas were acted out.

These scenarios lend themselves nicely to Victor Turner's (1968)
extended case study method, which promises not only to reveal something of the structural roots of disputes and schisms in this and similar
churches, but also to shed some light on questions of even more general concern in the anthropology of religion.

Ever since French social theorist Emile Durkheim (1915) argued
that religion provides the moral and conceptual framework that a
society requires to function, anthropologists have focused most of
their analytical attention on the contribution made by systems of religious belief and action to the stability of social systems. Shared religious ideology and common ritual interaction have been typically
understood to knit together the social fabric, most especially when it
threatens to unravel. Thus, for example, the life crises that interrupt
the order of social and personal life are marked by "rites of passage"
(Van Gennep 1960) that assert the ability of the culture to control
these processes. Further, group and individual conflicts that arise in
all realms of human experience may often be resolved by religion,
especially on the ritual stage, according to the analyses of numerous
anthropologists (see esp. Turner 1968). By actively reaffirming the
ideal moral order, ritual functions on a psychological and social level,
simultaneously providing both the individual and the group with a
conceptual order that guides and makes sense of experience and interaction.

Religion is often enough perceived to fulfill such functions for ethnic
Americans, but the differences among religious groups provide a variety of opportunities for the expression of ethnic or communal definition. Anthropologists, with their penchant for ritual, have been more
interested in Catholics and Orthodox Christians than Protestants. The
religious traditions of the former certainly possess many rituals replete
with symbolic objects and actions that, even if their explicit referents
are religious, may carry more secular meanings as well. Among such
nonsacred characteristics of religious symbols the ethnic loom large.

Among the Catholic immigrants in America, Italians and other
Mediterranean groups come particularly to mind in this connection.
In a church called St. Rocco's with a largely Calabrian population, for

example, we would expect a saint's day festivity complete with procession, perhaps with Rocco himself being transported along the avenue, his garments pinned with money. In this case, and it is a fairly typical one, a ritual that expressed localism in an Italian context retains its communal associations in America but adds a more general ethnic one, particularly if the group in question is surrounded by non-Italians.

Interestingly enough, not all Catholic groups in America seem to equally avail themselves of the opportunity of ethnic and communal expression. The Irish-Americans have their saints, but, Patrick aside, Irish saints do not seem to play the same role in ethnic or local group definition. Looking only at the American case, one might be tempted to conclude that the Irish dominance of the American Catholic church has made the need for separate definition less marked and, further, that the relative lack of difference between Irish culture and that of the surrounding American environment (as compared to Mediterranean cultures) has created less of a need for such local pageantry. Yet even in Ireland, such use of saints for local or regional expression is far less pronounced than in southern Catholic Europe. One possible reason may be the very different historical relation of Catholicism in Ireland to the state and the ethnic identity of the people. While regional differences are certainly not absent from Ireland, they are nothing like those of such countries as Spain or Italy. Irish identity was forged in opposition to British culture, with Catholicism playing a major distinguishing role in the binary opposition—considerably muting the need for local and regional identification through saint cults in mutual opposition. And so just as Ireland lacks important local saints' cults, it is, arguably, possessed of a stronger national ethnic symbol in Saint Patrick than is Italy or Spain (or even Poland). This has its ramifications for American ethnic identity. Indeed, there is an interesting inverse relation between the Irish and Italian cases. Among the Irish-Americans, St. Patrick symbolizes Irishness, but other saints do not carry strong local or regional Irish identities, and hence are less useful for symbolizing and reinforcing local communities. Among the Italian-Americans, local saints continue to be important group identifiers, but a secular hero—Columbus—is needed for expressing general Italian identity.

What about Protestants? It has been pointed out that Protestants, even those who theologically eschew "popery," have rituals, and important ones at that. The Reformed Christians who are the subject of this essay certainly indulged in symbolic and ritual behavior. There was the crucial rite of passage, the baptism, and the regular sacrament of the Lord's Supper. What makes these sorts of rituals different from those of the Catholic church, aside from their respective dogmas, is their relative lack of symbolic content. There are simply not as many things or actions involved: no saints, no costumes, no painted eggs— fewer anchors, therefore, for ethnic or distinctive communal associations. It is thus not surprising that among Dutch-Americans religious ritual provides few opportunities for direct expression of ethnicity or even local communal identity, yet it is just these "deficiencies" that make the study of religion in a Protestant immigrant community a compelling case for the understanding of both ethnicity and theories of the communal function of religion. For, when asked what is distinctive about being Dutch, the people of West Sayville typically mentioned religion as of paramount importance.

To judge from written memoirs and current oral sources (see Taylor 1983), the religious dogmas of the Reformed churches equipped the Dutch immigrants of West Sayville with a means of making sense of disparate experiences. The relationship of religious belief and practice to social interaction in a community like West Sayville, however, presents a challenge to social anthropological theories of religion in two respects.

First, the beliefs of the Reformed faith entailed a central contradiction, or at least conflict, pitting the notions of predestination and personal salvation against the absolute moral authority of the church-community. While the latter may have been a centripetal force in the community, the former was equally centrifugal. Several of the early immigrants expressed their desire to seek the fellowship of other Christians, but the tireless self-concern, arising from self-scrutiny for signs of predestination and the impossible quest for perfect Christians, made cooperation with newfound fellows difficult. They raged with self-doubt even as they condemned their profligate neighbors. Church dogma seems, therefore, to have been potentially as much a source of antagonism as of social solidarity.

This apparent contradiction between the independence of the individual in theological (as well as economic and social) affairs, and the moral authority of the church community, was addressed in the ideal realm through the Calvinist doctrine of the "Covenant," a union of free, saved individuals bound together by a kind of holy contract that was affirmed in stages. The confession of faith was a rite of passage that made the adult a full member of the congregation, binding him or her finally and completely to the God-directed will of the community, a bond that was periodically reaffirmed by the communal ritual of the Lord's Supper. Authority in this community of believers was invested in a "consistory" of elders and deacons, elected by the assembled congregation. That congregation of household heads also "called," or elected, a dominie from a slate of candidates furnished by the classis, the regional governance body. These consistory officials were supposed to have absolute authority over those who covenanted with them.

Moreover, the bond of the covenant further implied the right and duty of each member of the community to report the moral transgression of fellow members. Anyone's sin, after all, threatened the moral integrity of the group and therefore had to be expunged. One might imagine that such independent-minded people would not always have been happy to bend before the communal will, especially when embodied in a particular neighbor. One might expect conflicts to ensue.

That brings me to the second challenge that this religious form presents to analysis. As has already been noted, anthropologists expect that wherever conflict arises, religious ritual should provide a formal means for its symbolic resolution, or at least suspension. But ritual was not an obvious feature of the Reformed faith. In challenging Roman Catholic practice, nearly all the Protestant creeds removed authority in varying degrees from the ritually sacred altar and placed it in the deritualized, secular pulpit. This amounted to an attack on the symbolic separation of sacred from secular time and place. Calvinistic creeds were especially concerned with breaking down this barrier and bringing every action and thought under the governance of a deritualized religious faith.

Calvinist idealization and Calvinist practice, however, may be two different things. To discover when and how dogmatic contradictions produced conflict, and what sorts of resolutions religious practice offered, the best strategy is an ethnographic one. A researcher must look at what people actually do, not only what they say they should do. A close analysis of what actually went on in one particular church-community should reveal aspects of the dynamic social character of this religious faith not apparent in textual or statistical studies.

The Dutch Reformed Church

The Sayville Dutch Reformed congregation was formally organized in 1866, and the consistory records reveal that serious difficulties were not long in arising. Dealing with even the simple matter of Sabbath violation, the most common offense brought to the consistory's attention, rarely proceeded smoothly.

An entry in the consistory records for 2 April 1868 reads:

Special meeting was held; the Consistory learned that the following members [five names followed] were guilty of violation of the Sabbath day, by going to the bay on Sunday, March 22, to be at work at their boats. Notice was given to these members to appear before the Consistory.

As it turned out, two of the culprits "acknowledged their guilt and confessed that they had not done well." A third man informed the consistory that he was unable to attend the meeting but would be at the next. As for the other two, they were issued the following letter:

Sir:
I have to inform you that at the meeting of the Consistory . . . it was resolved to give you notice that you are not permitted to partake of the Lord's Supper and that for the following reasons: I. You are guilty of profanation of the Sabbath, II. Because you have refused to appear before the Consistory, notwithstanding you were ordered to do so. In case you have something to say in defense or excuse, opportunity is given you to do so, before a meeting of the Consistory.

By the Will of the Consistory,
L. G. Jongeneel, Pres.

These two men remained unregenerate for quite some time, even under threat of exclusion from the Lord's Supper. This sort of escalation of what began as a relatively minor offense, with the incurring of greater and greater acts of censure on the part of the consistory, was far from rare.

Ideally, fear of exclusion from the community should have brought the various offenders around, but if the offender could not contest the right of the community to enforce its will on him, he could question either the validity of the accusation or the fitness of the particular officers to represent the communal will. In resisting the orders of the consistory, he might claim either that he was not guilty of the crime or that the consistory or any one of its several members was not morally pure himself. In the first case, the accused took the charge of misconduct as an opportunity to turn communal attention on his accuser, so that what might conceivably have begun as competition or private argument between two individuals was soon raised to the rank of a public religious contention with suit and countersuit. In the second case, by questioning the right of the consistory to act in the community's behalf, the violator in effect claimed that the whole covenant was in a sorry state, as evidenced by the character of its officers. He was, furthermore, likely to find supporters in that claim, for various circumstances ensured that a portion of the community was always unhappy with things as they were.

In the Dutch Reformed congregation, however, it was the minister, or dominie, who was most often eventually found to be the underlying cause of whatever ailed the moral community. Today the ministers may be remembered as an unbroken line of eminent elders whose passage down the village streets was faithfully met with doffed hats and respectful nods, but the early church records reveal a different picture.

The first minister, a Reverend Jongeneel, arrived at the founding of the church in 1867 and remained until 1871. In those few years he was the frequent subject of open and angry accusations. In particular, the dominie was found wanting in the strictness of his interpretation of God's word. Early in his tenure one of his elders reprimanded Jongeneel for "preaching wrong doctrine" and for approving of the dropping of the word "Dutch" from the title of the national church. Later he was found to be teaching "false doctrine" by a whole coterie of congregation members; even one of his own elders was heard to remark that the reverend "was better fit for farming than for preaching."

Jongeneel was replaced by Van Emmerick in 1871, but the new dominie faired even worse than his colleague. On the evidence of a young girl, Van Emmerick was accused of sexual adventures with a local teenage girl. While officially cleared by a classis committee, the minister was never to recover from the suspicions unleashed by that case. He was the subject of constant complaints concerning doctrinal matters, and many began to withdraw from the congregation. On the occasion of a visitation from an elder, one dissatisfied woman remarked, "So long as that guy is minister here, I am not going to step into that church." Van Emmerick was vilified for every possible offense, but most of them were linked once again to what some members of his congregation viewed as the growing laxness of the moral bonds of the community. In 1866 he left the church, having finally secured the salary he was owed by the congregation. His replacement was a Reverend Crousaz, who fared no better than his predecessors. Reverend Schilstra, dominie from 1900 to 1910, recorded these remarks about both Van Emmerick and Crousaz:

> Rev. Crousaz behaved indecently and came home drunk now and then from Sayville. He held company with persons in Sayville and spent the evening playing cards and drinking. Afterwards it came out that the minister had a debt of $700 for beer and drink. When this unexpected behavior came out the love and respect for the minister was lost and then they let him go from the church. He went west and we never heard from this unlucky family. Dominie Crousaz was a principal in the Netherlands and probably had to leave that country because of his behavior. This was

now the second minister who behaved in this church in the same bad way. This is what happens when runaway vagabonds and bandits like Van Emmerick and Crousaz can come here without decent preparation and looking into and are put for candidates by the classis.

As Reverend Schilstra argued, the problem of the early ministers cannot be attributed to their personalities alone. Schilstra blamed the classis for sending "vagabonds and bandits" to the immigrant churches, and some of the local congregations' trouble certainly arose from their position as immigrant churches uneasily incorporated into an established American Reformed hierarchy. Although the language of church dispute was always religious, the underlying issues often seem to bear out this interpretation. There was, for example, the problem of money. According to the ideals of the Reformed church, the congregation should have been financially independent, paying the salary of its minister and building its own churches and facilities from the subscriptions and special donations of its own members. Poor immigrant communities, however, were rarely in a position to do so, and West Sayville was no exception. While the arguments between members were typically phrased in a religious idiom, the occasion for such fights could be the raising of money for the dominie's salary or other church expenses. Resentment was felt for the minister, a man who, after all, was living off a financially embattled and very hard-working congregation.

Again in common with many other immigrant congregations, the West Sayville Dutch found themselves uneasily placed in an American hierarchy of classes and synods on which they were financially dependent and from which they were separated by sometimes considerable cultural differences. Language was both an element and symbol of this cultural gap.

By the mid–nineteenth century the Reformed church in and around New York City was English-speaking, and the classis officials who oversaw the installation of the fledgling congregation in West Sayville expected the consistory minutes to be submitted in English. That was difficult enough, but when the classis officials further demanded that these English minutes be signed by the members of the consistory, the Dutchmen absolutely refused, saying, "How can we sign something we do not understand?" Such a protest may seem reasonable, but at several points it becomes obvious that in not signing, the immigrants were expressing a more generally felt resentment against the English language—not so much as the tongue of the society into which they had moved, for that they could understand, but as a language of the church and religion.

In the context of the church, language and doctrinal issues were inseparable. The Reverend Jongeneel was the subject of considerable criticism for having supported the national church's intention to drop the word "Dutch" from its official title. But Jongeneel was also accused, in almost the same breath, of preaching "false doctrine." Language and the title "Dutch" were evidently more than ethnic flags; many suspected that the pure Reformed doctrine could be preached only in "the Holland tongue." The defenders of the language were of course correct in assuming that the use of English would open their church to the influence of other doctrines, for once the Dutch Reformed congregation began holding services in English, relations with neighboring religious bodies, like the Congregationalist church, became possible and, in fact, took place.

The most threatening source of doctrinal pollution, however, was not any of the surrounding American congregations but the mother church into which the young Sayville congregation was incorporated. The tension along this cultural boundary served only to aggravate the issue of financial dependency, having the cumulative effect of creating and maintaining a hostility and resentment between the hierarchy and the local congregation into which any uneasiness the immigrants might feel toward their surrounding American environment could be channeled.

No wonder the minister got the worst of this tension, for he stood in an unenviable mediatory position between the local congregation and the hierarchy, both of which demanded obedience to conflicting doctrinal and cultural standards. Early ministers were always too Dutch for the tastes of the classis, while for the congregation they were never Dutch enough.

This sort of structural tension between the immigrant congregations and their American church was naturally also felt among the other Dutch communities in the Midwest and the East. As soon as the hardships of the earliest years of settlement were overcome, widespread dissatisfaction with the American Reformed church began to be felt. That church, the immigrants discovered, had fallen as far from the strictest standards of doctrinal purity as had the state church back in the Netherlands. If other, more secular, difficulties were behind this uneasiness, as was the case in West Sayville, it was nevertheless in the language of religious practice and dogma that these problems always found expression.

What most of these doctrinal issues had in common was a concern for the authority and boundedness of the covenant community. They bespoke a desire to withdraw from the nefarious influences of the outside world as represented most directly by the American version of

Reformed Christianity but as embodied more generally in American culture. To withstand these enemies, a tighter covenant had to be formed, a new church of more inwardly focused communities, each protected from the surrounding cultural wilderness by walls of non-association. Accordingly, as I have noted, in 1857 a number of immigrants withdrew from the Reformed Church in America to form the True Holland Reformed church, whose name was changed eventually to the Christian Reformed church. In West Sayville the split came in 1876. In the Netherlands, however, other schisms took place through the latter part of the century, and there, too, tighter covenants were formed by the seceders. In either the Dutch or the American case, the schisms can be interpreted following Swierenga (1980) as reactions by "locals" to the pressures of modernization, industrialization, and urbanization. The fact that in both nations this reaction could find religious expression may be attributed to the existence of a dogmatic form that lent itself to such uses.

What about the West Sayville immigrants? Certainly the pattern of cultural withdrawal is apparent from the outset, and the respective church records reveal that the Dutch Reformed congregation was more cosmopolitan in its cultural orientation than the Christian Reformed group. Attributing this difference of orientation to the regional origin of the communicants, however, is problematic. The early immigrants were mostly from Zeeland, in fact, from the two villages of Yerseke and Bruinisse. These towns were certainly influenced early on by markets and other modernizing influences, especially later in the century. At the time of the early immigration, however, there were potential seceders among the first settlers. Furthermore, it was in the wake of the boom of cosmopolitan influences in Yerseke late in the century that the more reactionary churches there made such headway.

Even after the West Sayville colony was joined by immigrants from other areas of Holland, particularly Texel and Friesland, church membership records do not reveal any significant tendency to join one congregation or another according to point of origin in Holland. Zeelanders and Frisians are found on both sides, and, what is more, not a few families and individuals changed congregations or, in the case of families, split between them.

The difficulty with Swierenga's theory is that it, like the American-adaptation explanation of the schism, blames the conflicts within the church, and the ultimate separation of the two churches, solely on external influences. The implication of his reliance on the "cosmopolitan"-"local" dichotomy is that this sort of church or institution is inherently conservative unless disrupted by the external forces of social change, which are seen as emanating from the city. But if the Reformed faith's emphasis on the covenant made it essentially conservative, did not its equal stress on individual predestination contribute directly, as Weber (1958) argued, to the entrepreneurial ethos of the city (see Taylor 1983)? In other words, do not these "cosmopolitan" forces find as much support in this variant of the Protestant ethic as do the forces of "localism"?

Certainly the community in West Sayville produced its own "cosmopolitans"; they did not have to be imported. As soon as various individuals found that their economic or social interests required a wider circle of associates, they managed a liberal enough interpretation of the covenant. Jake Ockers, the immigrant who founded the most successful oyster shipping business, was the most extreme case, for he married an American Methodist and joined her congregation. The other big shippers, Westerbeke and Vander Borgh, remained in the Dutch Reformed Church, and both families produced a series of "pillars" in that congregation. When the split came, however, a portion of the community sought a more restricted church, and this more closed and more visibly Dutch church attracted many among the newer immigrants arriving toward the end of the century.[3]

If it is correct to suppose that entrepreneurial cosmopolitanism is an internal product of this sort of community, then the separation of the two congregations should not have produced anything like perfect harmony or stasis among those who withdrew into the True Holland Church in 1876. There, too, the internal contradictions of orthodox Calvinism should have produced their very own disruptions, schisms, and threats of schisms as new cosmopolitans arose with their more open attitudes, and their opposition retreated behind even stronger covenantal walls. Further, as will be shown, the interactional character of this more convenantal church assured that conflict would be even more frequent than it was in the Dutch Reformed congregation.

The Christian Reformed Congregation

Two structurally based sorts of conflict within the Christian Reformed congregation can be distinguished.[4] One genre may be called "problems of boundary maintenance." Fights arose from a kind of border tension developing between those who responded to the more individualistic teachings of the church and those who sought tighter bonds in a closed community. The other type of conflict arose from the same structural opposition and typically followed the occurrence of boundary disputes. These "crises of authority" were more frequent in this congregation than among members of the Dutch Reformed Church. Ideally their reaffirmation of the absolute moral authority of the community should have readied such transgressors as were reported to accept the communal will as represented and expressed by the consistory. While in this regard the rights of the Christian Reformed Church were more authoritarian, its doctrine was also more democratic, so that the sinner might always suspect that, after all, he himself was right and the particular individuals holding office were sadly unfit for their sacred responsibility. In this church, those individuals were less likely to include the dominie.

The dominie was less important in the Christian Reformed congregation, first because for much of the time there was no one resident. From 1876 until 1890 the small, financially struggling congregation made do with periodic visits from New Jersey ministers whose authority in disputes was minimal. From 1894 until 1899, the communicants were once again without a religious leader, during which time political as well as financial difficulties made the "call" of a new dominie difficult. Even when the dominie was resident, his reduced role is evident in two opposite but mutually dependent ways: he was less powerful politically, and he was less likely to be used as a scapegoat for the conflicts of the community or to be perceived as the source of moral corruption. The dominie's relative lack of authority is precisely what made him less useful for that sort of symbolic role than his counterpart in the Dutch Reformed Church. That being the case, large-scale conflicts were more likely to find their way to the other consistory officers, as the only suitable symbols of the collective authority of the community.

The greater concern of the Christian Reformed Church with one's neighbor's behavior is evidenced in the consistory records by a far greater number of reported sins. One must conclude that the Christian Reformed community contained either more sinners or more "reporters" than the Dutch Reformed. Given the covenant ideology, one inclines toward the latter explanation.

Whereas the Dutch Reformed consistory concerned itself most often with very public Sabbath violations, the Christian Reformed consistory was somehow able to gain knowledge of far more private infractions. The very intention to get a job that would lead one to work on Sunday, if heard of in private conversation, would somehow turn up at consistory meetings. Thus, for example, were John, Willem, and Leendert brought before the consistory on three separate occasions because one church officer or another had heard that these men intended to "go yachting" (as crew members) in the summer, which employment "would lead them to violate the Fourth Commandment" (by working on the Sabbath). On an earlier occasion yet another communicant was brought in and asked, "Is it true that a drunken tailor entered your house last Sunday?" The accused man replied, "That is true, but the tailor was let in by my son Jan while I myself was taking a Sunday afternoon nap."

Reported infractions of the commandments were by no means limited to Sabbath violations. No less than five separate cases of adultery were brought up between 1890 and 1910, as well as several cases of theft (always involving shellfish) and a large number of such minor lapses from moral purity as drunkenness and card playing. A committee was even sent to investigate reports that well-respected members of the community had "behaved badly on the occasion of celebrating their daughter's wedding—there was dancing in the house until the early hours of the morning." Neither were the difficulties between married couples only their own affair. Twice the consistory assumed a mediatory position between estranged couples, attempting to reconcile them for the good of the community. What distinguishes all these cases from those reported in the Dutch Reformed Church records is the greater penetration into the domestic domain of the Christian Reformed consistory. Nearly all the sinners brought to account in the Dutch Reformed Church had transgressed in public. Members of that community were less likely to report lapses within the household, and their consistory was evidently less prone to penetrate into that inner domain.

The most significant incidents the Christian Reformed congregation felt it their duty to handle were those interpreted as "border violations," actions that threatened to blur the line of nonassociation that ideally separated the covenanters from the outer, sinful world and thus threatened the covenant in another way. The most obvious of these, and one of the most troubling to the West Sayville congregation, involved "secret societies." In particular, the Forresters lodge had attracted a number of communicants, who were forced to choose between membership in the church and membership in that society. A short-lived oysterman's union, though not officially forbidden by the consistory, was actively discouraged. The question was raised for the first time in March 1902: "Is it permitted to be a member of the Church and a member of the union at the same time?" The dominie responded, "This has been discussed many times at classis and synod meetings, and one has to take into account how and why the union originated and manifests itself, but that the consistory holds as its opinion that it shouldn't exist and it is extremely condemnable if violence is used."

Even when members of the community did not join secret societies but merely associated with groups whose interests were seen as opposed to those of the congregation, they might be censured. One man was known to have gone "on quite a few occasions" to services at the nearby Congregationalist church. There was, as well, the ambiguous issue of membership in "insurance associations," which were objectionable both on grounds of association and because subscription was understood, by some at least, to evince "a lack of faith in God's help." Closely related to the issue of preventing association with outsiders was that of keeping up the internal associations of community members. The consistory was particularly concerned with church attendance, of course, but also frequently reprimanded those whose children were not showing up for religious instruction.

In all the cases of reported lapses, the consistory's policy was to send a committee to investigate the matter and/or require the presence of the alleged transgressor(s). As with the Dutch Reformed Church, the procedure was to require a confession of guilt from the sinners, in lieu of which they would be placed under greater and greater stages of censure. Rarely did major offenders merely submit to the will of the consistory without any sort of fuss, but one can usefully distinguish between those crimes whose punishment incurred some conflict because of the individual's unwillingness to bend before communal authority, and those that were in fact only ammunition in continuing conflicts between individuals and factions. The latter conflicts are the more anthropologically instructive, because they offer occasions through which to view both the structural strains besetting the community and the kind of authority that existed to resolve those strains.

A particularly revealing case is that which involved a member of the consistory, whom I shall call Jan Smit. The trouble began when Elder Smit was renominated for that office in the annual election of 1891. Several families were reported to be "unsatisfied" with Smit's candidacy, and the dominie had accordingly gone with Smit to visit them at home and hear their objections. The first of these visits went very badly indeed, for the family in question, whom I shall call the S——s, sent Smit and Dominie DeVries from their door. The H——s were "more calm" and managed to communicate their objections to Smit in the appropriate religious idiom: "Is a member of the church, and an officer, allowed to do nightwatch work during the nights before and after Sunday?" This ambiguous question of Sabbath violation was brought by the minister to the classis, who decided that Smit's behavior as a night watchman was compromising enough to render him unfit for the eldership. Smit confessed his guilt in "sinning against his elderly profession" but did not want to be conceived a

"Sabbath violator." That, however, was far from being the end of the matter.

A year later, in the autumn of 1892, once again the election for church officers came around, and once again Smit was nominated. The same two men who had complained the previous years raised their voices again and were joined by a third, a deacon by the name of K——. In addition to the fact that too little time had elapsed since his confession, these men felt Smit was unqualified for eldership because he had in the past divulged consistory secrets to nonchurch members and because he had spread slander about the dominie. This time Smit "accepted nothing of what they brought up against him." A big fight ensued, splitting the consistory, and once again recourse was had to the classis officials. Smit confessed that he was wrong, but he was allowed to stand for the eldership and was once again elected. The other elder and the deacon who were elected, however, declined their posts. Their replacements evidently accepted Smit, because the records note "no further objections among the Consistory, but there are some problems in the community, some are unsatisfied about Smit's eldership and the Consistory has decided that the Dominie should announce from the pulpit that the Consistory wishes to be spared from unsigned letters."

Smit was at the center of various controversies over the next few years, sometimes as elder and sometimes as member, but in every case he was identified with a more "cosmopolitan" interpretation of church doctrine, and his opponents, to judge by their alignments on other issues as well as against Smit, can be characterized as "locals." He was, for example, accused by one couple of having advised their daughter to go out to one of the American churches on Sunday evening, and of having complained to her of the "coercive" nature of their own church.

The full assault on Smit came when he was re-elected to an eldership in December 1896. The consistory meeting of that 18 December began with Smit's announcing that some people would come to raise objections. Three men then entered the room, all of them strict interpretationists on doctrinal issues. S—— began, "When a man's wife goes to another church, can that man become an elder in his church? Also, is it Christian to ask money for serving as elder, as Smit has done in the past? Can any man be trusted who has been accused and confessed so many times?" K—— repeated these charges, but added that "Smit visits the Congregational church on Sunday nights and kneels there like the others." The final charges came from Van Y——, who referred to a letter he had already given the consistory to protest Smit's election. In that missive, Van Y——

had cited the biblical passage 1 Tim. 3:1–7, which relates the qualities necessary to be a bishop in the church and states: "He must manage his own household well . . . for if a man does not know how to manage his own household, how can he care for God's church?"—evidently referring to Smit's wife's not being a member of the church.

Things got hot enough for the visiting Reverend Koster to say "that he will conclude and leave and that he doesn't want to get ill here." Referring to the problem Smit's wife was said to have in understanding Dutch, Koster pointed out that it was not unusual for the wives of functionaries not to be members. It seems, however, that although Mrs. Smit was American-born, she had grown up with her Dutch-speaking grandfather in Grand Rapids, Michigan, so that it was unclear to Smit's opponents why she would be unable to understand the service. The dominie tried to mollify Smit's accusers on the Congregationalist church issue also, whereupon he earned the vituperative response from Vander E——, "Do you believe that these 'Children of God' follow the hints of the devil, and if they do so premeditatively, are they not even more sinful?" More angry words were exchanged, and once again Dominie Koster threatened to leave them to their own devices.

The final issue against Smit was one that especially raised the hackles of the contenders. Van Y—— said that Smit was "an agent for a life insurance company." He added, "Isn't it terrible that everything is allowed to take place in our Church? If I had known beforehand that such a thing would be approved of I wouldn't have become a member." Smit, meanwhile, explained that he did not sell insurance, but merely acted as an interpreter for the company. That was a distinction too subtle by far for his opponents. On this issue the dominie and another consistory member were, however, even more supportive of Smit. The latter fellow allowed as how he was considering taking out insurance himself, while the dominie asked Smit's enemies to show him "where in the Bible or in the Church order it is forbidden." "Our ancestors," Vander E—— replied, "couldn't have imagined such a thing. If everything is tolerated I will ask for my 'attest.'" Insurance, according to Smit's opponents, was a sign of lack of faith in God. The God-fearing member of the covenant, after all, need not fear want, for the "deserving poor" (to borrow a more contemporary phrase) are always well provided for. The recorder tells us that the dominie decided at this point that he was unwilling to "sicken himself any longer in Sayville. He foresees a schism and regards himself as unable to set right this case. He doesn't want to become the cause of a schism." The schism, in fact, would not come for some time. Smit retained his office after all, and the controversy subsided for another two years. When Smit was up for re-election in the fall of 1899, however, the whole process began again.

It will not have escaped the reader's attention that the crimes of which Smit was accused in these various confrontations nearly all involved perceived violations of the integrity of the covenant: "border violations" by a "cosmopolitan" that threatened to destroy the barrier between the closed Dutch community and the outside American world. The fact that Smit was periodically re-elected to eldership testifies to the existence of a fair number of "cosmopolitans" who shared his view, as the constant and concerted opposition he met shows the strength of the reactionary "localist" element in the community. The Smit disputes constitute a particularly glaring example of this sort of attack and counterattack (for Smit was able to take advantage of some embarrassing lapses in the families of his opponents), but it is by no means the only lengthy contretemps. "Cosmopolitans" were pitted against the "locals" individually or severally any number of times and over any number of issues.

If one judges by the language of the conflicts alone, then one is led to believe that Smit's opponents were simply religious people appalled at their neighbor's transgressions. Could their close attention to Smit in particular be explained by the fact that he alone was so often sinful? More likely it was because of his structural position as an elder who represented in his actions one particular internally produced danger to the covenant community. The two opposing world views and social strategies represented in these disputes were equally the product of this particular variant of the Protestant ethic. Further, the democratic-authoritarian government and idiom of the Christian Reformed Church made it certain that neither variant would lose sight of the other, and the lack of a strong minister further assured that the consistory officers, directly elected by factions within the community, would be left as the principal actors and targets in the resulting disputes. According to this theory, the other congregation—the Dutch Reformed—suffered fewer upsets after the 1890s not because it contained fewer sinners but because the private behavior of its members was less threatening to the community's vision of its own sanctity, and because the more symbolically important dominie provided a convenient target for all manner of scrutiny and accusation. The Dutch Reformed Church could see itself through a very difficult period by periodic purgings of its minister. The Christian Reformed Church, on the other hand, was constantly riven by individuals and factions pitted against one another.

Ritual Resolution

Might not such conflicts, even if abetted by religious ideology, have been overcome in communal rituals that reaffirmed the solidarity of the group? There was, after all, the Lord's Supper, the Communion rite that symbolically and dramatically acted out the sacred bond that ideally linked all communicants together and separated them from those outside the covenant. The record reveals, however, that the rite presented an opportunity to express hostility as often as solidarity. There were, first of all, communicants who were conspicuous by their absence, who by hint of consistory censure were barred from the Lord's Supper until they had confessed their sins. There were also those not kept away but choosing to stay away, thus demonstrating by their absence disapproval of the current moral state of the community, and particularly of its symbolic representatives, the consistory. In a community of this size and constitution such a strategy was quite effective. If someone stayed away from the communal ritual for long enough, that person would be assured a visitation by a consistory committee, on which occasion he or she would be provided with an opportunity to express disapproval dramatically in the appropriate idiom, replete with biblical allusions. Even presence at the Lord's Supper did not assure a person's ritual "oneness" with the community, for if someone did not approve of the day's sermon (or was simply seeking an opportunity for a public attack on the minister), he or she was always free to express that disapproval by not shaking hands with the dominie on the way out of church.

The shaking of hands was a religious ritual in itself, a symbolic reaffirmation of the binding covenant, the Holy Contract. When two individuals fought and then repented, the consistory officers would direct them to shake hands, or, in the language of the church, "to give one another the brotherhood." If the intention of this act was to apply a little ritual glue to such social bonds, the adhesive did not prove strong. Those who gave one another the brotherhood one month were likely to be at each other's throats again a month or two later. Many were these ritual confessions of guilt, but the deep-rooted conflicts, as has been described, outlasted a hundred such confessions.

If all these more or less official church rituals were of so little effect in counteracting the conflicts so often pitting the covenanters against one another, by what means did religion resolve these self-generated difficulties? By no means, one is tempted to answer. After all, the difficulties in the Dutch Reformed congregation led to fission—the schism of 1876 that split the church community into two antagonistic camps. Further, within the Christian Reformed Church, at least, schism seemed always imminent, and in fact did finally come to pass in 1911, when a number of communicants from that church founded the Netherlands Reformed congregation of West Sayville. For if the Dutch Reformed had their shared dissatisfaction with whomever happened to be dominie to hold them together, the Christian Reformed were only later supplied with dominies, and even then such men were not as symbolically or politically powerful as their Dutch Reformed counterparts. Without such scapegoats the unfortunate congregation was left with only one another, but most especially with their neighbors who had been raised to the religious ranks of elders and deacons.

Was schism, however, tantamount to the permanent fission of the community and thus a signal of the final failure of the religious form to contribute to the solidarity of the local social system? To answer, it is necessary to take a closer look at the character of association both across sectarian lines within the community and between persons within them. Following Georg Simmel (1955), one must be careful not to mistake conflict for nonassociation. Nor should one exclude the possibility that conflict itself can exist as a kind of ritual, both formal and informal. Ritual combat, after all, may be as ancient a form as ritual communion, although the latter has certainly received the most scholarly attention.

Let me first take up the matter of the schisms. What sort of continuing relations marked the two congregations after the split in 1876? There was, of course, the hostility one might expect to issue from such a schism. The Dutch Reformed congregation saw the newer church as composed of dangerous heretics and troublemakers, malcontents who separated themselves artificially with "man-made laws." The Christian Reformed Church, on the other hand, perceived the others as reprobates who had fallen away from the covenant under the evil influence of the surrounding liberal environment. A few older locals still remember confrontations between the two congregations: "If a crowd was goin' down the road on a Sunday to the one church, and another group was comin' up by them toward the other, they'd each stick to their path and so try to force the others off the road. They'd fight with their choirs as well—the one trying to drown out the other." These near-ritual confrontations do not seem to have ever become violent, nor indeed should they be taken as an indication of a necessarily strong hostility between the individual members of the respective congregations. While separated on Sunday, members of the two congregations mixed on other days and in other contexts, and there is no indication, for example, that the oyster houses that employed many local men were segregated according to church membership.

Beyond that, however, individuals not infrequently shifted their allegiance from one church to another. It is difficult to separate religious from nonreligious motivations for these shifts. One old woman whose marriage left her outside and somewhat embittered toward both Dutch churches commented, "They're just like hoppy-toads down there—goin' from one church to the other. Why there was one fella, a carpenter, who was in the one church and when he didn't get the job of doin the roof on that church, he left and joined the other."

Whatever the individual motivation for moving between the two congregations, their existence within the bounds of a single isolated ethnic community permitted a strategy of internal adjustment, both to the pressures and attractions of the surrounding American environment and to the interactional difficulties arising from the confined and competitive life of the community. Although relatively more "cosmopolitan," the Dutch Reformed Church was still, up through World War I at least, very much an immigrant church, and communicants could certainly feel anchored in the Dutch community there even if their field of activities brought membership in the Masons or the Forresters as well. As an alternative, the Christian Reformed congregation offered the refuge of further withdrawal from the outer world.

But what of further schism within the Christian Reformed congregation? It is first important to note that even with the intense quarreling that beset the congregation from its organization in 1876, and despite the fears of visiting dominies, the schism resulting in the Netherlands Reformed group was more than forty years in coming. Many of the more conservative members of the Christian Reformed congregation threatened to leave when things were not going their way, and some withdrew individually or as families from the church. But many of them returned after a brief interim, and the fact remains that in cases of conflict like those involving Smit, the combatants seemed quite willing to wage a constant seesaw battle over the decades with no victory for either side.

In fact, those who did finally leave to form the Netherlands Reformed group were very few in number, a mere handful of men who ostensibly departed over the appointment of a dominie of whom they evidently did not approve. Far from creating a permanent rift between those who left the church and those who remained, the division left the wives and children of the men who "separated themselves" in the Christian Reformed Church. That is not to say that this was not troublesome for at least those families. For them especially, the Sabbath became a day of combat rather than communion. The son of one of the Netherlands Reformed vividly remembers that

Sunday was the day I dreaded. All week it wouldn't be that bad, but on Sunday my father would get up in a foul mood and everyone in the house would be upset, waiting for the time for church, when my mother and us children would go off in one direction and my father would go off in the other. Sometimes my parents would fight dreadfully over the church and sometimes they would just be silent with each other. My father held to that church until his dying day, but then, thank God, he repented his ways. . . . He said he realized that it was the devil leading him that way, and we were joined together in the end.

While thus traumatic enough within the few families so affected, that schism hardly fissioned the entire community as the first had done. More important was the threat of schism that seemed always to hang over the proceedings of the Christian Reformed consistory. Schism was the ever-possible event; enemies could be accused of abetting it, or it could be used as a threat to curb the hubris of those in office. To withdraw from the covenant when it had lost its sanctity was an understood right within the contractual idiom of the church community. "Protestants," in the words of one battling deacon, "were allowed to protest"—that is, to voice independent religious opinions and interpretations.

Indeed, in this religious form at least, Protestants were not only allowed to protest, but they availed themselves so often and in so many contexts of this right, it must be concluded that the religious conflict itself was a major ritual form. Not only on church grounds, before the members of the consistory, but anywhere in the community, the individual was able to turn a secular situation into a sacred one merely by using the appropriate language. The prospective combatant turned to his textual repertoire as provided by the Bible and church law and found within them the appropriate passage to turn whatever problem he faced into a moral and religious one. As the church records indicate, once this religious idiom was initiated, the combatants were constrained to remain within it. Thus, if formal rituals in the church did little to relieve the conflicts of the community (the Lord's Supper was, in fact, not even held during periods of intense strife), then the absence of a sacred arena for acting out religious values only succeeded in turning the entire village into a religious forum. In breaking down the boundary between the sacred and the secular, the Calvinistic creed left each man and woman to his or her own theological devices and made all the world a stage for their confrontations. The ritual nature of these confrontations is evident not only in their symbolic expressions and adherence to understood rules,

but also in the people's ability to live with and between these often
fierce battles.

Even when faction and schism were the apparent result, confrontation acted to draw the community together in that "honest war," as
an early minister called it, whose contenders knew that the greatest
gulf lay not between opposing combatants but between soldiers and
civilians. It is thus possible to see an integrative dimension to these
conflicts; with the aid of church doctrines and associations, entrepreneurial attitudes and clannish communalism could exert their
opposing forces as long as the ensuing conflicts were allowed open
expression in religious language and on the broad religious stage.

Religion continues to be important in West Sayville, but that does
not mean that even the Christian Reformed Church is unchanged;
rather, the covenant survived by always adjusting the symbolic threat
to one appropriate to the times. That is a very elastic sort of conservatism, and one that struck me most clearly in the course of conversation with an elderly immigrant woman. "So you live in Pennsylvania," she said. "I went there once on a trip organized by the church
[Christian Reformed], to the Amish country. Those were very godly
people, but I don't understand why they have to be so backward.
Why, I have a cousin out in Michigan who's a farmer, and he's got the
latest kind of tractor with all the gadgets—and I'm sure he's as good a
Christian as anyone."

Notes

1. The American commentators on the religious scene were prone to counting up
the number of churches—the higher the number, the greater the presumed religiosity
of the community.

2. For a summary of the religious issues and the complicated series of events involved in the schism, see Lucas (1955, 511–12). A more detailed treatment of the
Christian Reformed church can be found in Kromminga (1943) and Zwaanstra
(1973).

3. Commenting on the social context of the schism and of the further explosion in
1882, when many more joined the Christian Reformed Church in America, Arnold
Mulder (1947) wrote, "During those years more congregations, in Michigan, in Iowa,
in Wisconsin, and in nearly every community where Hollanders had settled, had
joined the movement and the Christian Reformed denomination had become firmly
established." For the present argument, the important point is that splits tended to
bifurcate small communities and hence should be examined from the point of view of
village dynamics as well as personal attributes and religious issues.

4. Quotations are from Hendrickus Taatgen's translation of the Dutch manuscript
records of the Christian Reformed Church in West Sayville. The consistory of that
church is to be thanked for making it available.

References

Durkheim, E. 1915. *The Elementary Forms of the Religious Life*, translated by J. W. Swain. New York: Free Press.

Kromminga, D. H. 1943. *The Christian Reformed Tradition: From the Reformation to the Present*. Grand Rapids, Mich.: William B. Eerdmans.

Lucas, S. 1955. *Netherlanders in America*. Ann Arbor: University of Michigan Press.

Merton, R. 1949. "Patterns of Influence: Local and Cosmopolitan Influencials." In *Social Theory and Social Structure*, edited by R. Merton. New York: Free Press.

Mulder, A. 1947. *Americans from Holland*. Philadelphia, Pa.: J. B. Lippincott.

Simmel, G. 1955. *Conflict and the Web of Group-Affiliation*, translated by K. Wolff. New York: Free Press.

Swierenga, R. 1980. "Local-Cosmopolitan Theory and Immigrant Religion: The Social Bases of the Antebellum Dutch Reformed Schism." *Journal of Social History* 14:113–35.

Taylor, L. J. 1983. *Dutchmen on the Bay: The Ethnohistory of a Contractual Community*. Philadelphia: University of Pennsylvania Press.

Turner, V. 1968. *Drums of Affliction*. Oxford: Clarendon Press.

Van Gennep, A. 1960. *The Rites of Passage*, translated by M. B. Vizedom and G. L. Caffee. Chicago: University of Chicago Press.

Verrips, J. 1973. "The Preacher and the Farmers: The Church as a Political Arena in a Dutch Community." *American Anthropologist* 75:852–67.

Weber, M. 1958. *The Protestant Ethic and the Spirit of Capitalism*, translated by R. H. Tawney. New York: Charles Scribner.

Zwaanstra, H. 1973. *Reformed Thought and Experience in a New World*. Kampen, Netherlands: J. H. Kok.

Contributors

DAG BLANCK is the director of the Swenson Swedish Immigration Research Center at Augustana College and is a doctoral candidate in the history department at Uppsala University. He is the author of several articles on Swedish-Americans and is the coeditor (with Harald Runblom) of *Scandinavia Overseas*.

PETER KIVISTO is an assistant professor of sociology at Augustana College. He has contributed numerous articles on race and ethnicity, including several on Finnish-Americans. He is also the author of *Immigrant Socialists in the United States: The Case of Finns and the Left*.

PETER RACHLEFF is an associate professor of history at Macalester College. Trained as a labor historian, his research has focused on the interplay between race/ethnicity and class. This is evident in his book *Black Labor in the South* and in his recent work on Croatian-Americans.

ALICE SCOURBY chairs the sociology and anthropology department at the C. W. Post campus of Long Island University. She also directs the women's studies program there. In addition to several articles on Greek immigrants, she is the author of *The Greek Americans* and editor of *The Greek American Community in Transition*.

LAWRENCE J. TAYLOR is an associate professor of anthropology at Lafayette College. He is the author of *Dutchmen on the Bay* and a number of articles based on his fieldwork in Ireland, as well as his work on the Dutch Calvinist community in the United States.

DONALD TRICARICO is an associate professor of sociology at Queensborough Community College. In his book *The Italians of Greenwich Village: The Social Structure and Transformation of an Ethnic Community* and in numerous articles he has sought to explore the shifting character of ethnic-group affiliation across generations.

BELA VASSADY, JR. is a professor of history at Elizabethtown College. His scholarly interests focus on African history and on Hungarian migration to the United States. His articles on the latter have appeared, among other places, in the *Journal of American Ethnic History*.

Index

Abramson, Harold, 11
Acculturation, 51, 83
Adamic, Louis, 14, 106
Alba, Richard, 36
Alexander I (king of Yugoslavia), 105, 107
All-American Slavic Congress, 102
All Croatian Congress, 106
American Action program, 60, 63
Americanization, 17, 70, 76, 97, 105, 134, 139; campaigns for, 20
American Jugoslav Association, 102
American Youth Congress, 102
Anderson, Charles, 136, 140
Appalachia, 82
Archdeacon, Thomas, 20
Assimilation, 14, 24–25, 26, 32, 51, 52, 55, 100, 125, 131, 134, 139, 150; straight-line, 68; theory of, 12, 15, 16
Association of Italian American Faculty, 33
Attenzione, 29, 37, 41
Augustana Synod, 138, 147, 149
Austro-Hungarians, 47, 57, 58, 103, 104

Balch, Emily, 54
Banfield, Edward C., 117
Beebe, Arie, 154
Beijbom, Ulf, 138
Bender, Thomas, 20
Bernstein, Irving, 73
Berta, John, 49
Bilingualism, 51, 55. *See also* Language loyalty
Bjursten, Herman, 140
Bodnar, John, 19, 121
Böhm, Károly, 62
Boundary maintenance, 32, 85, 163
Butkovich, John D., 95, 97, 108

Campisi, Paul, 26
Canute (king of England, Denmark, Norway), 144

Carpatho-Rusins, 48, 49
Casa Italiana, 28
Central Cooperative Wholesale, 71
Chalupa, Mirko, 108
Charles XII (king of Sweden), 142
Chicago School, 12
Chinese immigrants, 41
Cinel, Dino, 11
Citizenship, 20, 104, 105, 143
City University of New York (CUNY), 33
Cochran, Bert, 73
Common Council of American Unity, 102, 103
Communists, 107
Congress of Industrial Organizations (CIO), 73, 108
Congress of Italian-American Organizations (CIAO), 31
Consumer cooperatives, 70–72
Contadini, 115
Cooperative Builder, 71
Co-op Weekly, 71
Copeland, William, 81
Cornish-Americans, 82
Crèvecoeur, J. Hector St. John, 13, 17
Crispino, James A., 25
Croatia, 97, 98
Croatian-Americans, 48–49, 54, 89–113
Croatian Catholic Union, 91
Croatian colonies, 105, 106
Croatian Day, 108
Croatian Fraternal Union, 97–103, 105–10
Croatian National Council, 106
Croatian Peasant Party, 104
Croatian Republican Peasant Party, 104–6
Crousaz, Rev., 161
Cuomo, Mario, 39
Czech immigrants, 56
Czech-Slovak connection, 54

Danish-Americans, 77
Democratic party, 106, 107
Dénes, Ferenc, 58, 59, 60
DeVries, Dominie, 168, 169
DeWall family, 153
DiDonato, Pietro, 29
di Leonardo, Michaela, 114
Diner, Hasia, 114
Diocese of Kassa, 56, 58, 60, 61
Discrimination, 39, 137. *See also*
  Prejudice
Doby, Harry Rickard, 84
Domobran, 107
Douglass, William, 16
Duma, 105
Durkheim, Emile, 156
Dutch-Americans, 153–76

Ebony, 29
Ecological factors, 38
Educational attainment, 28, 33, 37–38
Elo, Taisto, 73
Emergent ethnicity, 16, 82
Employment, 37–38, 120, 122, 137
Enander, Johan Alfred, 142, 145, 146,
  149, 150
Ericsson, John, 144
Eriksson, Leif, 146
Ethnic generations, 15, 25, 34, 37, 40, 71,
  78, 80, 84–85, 92, 97, 98–102, 110,
  115, 120, 121, 124–27, 135–36
Ethnic Heritage Act, 40
Ethnic identity, 11, 27–41, 86, 97–103,
  114–19, 130–31, 134–50; mixed, 47–
  65
Ethnic leadership, 54, 136
Ethnic mobilization, 27
Ethnic mosaic metaphor, 11
Ethnic organizations, 31–33, 41, 69–77,
  89–110, 138
Ethnic revival, 67–68
European immigrants, 17, 19, 36, 37
Ewen, Elizabeth, 114

Families, 27–28, 35, 115–17, 122–31
Festival of Nations, 102
Finnish-Americans, 67–88
Fishman, Joshua, 67, 77, 135, 136, 145,
  150
Francis, E. K., 16
French-Americans, 82

Gans, Herbert, 21, 42, 67, 68, 83, 130
Geertz, Clifford, 19
Gender identity, 20, 33, 114–31
Geographical mobility, 79–83
German-Americans, 77, 79
Giddings, Franklin, 12
Gjerde, John, 18
Glazer, Nathan, 12, 15
Glettler, Monika, 64
Gödecke, P. A., 141
Gordon, Milton, 16, 114
Gouze, Matt, 101
Greek-Americans, 63, 114–33
Greek Orthodox church, 115, 120, 124
Greeley, Andrew, 12, 35, 67, 83
Greene, Victor, 136
Greenwich Village, 40
Gusfield, Joseph, 70
Gustavus Adolphus (king of Sweden),
  142, 148
Gustavus Vasa (king of Sweden), 142
Gutman, Herbert, 15, 20

Hage family, 153
Haitinger, Imre, 58, 59
Handlin, Oscar, 15, 17–19, 134
Hansen, Marcus Lee, 15, 16, 67, 135
Hansen's thesis, 15, 67
Harney, Robert, 48, 52, 54
Hasselquist, T. N., 139
Hayes, David, 84
Heikkila, William, 73
Hemlandet, 139, 142
Higham, John, 15, 136, 150
Hobsbawn, Eric, 149
Hoglund, William, 84, 86
Homeland issues, 63–64, 103–9, 155
Hoover, Herbert, 106
Horvath, Michael J., 94, 98, 99
Howe, Irving, 67
Hrvatski Domobran, 107
Hrvatsko Kolo, 105–7
Hungarian-Americans, 47–66

Iacocca, Lee, 38, 40
Ibson, John, 11
Ideology, 13, 150
Immigration, 26, 31, 50, 110, 119–22;
  restriction on, 12
Independent Order of Svithiod, 138
Individualism, 115

Indo-European, 50, 77
Industrialisti, 74
Industrial Workers of the World (IWW), 73
Institute of Italian Culture, 28
Intermarriage, 20, 24, 36, 49, 78–79, 122–25
Irish-Americans, 35, 36, 38, 114, 157
Italian-American Bar Association, 33
Italian-American Historical Association, 33
Italian-American Institute to Foster Higher Education, 33
Italian-Americans, 18, 24–46, 82, 114, 156, 157

Jăskovič, Ignác, 56, 57
Jednota, 57
Jewish-Americans, 38, 126
Jobs. *See* Occupations
John Lackland (king of England), 144
Jongeneel, Rev., 161, 163
Jugoslav Fraternal Federation, 102

Kalevala, 86
Kallen, Horace, 14
Kann, Robert, 54
Karni, Michael, 70
Katekismus, 76
Kazinczy, Béla, 58
Keynesian economics, 89
Kivisto, Peter, 135
Klehr, Harvey, 72
Kohányi, Tihamér, 57, 62
Kolehmainen, John, 78, 79
Kossalko, Josef, 56, 57, 59
Kossuth, Louis, 64
Koster, Rev., 170
Kourvetaris, George A., 122

Language loyalty, 77, 162–63. *See also* Bilingualism
League of Nations, 106
Lehtinen, Donald, 71
LeRoy Ladurie, Emmanuel, 13
Levi, Carlo, 29
Lincoln, Abraham, 145, 148
Lindmark, Sture, 137
Little Italy Restoration Association (LIRA), 32
Locals and cosmopolitans, 155–56, 164–65

Loukinen, Michael, 80, 85
Luther, Martin, 76
Lyman, Stanford, 16

Macartney, Carlile, 54
McCarthyism, 110
Maček, Vladko, 107
McNall, Scott G., 118
Mafia, 39
Magyars, 47–66
Marginality, 61
Mass culture, 20
Matthews, Fred, 14
May, Arthur, 54
Melting pot, the, 11–15, 31, 71, 123
Merton, Robert, 155
Mogyorossy, J., 57
Morawska, Ewa, 19, 47, 49
Morton, John, 146, 148
Moynihan, Daniel P., 12
Mussolini, Benito, 106, 107
Mutual aid societies, 120, 137; insurance associations, 168

Nahirny, Vladimir, 67, 135, 136, 145, 150
National Association for the Advancement of Colored People (NAACP), 41
National Fraternal Congress, 102
Nationalism, 61, 162
National Italian-American Foundation (NIAF), 33, 41
National Organization of Italian-American Women (NOIAW), 33
Nelson, Lowrey, 78, 79
Neurwirth, Lásjló, 60
New Deal, 108
New Deal Coalition, 106
New York Times, 30, 40
Nikander, J. K., 76
Norelius, Erik, 139
Norwegian-Americans, 18, 83
Novak, Michael, 12, 67

Occupations, 28, 37
Ockers, Jake, 165
Olin-Fahle, Anja, 85
Olson, Ernst W., 147–50
Olsson, Olof, 139–40
Order of the Vikings, 138

Pan-Slavism, 57, 63, 104
Park, Robert, 14
Patrick, Saint, 86, 157
Patterson, Orlando, 12
Pavelić, Ante, 107
Peasant International, 105
Peasant party, 107
Persephone syndrome, 126
Person, Johan, 134
Petrakis, Harry Mark, 125
Phrenokosmian Society, 141, 148
Pilli, Arja, 78
Pluralism, 27, 31, 32, 34, 42; cultural, 14, 16
Polakovič, Ján, 58, 65
Polish-Americans, 82
Political organizations, 72–74
Politics, 30–34, 39, 41, 58–59, 92–96, 103–9; radical, 73–74
Prejudice, 39–40, 137. *See also* Discrimination
Puskás, Julia, 52

Raamataa Historiai, 76
Race relations cycle, 14
Radić, Ante, 104–5
Radić, Stjepan, 104–6
Raivaaja, 74
Regional identities, 20, 82
Religion, 20, 55–65, 74–77, 115, 120–21, 124–25, 138–39, 149, 153–75
Rietdyk, Rev., 154
Rocco, Saint, 157
Roosevelt, Franklin D., 93, 95, 106, 108
Rosen, Bernard, 126
Rovnianek, Peter, 57, 59
Runeberg, Johan Ludvig, 140
Rusin Catholic, 63
Rydberg, Niktor, 141

Saarinens, Eilel and Eero, 86
Saloutos, Theodore, 120, 122
Scandinavian Fraternity of America, 138
Schiick, Henrik, 147
Schilstra, Rev., 161, 162
Schoefor, John, 83
Serbian-Americans, 48, 49, 104, 106, 108
Serbo-Croatians, 49
Seton-Watson, Hugh, 54
Shils, Edward, 114–15
Sibelius, Jean, 86

Simmel, Georg, 20, 173
Slavic-Americans, 48, 64, 104, 106
Ślebodni Orel, 60
Slovak-Americans, 47–66, 104, 108
Slovenian-Americans, 48
Smit, Elder, 168–71
Smith, Anthony, 68
Smith, John, 145
Social class, 20, 80, 122; middle, 25, 27–30, 33–34, 37–38, 42, 84, 121, 126, 138; working, 27–28, 79, 91, 94
Social history, 13, 20, 134
Sollors, Werner, 67
Southern Living, 29
Sowell, Thomas, 12, 37
Steel Workers Organizing Committee (SWOC), 95
Stein, Howard, 49
Steinberg, Stephen, 12, 28
Stolarik, Mark, 49, 54
Svenska Vitterhetsäleskepet, 140
Swedish-Americans, 15, 77, 79, 134–52
Swidler, Ann, 19–20, 83
Swieregna, Robert, 155, 164
Symbolic ethnicity, 42–43, 68–69, 86, 130
Symphonic orchestra metaphor, 11
Szabadsáq, 57, 62, 63
Szabó, Gyula, 60

Taylor, Ronald, 34
Tegnér, Esaias, 140–41
Temperance societies, 69–70
Thompson, E. P., 15
Tilly, Charles, 13
Transmuting pot metaphor, 11
Transplanted thesis, 19–20, 61
Turner, Victor, 156
Työmies-Eteenpäin, 74

Uhru, Saint, 86
Ukrainian-Americans, 49
Unions, 73, 93–96
United States Census Bureau, 78
Uprooted thesis, 17–18
Uštaša, 107

Vanden Bosch, Rev., 154
Van Emmerick, Rev., 161
Vasa Order of America, 138
Vecoli, Rudolph, 11, 17–18, 115, 134

Verrips, J., 155
Virágh, Pál, 60–61
Virtanen, Keijo, 80
Von Schéele, Bishop K. G., 147

Wagner Act, 108
Ware, Carolyn, 37
Wargelin, John, 76
Washington, George, 145–46
Weber, Max, 11, 165
Wilson, Woodrow, 90, 104

World War, First, 51, 56, 92, 104
World War, Second, 24, 39, 72, 78, 121

Yancey, William, 16, 34
Yans-McLaughlin, Virginia, 18
Yugoslavia, 105–6
Yupper, 82

Zajedničar, 91–102, 108
Zangwill, Israel, 13–14
Zunz, Olivier, 15, 80